THE ONTOGENESIS
OF GRAMMAR

THE CHILD PSYCHOLOGY SERIES
EXPERIMENTAL AND THEORETICAL ANALYSES OF CHILD BEHAVIOR

EDITOR
DAVID S. PALERMO
DEPARTMENT OF PSYCHOLOGY
THE PENNSYLVANIA STATE UNIVERSITY
UNIVERSITY PARK, PENNSYLVANIA

The Perception of Stimulus Relations: Discrimination Learning
and Transposition, HAYNE W. REESE, 1968

Cognitive Development: The Child's Acquisition of Diagonality,
DAVID R. OLSON, 1970

The Ontogenesis of Grammar: A Theoretical Symposium, DAN I.
SLOBIN, ED. 1971

THE ONTOGENESIS OF GRAMMAR
A Theoretical Symposium

Edited by

Dan I. Slobin
Department of Psychology
University of California
Berkeley, California

1971

ACADEMIC PRESS
New York and London

A Subsidiary of Harcourt Brace Jovanovich, Publishers

ACADEMIC PRESS, INC.
111 Fifth Avenue, New York, New York 10003

United Kingdom Edition published by
ACADEMIC PRESS, INC. (LONDON) LTD.
24/28 Oval Road, London NW1

LIBRARY OF CONGRESS CATALOG CARD NUMBER: 79-154400

Second Printing, 1973

PRINTED IN THE UNITED STATES OF AMERICA

Contents

List of Contributors

Numbers in parentheses indicate the pages on which the authors' contributions begin

MARTIN D. S. BRAINE University of California, Santa Barbara, California (153)

V. LYNN EBERHART University of Iowa, Iowa City, Iowa (225)

SUSAN ERVIN-TRIPP University of California, Berkeley, California (189)

DAVID McNEILL University of Chicago, Chicago, Illinois (17)

DAVID S. PALERMO Pennsylvania State University, University Park, Pennsylvania (41, 225)

I. M. SCHLESINGER Hebrew University and Israel Institute of Applied Social Research, Jerusalem, Israel (63)

DAN I. SLOBIN University of California, Berkeley, California (3, 215)

ARTHUR W. STAATS University of Hawaii, Honolulu, Hawaii (103)

Preface

This book gradually grew out of a symposium which I organized for the December 1965 meeting of the American Association for the Advancement of Science, held in Berkeley, California. That symposium, sponsored by the Western Psychological Association and the Society for Research on Child Development, sought to bring divergent theoretical approaches to bear upon the same body of language acquisition data. This goal, with broadened theoretical scope, underlies the present book. The original symposium included David McNeill and David S. Palermo, with Susan Ervin-Tripp as discussant. That group has been expanded to include I. M. Schlesinger and Arthur W. Staats; and Martin D. S. Braine contributed a paper after the four symposium participants had completed their work. The book thus spans a half decade of thought. The contributors were given a last chance in 1970 to revise their positions, and only Dr. Palermo had moved far enough from his original contribution to add a strong disclaimer (see the footnote to his chapter).

By late 1965 the impact of modern linguistics on child language studies had given rise to a rich and suggestive body of developmental data. Detailed information on early stages of grammatical development in about ten English-speaking children, based on intensive longitudinal study, emerged from independent but convergent investigations at Harvard, Berkeley, and Walter Reed.[1] At the same time, the theoretical literature flowered with controversy.[2] By and large, however, theorists do not address themselves to precisely the same body of data. It is the purpose of the symposium, published in this volume, to bring several

---

[1] This work is described in the following references, listed in the bibliography of this volume: Bellugi, 1964, 1965, 1967; Braine, 1963b; Brown, 1970; Brown and Bellugi, 1964; Brown, Cazden, and Bellugi, 1969; Brown and Fraser, 1963; Cazden, 1968; Ervin, 1964; Klima and Bellugi, 1966; W. Miller, 1963; W. Miller and Ervin, 1964.

[2] See Bever, Fodor, and Weksel, 1965a, 1965b; Braine, 1963a, 1965b; Brown and Bellugi, 1964; Chomsky, 1959, 1962, 1965; Ervin, 1964; Fodor, 1966; Jenkins and Palermo, 1964; Katz, 1966; Lenneberg, 1962, 1964, 1966, 1967; McNeill, 1965, 1966; G. Miller, 1964, 1965; Miller, Galanter, and Pribram, 1960; Osgood, 1963; Slobin, 1966b; Staats, 1963.

divergent theorists together to discuss the same body of data and each other's interpretations of those data.

The data are presented in the introductory chapter, which served as the Introduction to the December 1963 symposium. Because grammar has been the aspect of language development most thoroughly studied, only grammatical data are offered. After nine years of intensive research on child language, those data have, of course, been enriched. I have found it necessary to add an addendum modifying the analysis of two-word utterances presented in the introductory chapter. With the excep tion of "pivot constructions," however, the phenomena summarized in that chapter have found confirmation in more recent studies,[3] and are still in need of theoretical explanation. The papers in this volume make it clear that much work remains to be done on the collection, analysis, and explanation of data of language acquisition.

The plan of the book is as follows: the introductory chapter presents the data for discussion, as drawn from the work of Bellugi, Brown, and Fraser at Harvard, Ervin-Tripp and W. Miller at Berkeley, and Braine at Walter Reed. These data are then interpreted by McNeill, Palermo, Schlesinger, and Staats. Each of the four theorists was given the opportunity to read and comment upon the collection of papers, and each has offered additional remarks on the positions of his three co-contributors. Martin Braine has contributed a more recent theoretical paper, completed after the written symposium between the first four theorists. Finally, Susan Ervin-Tripp comments on the five theoretical discussions and sets forth guidelines for needed further research. (For the record, her paper, reflecting our collective work at the Language-Behavior Research Laboratory at Berkeley, is closest to my own position.) Beyond the foregoing parenthetical remark, I step outside of my editorial neutrality only in the Appendix, where I feel compelled to comment on the sort of laboratory investigation of grammatical development proposed by Palermo and by Staats. Palermo and his co-worker Eberhart have the last word in the Appendix; and the book moves on to a final biblio-

---

[3] For recent studies of language acquisition see: Bloom, 1970; Blount, 1969; Bowerman, 1970; Brown, 1968; C. Chomsky, 1969; Cromer, 1968; Ervin-Tripp, 1970a; Kernan, 1969; McNeill and McNeill, 1968; Menyuk, 1969; Mikeš, 1967; Shipley, Smith, and Gleitman, 1969; Slobin and Welsh, in press; Smith, 1969. A compendium of classical and recent studies of language development can be found in Ferguson and Slobin (in press); and Slobin (in press b) offers an exhaustive bibliography of work in the field from the earliest studies through 1967. Current research published in journals is regularly abstracted in *Language and Language Behavior Abstracts*. For reviews and discussion of cross-linguistic similarities in child language see Braine, in press a; Ervin-Tripp, 1966; and Slobin, 1970, in press a.

graphical flourish embracing all of the defendants, witnesses, and aides called upon by all of the contributors.

The task of coordinating a written exchange of views has been time-consuming, and I wish to thank the contributors for their patience in waiting for each other and for me to finish writing various parts of the book.

THE ONTOGENESIS
OF GRAMMAR

INTRODUCTION

Data for the Symposium[*]

DAN I. SLOBIN
University of California
Berkeley, California

Perhaps the basic fact which faces investigators of child language is the speed of language acquisition. In the brief course of three or four years, during which very early levels of cognitive development are traversed, the child succeeds in mastering the exceedingly complex structure of his native language. What is more, each child, exposed to a different sample of the language, and generally with little or no conscious tuition on the part of his parents, arrives at essentially the same grammar in this brief span. By the end of the preschool period the normal child is—at least on the grammatical level—almost a full-fledged member of his language community, able to produce and comprehend an endless variety of novel sentences of the language he has mastered.

The facts dealt with in this book have to do with one aspect of the course of language acquisition: the process of grammatical development. And the basic facts, in regard to the ontogenesis of grammar, are: that combinations of words and parts of words in child speech seem to be systematic rather than random, and productive rather than merely imitative or rote learned. In this chapter an attempt is made to demonstrate that child language is structured from the start, that it soon takes on a hierarchical structure, that it tends to be regular, that the structures change in the course of development, and that they do not always correspond to adult structures.

[*] This chapter, with the exception of the Addendum following Section 1, presents the basic data offered to Professors McNeill, Palermo, Schlesinger, and Staats for theoretical discussion.

1. Two-Word Utterances[1]

While it is possible, at the one-word stage, to speculate about the child's underlying grammatical knowledge, at the two-word stage one can ask whether there are any formal regularities in the structure of utterances. Several investigators have dealt with this stage (Braine, 1963b; Brown & Fraser, 1963; W. Miller & Ervin, 1964), and since their findings have been remarkably similar it is possible here, for descriptive purposes, to speak of the generic, typical, two-word-utterance child. This child is found during a fairly brief stage of development, at about 18 months of age, during which there seems to be a length limitation of two morphemes upon utterances. In the course of several months large numbers of new two-word utterances are produced. For example, the following are figures from the speech of one child studied by Braine (1963b): the cumulative number of *different* two-word combinations recorded in successive months was 14, 24, 54, 89, 350, 1400, 2500+.

Braine analyzed the distribution of words in such utterances, and discovered that the utterances are not random or unstructured juxtapositions of two words. His analysis reveals two distributionally defined word classes: a small class of "pivot" words [cf. Miller and Ervin's "operators" (1964)] and a large, open class of words, many of which were previously one-word utterances. Pivots occupy fixed utterance position; that is, a given pivot word always occurs in either first or second position. One first-position pivot, for example, is *allgone*, as in utterances such as *allgone shoe, allgone bandage, allgone outside, allgone pacifier. Allgone* thus occupies a pivotal position, followed by a large collection of words which can occur in either position. A common second-position pivot is *on*, as in utterances such as *shoe on, bandage on, fix on, take on.* Words such as *allgone* and *on* are defined as pivotal, while words such as *shoe* and *bandage* fall into the residual "open class" of words, freely occurring in combination with both first and second position pivots. The class of pivot words is small and expands slowly, while the open class is large and rapidly growing. All of the words in the open class can occur as single-word utterances, but some of the pivot words never do. Table 1 presents a sample of part of the pivot grammar of one child (McNeill, 1966, p. 22). On the left is the total list of first-position pivots (there are nine of them); on the right is a partial list of the open class (which may contain hundreds of words). Generally

[1] Recent studies have cast doubt on the universality and the usefulness of the analysis presented here, as clarified in the Addendum which follows this section (Section 1.1).

TABLE 1   Fragment of Pivot Grammar
of One Child

First-position pivots		Open class words	
allgone	my	boy	vitamins
byebye	see	sock	hot
big	night-night	boat	Mommy
more	hi	fan	Daddy
pretty		milk	.
		plane	.
		shoe	.

(with some few exceptions), any of the words on the left can be combined with any of the words on the right to form a sentence in this child's language.

Somewhat later, words from the open class can also be combined in two-word sentences, but the sentence position of these words is not fixed. That is, taking the word *car* as an example (Braine, 1963b), one can find utterances like *man car* (with *car* in second position), meaning, "A man is in the car," and also *car bridge* (with *car* in first position), meaning, "The car is under the bridge."

To summarize the child's system at this stage, as shown in Table 2, one can say that there are two word classes: pivot and open class; that the pivot class can be subdivided into two subclasses: first- and second-position pivots; and that there are three sentence types: pivot–open, open–pivot, and open–open.[2]

An important datum at this stage (and later stages) is the fact that many of the child's utterances—although consistent with *his* system—do not directly correspond to adult utterances, and do not look like reduced imitations of utterances he has heard. Braine (1963b) offers many exam-

---

[2] As Braine (1971) correctly points out, it is an oversimplification to speak of a beginning stage of grammatical development in which the major structures are P–O, O–P, and O–O. He notes:

"First, there is no evidence that there is ever a generative rule O + O as such: by the time enough apparent 'O–O' forms have developed to permit analysis, it becomes clear that they are a set of fairly complex structures to which the formula O–O does not begin to do justice. . . . Second, the suggestion [that the first utterance structures are P–O, O–P, and O–O] obscures the temporal course of events, i.e., the existence of an early period when the P–O and O–P formulae are clearly the dominant forms of a sparse output, and of a later period when they are minor modifier–head structures within a very productive grammar generating a host of 'O–O' and other forms." [Braine's notation of formulas has been adapted to that employed in this book.]

TABLE 2   A Sample of Two-
Word Grammar

$$ S \rightarrow \left\{ \begin{array}{c} P_1 + O \\ O + P_2 \\ O + O \end{array} \right\} $$

$P_1 \rightarrow$ *allgone, byebye, big, more*, . . .

$P_2 \rightarrow$ *off, on,* , , ,

$O \rightarrow$ *boy, sock, Momma,*

also of following utterances in the pivot-open grammar (Anton washing hands), *allgone outside* (said when door was shut, apparently meaning, "The outside is all gone"), *more page* (meaning, "Don't stop reading"), *more wet, more car* (meaning, "Drive around some more"), *more high* (meaning, "There's more up there"), *there high* (meaning, "It's up there"), *other fix* (meaning, "Fix the other one"), *this do* (meaning, "Do this").

The evidence is that even at this early stage children can produce and understand an endless variety of sentences, most of which they have never heard before.

1.1 Addendum: Reservations about Pivot Grammars

Recent work has raised a number of reservations about the adequacy of pivot constructions as descriptive of the two-word stage of grammatical development (Bloom, 1970; Bowerman, 1970; Brown, 1970; Ervin-Tripp, this volume; Kelley, 1967; Kernan, 1969; Schlesinger, this volume; Slobin, 1970). The classic definition of pivots as fixed in position, never occurring in isolation, and never occurring in combination with other pivots does not apply to all children studied [see Brown (1970) for details]. For example, the "operators" (cf. pivots) of Miller and Ervin's (1964) subjects showed only a *tendency* to occupy first or second position; and Bowerman (1970) found pivot-like words (defined by high frequency of occurrence and operator-like meaning) freely occurring in both positions in the two-word utterances of a Finnish child. Bowerman also points out that "pivot" and "open" are not undifferentiated classes, because particular "pivots" only occur with particular subgroups of "open class" words—e.g., the pivot word *here* occurs only with nouns and the pivot word *Rina* (the child's name) only with verbs. Braine also noted in his original paper (1963b) that, in one child's speech, the pivot *it* was only preceded by verbs. Thus the general rule, $S \rightarrow P + O$, is too simple. Bloom (1970) has also failed to find classical pivots in two of the three children she studied. Thus it appears that not all children develop a grammar of two-word utterances with fixed-position pivots and initially unsubdivided pivot and open classes, as described above. Perhaps the most that can be said is that a small class of frequently occurring operators or functors is present at the two-word stage, and that these operators combine with content morphemes in restricted and selective ways to signal particular semantic relations.

Considerations of expression of semantic relations cast new light on the entire analysis of two-word utterances (as indicated, especially, by Schlesinger in this volume). The analysis of utterances as pivot–open and open–open is a surface description of positional occurrences of words. As soon as the child's *communicative intent* is taken into regard, it becomes clear that the underlying structures—be they described as syntactic or semantic—are far more detailed than the surface description reveals. A description of a two-word utterance as "open-open" ignores the fact that it could represent any one of a number of semantic relations. For example, Bloom (1970) has noted that noun–noun utterances in child speech can express a number of different relations: conjunction (*boot umbrella*), attribution (*party hat*), possession (*daddy hat*), subject–locative (*sweater chair*), and subject–object (*mommy book*). Indeed, one utterance, *mommy sock,* was produced in two different situations with clear evidence of two different meanings: (1) "mommy's sock" and (2) "Mommy is putting my sock on." A superficial description of these two utterances as open–open would fail to reveal the full linguistic competence of the child. Note also that such "open–open" sentences can also be based on order rules when semantic function is taken into account, such as possessor–possessed, subject–object, etc.

The grammatical representation in Table 2, therefore, while appealing in its simplicity and clarity, can no longer serve as a representation of the child's competence at the two-word stage. The basic claim that early speech is grammatically structured, however, takes on added force in the light of more recent work. Newer analyses take account of both syntax and semantics, presenting "deep" and "surface" levels of analysis even in the case of two-word utterances (Bloom, 1970; Blount, 1969; Brown, 1970; Kernan, 1969; Schlesinger, this volume).

2. Hierarchical Constructions

Already at the beginning of the three-word stage it is possible to analyze sentences in terms of immediate constituents, or structured subunits. Braine (1963b) gives examples of pivot constructions serving as phrases in three-word utterances. For example, in the open–open sentence *man car, man* can be replaced by the pivot construction *other man,* resulting in the utterance *other man car,* meaning "The other man is in the car." A pivot construction with *other* can also replace the second word in that same open–open sentence, resulting in *man other car,* meaning "The man is in the other car." The sentences *other man car* and *man other car* are not simply strings of three words; rather, each of these sentences is a string of two units, one of which can be replaced by a phrase of two words. In formal terms these sentences are hierarchical, and could be represented by tree diagrams having minimal depth.

In later stages of development a number of word classes can be successively separated out on distributional grounds, and these can be combined into constituent phrases in increasingly complex hierarchical phrase structure sentences. An important example from a later period is the emergence of noun phrases or longer sequences of words which have the same privileges of occurrence as individual nouns in the child's speech, as shown in Table 3.

Note in Table 3 that the noun slot can be filled with a noun phrase, and that the resulting longer sentence is sometimes deviant from the point of view of adult grammar. There is, for example, no clear adult model for such utterances as *Put a gas in* or *That a your car*.

TABLE 3   Emergence of Noun Phrases[a]

Earlier samples	Later samples
That *factory*.	That *a factory*.
That *flower*.	That *a blue flower*.
That *car*.	That *a your car*.
Where *scissors* go?	Where *Mommy scissors* go?
Horsie stop.	*A horsie* stop.
Put *gas* in.	Put *a gas* in.
Put *hat* on.	Put *the red hat* on.

[a] Illustrative examples are based on Brown and Bellugi (1964), and on unpublished data of Brown *et al.* The utterances appearing together in the same column were not all produced at the same age; the important distinction for a given pair is "earlier-later."

Hesitations, according to Brown & Bellugi (1964, p. 150), also provide evidence that noun phrases function as units in the child's speech:

> The noun phrase has a kind of psychological unity. . . . Consider the sentence using the separable verb *put on*. The noun phrase in "Put the red hat on" is, as a whole, fitted in between the verb and the particle even as is the noun alone in "Put hat on." What is more, however, the location of pauses in the longer sentence, on several occasions, suggested the psychological organization: "Put . . . the red hat . . . on" rather than "Put the red . . . hat on" or "Put the . . . red hat on." In addition to this evidence the use of pronouns suggests that the noun phrase is a psychological unit.

The latter point is supported by examples of noun phrases replaced by pronouns (e.g., *Made a ship, Made it*) and pronouns and noun phrases used in the same utterances (e.g., *Mommy get it ladder, Mommy got it my ladder*) (Brown & Bellugi, 1964).

3. Regularizations[3]

Another area in which consistently deviant utterances appear is the overregularization of inflections. Anyone listening even briefly to child speech will hear forms such as *breaked, throwed, mouses, handses,* and the like. Overgeneralizations have been repeatedly noted by investigators of child speech in a number of different languages.

The case of English past tense inflections is instructive. In all of the children who have been studied (and these are children of homes where standard English is spoken, and are usually first-born children) the first past tenses used are the correct forms of the irregular verbs—*fell, broke, went,* and so on. (These are, incidentally, the most frequent past tense forms in adult English speech.) As soon as the child learns only one or two regular past tense forms—like *helped* and *walked*—he immediately replaces the correct irregular past tense forms with their incorrect overgeneralizations from the regular forms. In fact, in some cases, the correct irregular forms are replaced even before one hears the use of regular forms in the child's speech: apparently it is sufficient that a child hear and understand the regular past tense inflection. Thus children actually say *it came off, it broke,* and *he did it* before they say *it comed off, it breaked,* and *he doed it.* Even though the correct forms may have been practiced for several months, they are driven out of the child's speech by the overregularization, and may not return for years. This is just one example of a widespread phenomenon, noted by investigators of child speech in many languages (Slobin, in press a).

Another interesting example comes from the work of Ervin-Tripp and Miller. Their subjects, like most English-speaking children, regularized the plural of *foot.* Some children would say *foots;* others would say *feets.* Ervin-Tripp reports (Ervin, 1964, p. 175): "Very few of the children fluctuated between *foot* and *feet,* so although the word *feet* must have been heard by the children, we can clearly see a regularizing influence. If imitation alone were at work, we would have expected fluctuation between *foot* and *feet.*" At a somewhat later stage, these children learned syllabic plurals, such as *box-boxes,* and replaced the earlier plural *foots* with a new analogic form, *footses.* Or other children,

[3] Additional data on the development of inflections is presented in the Appendix to this volume.

upon learning the pluralization *glass–glasses,* replaced *foot* with *footiz.* Ervin-Tripp concludes that even highly practiced, familiar plurals may be temporarily changed in form by overgeneralization of new patterns" (Ervin, 1964, p. 177).

Similar phenomena are seen repeatedly in Russian child language, where the abundance of inflections allows for many more overgeneralizations than in English. Again and again a form which has been highly practiced will suddenly be driven out by another, more regular form, and only much later will a proper balance be achieved (Gvozdev, 1961; Popova, 1958; Slobin, 1966a, in press a; Zakharova, 1958).

4. Negation and Transformational Development

The growth of grammatical transformations has, as yet, been little investigated. Outstanding contributions to this difficult area are Bellugi-Klima's analyses of the development of the negative and the interrogative in the children studied by Brown's group (Bellugi, 1964, 1965, 1967).[4] Her description of negation serves as basic data in this section. The picture is complex, and is only sketched briefly here. Especially striking is the diversity of transitory sentence types, many of them quite different from adult forms of negation.

The earliest form of negation in English child speech, and in many other languages as well (McNeill & McNeill, 1968; Slobin, in press a), is simply affixation of a negative element such as *no* or *not* to a childish sentence, as shown in Table 4. These sentences are quite unlike

TABLE 4   Negation Stage I[a]

No . . . wipe finger.	Not . . . fit.	No mitten.
More . . . no.	No singing song.	No sit there.
	No wash.	No play that.
	No drop mitten.	Wear mitten no.
		No David fun play?

[a] All examples in this section are taken from Bellugi (1964), and are drawn from the recorded speech of two children ("Adam" and "Eve"). Adam was 29 months old at Stage I, and Eve 21. Periods between stages are from three to six months. Both children went through roughly the same initial stages. (Only data from Adam are available for Stage IV.)

[4] More detailed analysis of the earliest stages of negative development has recently been carried out by Bloom (1970).

anything in adult speech. Even those which superficially resemble adult negative sentences—like *No sit there*—are different in an important respect. *No sit there* has the same order of elements as the adult sentence, *No, I won't sit there*, but the intonation contours are different. The adult sentence has falling intonation on *no* and a pause between *no* and the rest of the sentence. The child sentence has no pause and a single intonation contour for the entire utterance. The other forms in Table 4 have no obvious adult model.

In the second period, three to six months later (depending on the child investigated), the early negation forms of the first period are still

TABLE 5   Negation Stage II

I can't see you.	Don't leave me.
. . . so you can't see.	Don't want wear it.
We can't talk.	Don't wait for me.
	Don't . . . wake me up . . . again.
I don't sit on Dick coffee.	
I don't want it.	That no fish school.
	That no Mommy.
I don't know his name.	There no squirrels.
Don't want me pull it?	No . . . Rusty hat.
Why not?	Book say no.
Why not me sleeping?	Touch the snow no.
Why not . . . cracker can't talk?	This a radiator no.
Why not you looking right place?	
Why not me can't dance?	I want not envelope.
Why not me get hit?	
Why not he eat?	

present, but there are many new forms as well, as shown in Table 5. Note the use of the negated auxiliaries *can't* and *don't* in Table 5. At this stage, however, these auxiliaries are used only in the negative; there are no affirmative sentences using *can* and *do* as auxiliaries. Table 5 also shows negative questions beginning with *why not*, often followed by a negative sentence. Double negatives of this sort are not found in the speech of the children's parents. At this stage there are also negative imperatives beginning with *don't*, and sentences like *That no fish school* and *There no squirrels*, which seem to be reduced versions of negative copular sentences occurring in adult speech, with the copula missing.

By the third stage, presented in Table 6, the early negation form of simply affixing *no* or *not* to a sentence has disappeared. Some sentences are now fully in correspondence with those of adult speech, even in regard to intonation: e.g. *No, it isn't; No, I don't have a book.* Negated auxiliaries are still used, but, at this stage, the auxiliaries also occur without negation. That is, the child says sentences like *I can see it* as well as sentences like *I can't see it.* Negation is used in copular sentences as before (e.g. *That not a clown*), but sometimes the copula is included at this stage (e.g. *I am not a doctor*). Note also the change in negative questions from the earlier period. The formula *why*

TABLE C Negation Stage III

No, it isn't.	Why you say, you don't want some bottles?
That was not me.	Why the kitty can't stand up?
I am not a doctor.	Why he can't play with it?
	Why he don't know how to pretend?
No, I don't have a book.	Why this doesn't work?
Paul can't have one.	I don't want cover on it.
I can't see it.	You don't want some supper.
This can't stick.	You didn't eat supper with us.
We can't make another broom.	I didn't see something.
	Paul didn't laugh.
This not ice cream.	
This no good.	Don't put the two wings on.
They not hot.	Don't kick my box.
Paul not tired.	Don't touch the fish.
They not wet.	
That not a clown.	I not see you any more.
	Ask me if I not made mistake.
I not crying.	Fraser not see him.
He not taking the walls down.	
That not turning.	No, I don't have a book.
	I gave him some so he won't cry.

not + *negative sentence* has been dropped. Questions like *Why I didn't see something?* and *Why he don't know how to pretend?* differ from the adult form only in that the order of pronoun and auxiliary remains to be inverted. Thus double negatives have dropped out (although a different sort of double negative appears in Stage IV). The first uses of indefinite determiners and pronouns with negation appear at this stage, as in *You don't want some sugar* and *I don't see something.* These are similar to affirmative sentences in the child's speech: *I want some sugar* and *I see something.* Negative imperatives remain as before.

For the fourth stage we only have data from one of the two children studied, the boy named Adam in the literature. Examples appear in Table 7. Note that many of the trends observed in Stage III continue, and that many sentences (though by no means all) are now in correspondence with those produced by the adult grammar. Double negatives appear again, but these are quite different from the double nega-

TABLE 7   Negation Stage IV

I can't push it back and forth.	I not going to cut myself on that.
You said you can't play with it.	I not peeking.
You don't say you can't have it.	Don't cry.
I hope he won't bother you.	Don't do it on me.
It's won't hurt.	
I can't get this thing in here.	I never used that color.
	I never have one.
I don't know how this goes.	I never seen her.
I don't know what is missing.	
I don't know what they are.	I can't do nothing with no string.
You don't know where you're going.	He can't have nothing.
You don't like to be rolled into clay.	I can't go nowhere.
It's doesn't fall out.	I can't punch no more.
He doesn't know where he's driving.	It's wasn't no chicken.
They doesn't cut my finger or anything.	Nobody won't recognize us.
I doesn't know how to put this together.	I don't want no people to recognize me.
Cars doesn't get on tracks.	I never had no turn.
You didn't put it all the way through.	I didn't put no paint on.
No, I didn't.	
	Why it won't go up?
No, I not big boy.	Why he can't drive very well?
I not big enough.	Why you won't let nobody recognize
I am not a toy.	you?
No, it's not.	Why I didn't live in Italy?
That's no wheel.	Why you say that, you don't have it,
That's not your deedee.	again?
That duck isn't a very good driver.	Why you couldn't find out?
Those are not your tires.	
It's not black.	Did I didn't mean to?
I wasn't talking 'bout it.	Do she don't need that one?
	Did you take no cooking?

tives of Stage II, which were negative questions beginning with *why not*. These disappeared in Stage III, where negative questions were formed with a simple *why*, rather than *why not*. The double negatives of Stage IV are based on use of negative indefinite pronouns and determiners (e.g., *nothing, nowhere, nobody, no*), and also sometimes reflect the fact that *some* is no longer used as a determiner and pronoun, as in *He can't have nothing*. This situation also leads to *triple* negatives, such as *I can't do nothing with no string*

It is clear that, in less than two years, the child's negation system has grown quite complex, and that it is not yet fully in accord with adult English. A similar picture emerges from Bellugi-Klima's analysis of interrogative development in these two children (Bellugi, 1967). There is a great diversity of sentence types, with many short-lived forms and many constructions which seem cumbersone and awkward from an adult point of view; change is rapid; and by the time the child reaches school age his grammar differs negligibly from that of his parents.

5. Conclusions

These facts are presented for theoretical discussion in the following four chapters:

1. Early two-word sentences are structured. The structure can be characterized as a pivot structure, and it is used productively by the child.

2. With the advent of three-word sentences, the structure of many sentences is hierarchical. This is to say that constituent phrases function as units in the child's language.

3. Regular forms are overgeneralized, even to highly practiced forms.

4. There is a succession of short-lived devices for performing grammatical transformations such as negation and interrogation.

The themes underlying these four points are the rapidity of change and the frequent lack of obvious correspondence between child and adult grammatical constructions.

THE SYMPOSIUM

The Capacity for the Ontogenesis of Grammar

DAVID McNEILL
University of Chicago
Chicago, Illinois

A basic assumption of this chapter is that the acquisition of language can be understood as an interaction between a child's linguistic experience and his innate linguistic capacities. The goal of a theory of language acquisition is set accordingly. Such a theory should provide a description of the innate capacities of children, their interaction with experience, and ultimately show in this way how knowledge of language develops automatically, naturally, effortlessly, and (as Slobin emphasizes) quickly.

One aspect of the problem is the tremendous speed with which language acquisition takes place. A large amount of syntax is known to four-year olds. Experimental studies of children show this (Berko, 1958; Slobin, 1966c) as well as ordinary observation. Of course, linguistic advancement continues long after age four, but these late developments involve such matters as style (Labov, 1964) and possibly semantics, but apparently not syntax.

A second aspect of the problem of language acquisition is the emergence of linguistic abstractions. Children develop structures that are abstract, never made manifest in the actual speech of adults, but nonetheless crucial to the communication of meaning.

One claim below is that these two problems—speed and abstraction—are intimately related, the speed of acquisition being possible because of the way in which children develop abstractions. But in order to present the argument, some preliminary issues must first be clarified. It is to these questions that we now turn.

A language is a relation between sound and meaning, expression and content, outer and inner form (Sapir, 1921). So describing language is probably the most general true statement one can make about it. Consider paraphrase, for example. One can always find two or more sentences that express the same meaning. Declarative sentences and their passive counterparts are merely the most obvious examples—*The junta horribly wrecked the economy* and *The economy was horribly wrecked by the junta* mean essentially the same thing. In paraphrase, the same content is expressed in different ways. The opposite phenomenon is ambiguity, where different content is expressed in the same way—for example, *outgoing tuna*, or *For some bad examples, see my previous paper*.

In the case of ambiguity and paraphrase, expression and content cannot be the same. But the entire phenomenon of language is precisely that expression and content are never the same, in any sentence. All sentences consist of a manifest part (expression) and an abstract part (content). The arrangement of the one is not the same as the other. To suppose otherwise is to commit Colonel Blimp's error—that English (for instance) is so marvelous because the order of words is the same as the order of ideas.

One of the major developments in recent linguistic theory bears on the distinction between expression and content. In the transformational generative grammars developed by N. Chomsky (1965) and others, the deep and surface structures of sentences are related to each other in a manner described explicitly by rules of transformation. The deep structure contains all the syntactic information necessary to place the correct meaning on a sentence—such as what the subject or predicate is, or whether the sentence is affirmative or negative—and the surface structure contains all the syntactic information necessary to place the correct pronunciation on a sentence—such as the order of morphemes, or the location of constituent boundaries. The deep and surface structures of a sentence, although differently arranged, always stand in a specific relation to one another—a relation described by one or more transformations. Thus, a child acquiring a language must acquire the transformational relations between the deep and surface structures of sentences.

We can now rephrase the problem of linguistic abstraction. In acquiring the transformations that define language, children learn to relate deep and surface structures; but the deep structures of sentences are never displayed in the form of examples, stimuli, responses, or anything else. They are abstract and, for one who does not already know the language, inaccessible. It is this simple linguistic fact, which every child faces and overcomes, that eliminates S–R theory as a serious explanation of language acquisition.

There is no form of S–R theory that can account for the emergence of a relation, one half of which is never manifested. The most fundamental ground-rule of behavioral analysis—that a phenomenon can be analyzed into responses paired with stimuli—is contradicted. Moreover, there is no conceivable elaboration of S–R theory, short of abandonment, that can apply to the acquisition of linguistic abstractions. Operant analysis, mediated S–R connections of any degree of complexity, all are inappropriate forms of analysis. It is not that S–R theory is wrong in the case of language acquisition, but that it is irrelevant.

Although S–R theories are inappropriate for explaining the emergence of linguistic abstractions other hypotheses can be considered. The one to be elaborated here fits into the general framework stated by Lenneberg (1967), and may be regarded as an attempt to develop further the biological point of view toward language that he urges.

Conceiving of language as a biological phenomenon, one naturally regards it as the product of evolutionary specialization. Given such a biological point of view a major problem is to describe the specialization, and this seems to come to a focus on two points: on the one hand, on language itself, and on the other hand, on the biological support for language. Descriptions of the first kind are given in linguistics; a transformational grammar will be taken here to be the best approximation to such a description currently available. Descriptions of the second kind are far less well studied, the problem only recently having been recognized, but the remarks below are to be taken as belonging to this category. What follows is a hypothesis about man's capacity for language and the way in which this capacity interacts with linguistic experience.

It will be helpful to approach the problem in a semiformal way. Let us consider, not children for the moment, but an abstract Language Acquisition Device (Chomsky, 1957), which we can call LAD for short. LAD receives a corpus of utterances and from the corpus produces a grammar—that is, a theory of the regularities that hold within the corpus. LAD thereby distinguishes grammatical from ungrammatical structures and develops an ability to understand and produce an unlimited variety of sentences. The arrangement can be diagrammed as follows:

$$\text{corpus} \rightarrow \boxed{\text{LAD}} \rightarrow \text{grammar}$$

If we understood the internal structure of LAD—the contents of the box above—we would understand how LAD develops a grammar from a corpus. The problem is analogous to the engineering exercise of inferring the structure of a "black box" from various input–output relations. In the case of LAD, the input is a corpus of utterances, the output is a transformational grammar, and the internal structure is what we wish to reconstruct.

One general consideration concerning LAD's internal structure is that it must be so arranged as to acquire any language. LAD's structure should not bias it in the direction of some languages and away from others. Whatever comprises the internal structure of LAD must be universally applicable—LAD may contain information bearing on the general form of language, but it must contain no information bearing on the form of any particular language to the exclusion of other particular languages.

The description of linguistic universals is the goal of the *theory of grammar* (Chomsky, 1965; Katz, 1966). As a linguistic enterprise, the theory of grammar states the conditions to be met by the grammars of individual languages—for example, that each grammar must be transformational. As an account of LAD, the theory of grammar can be offered as a description of LAD's internal structure. Whatever is in LAD is (or will be) in the theory of grammar. By offering the theory of grammar as a description of LAD in this way, we offer a *hypothesis* about LAD's internal structure. It is an empirical question whether or not LAD's structure can be so described.

LAD, of course, is a convenient fiction. The purpose in considering it is not to design an actual machine. On the contrary, the purpose is to isolate certain crucial points in the acquisition of language by real children.

Just as LAD is confronted with a corpus of utterances, some of which are grammatical sentences and some not, so are children. And just as LAD develops a grammar from the corpus on the basis of some kind of internal structure, so do children. Moreover, since children and LAD produce identical grammars from identical corpora, LAD and children must have the same structure, at least within the limits that different children may be said to have the same structure. A hypothesis about LAD is *ipso facto* a hypothesis about children's linguistic capacities. The connection between the theory of grammar and children's capacities for language is straightforward. Each generation of children automatically imposes those features on their language that correspond to their native capacities. Thus, these features appear universally, and the theory of grammar is possible.

What are the universals described in the theory of grammar? Some have to do with phonology. Every language, for example, employs consonant and vowel types and every language has a sound system that can be represented by various combinations of some 15 distinctive features (Halle, 1964).

Within syntax, a number of universals have to do with the deep structure of sentences (Chomsky, 1965). Thus, every language contains the same basic syntactic categories—sentences, noun phrases, predicate phrases, and so forth. Every language adheres to the same basic grammatical relations among these categories—subject and predicate, verb and object, modifier and head, and others. All such syntactic universals are aspects of the deep structure of sentences and all consist of syntactic information essential for the establishment of meaning.

In addition to these universals of the deep structure, every language maintains a distinction between deep and surface structure, and so every language is transformational. Although the transformations of each language are largely, if not exclusively, idiosyncratic, the *types* of relation between deep and surface structure are not. It is through the combination of universal types that transformational uniqueness arises.

These several considerations can be put together into a hypothesis about language acquisition, and in particular into an account of how children develop linguistic abstractions. Linguistic abstractions are described as the universal categories and relations that coincide with children's innate capacities, and they are *made* abstract through the acquisition of transformations. Children acquire a language by discovering the relations that hold between the surface structure of sentences and the universal aspects of the deep structure, the latter being a manifestation of children's own capacities. The interaction between children's capacities and their linguistic environment occurs then in the acquisition of transformations.

Although the number of different transformation rules in any language is large, the number of universal elementary transformations is a mere handful. A particular transformation may consist of a permutation, an addition, a deletion, or some combination of these. There may be a few other types of relation. But, for example, no surface structure contains the elements of the deep structure in reverse order, or in twice their numbers, or every other one—these being possible but nonexistent relations. This constriction to a few relations presumably is one outcome of the species-specific evolution that led to natural language.

We can now understand why the speed of language acquisition seems so great. It is learning of a highly specialized kind. Children apparently have the ability to learn new and often complex combinations of a few transformational relations and they can do this with great efficiency. But such learning, although it is universal among children, has never been studied by psychologists whose interests lie in the process of learning. There is a gap in the technical knowledge of how learning occurs, which neatly surrounds whatever children do to acquire transformations.

We can, at least, discuss the possibility that the universal features of the deep structure are a manifestation of children's capacities. If a language is acquired by discovering the transformational relations that hold between its various surface structures and the universal features of its deep structures, the latter must then be present in children's earliest grammatical speech.[1] Early speech is supposedly free of transformations and therefore should be a direct manifestation of children's capacities. In effect, early sentences should be the universal part of the deep structure of sentences, but pronounced directly. Evidence related to these conditions is contained in Hirsh's introductory chapter.

1 Grammatical Categories and Hierarchical Sentence Structures

In order to discuss the appearance of grammatical categories and hierarchical sentence structures in child language, it is necessary first to consider the so-called basic grammatical relations. My argument will be that the categories depend on the relations. The concepts of subject, predicate, main verb, etc., are all abstract relations, defined in the deep structure of sentences, and are all truly relational, not a fixed property of particular grammatical categories. The first of these characteristics means that the basic grammatical relations cannot be learned from a corpus of sentences, the second means that they cannot be associated with particular words or categories of words.

The subject of a sentence is a NP immediately dominated by S; the predicate of a sentence is a PredP immediately dominated by S. The subject–predicate relation, therefore, holds between a NP and a PredP when both are dominated by the same S. The main verb of a predicate is a V immediately dominated by a PredP, and an object of a verb is a NP also immediately dominated by a PredP. The verb–object relation is defined accordingly. Finally, a modifier is any determiner (Det) immediately dominated by a NP, a head is any N also immediately dominated by a NP, and the modification relation holds between a Det and a N when both are dominated by the same NP. Six grammatical relations do not of course exhaust the set of existing relations. Not included are possession and location, for example, which clearly are of significance in child language. However, the linguistic definition of these relations is so far from being settled that a discussion of them, aside from acknowledging their existence and significance, is really not possible.

[1] Except, of course, for the possibility that some aspects of children's capacities may mature later than others. Thus, we expect to find that the nontransformational features of children's early syntax are all described in the theory of grammar, but not that everything in the theory of grammar is present in children's early syntax.

The basic grammatical relations are contained in the theory of grammar. Since the basic grammatical relations are defined in the theory of grammar, according to the hypothesis sketched before, they describe an aspect of children's capacity for language. Since the grammatical relations can be consistently defined only in the deep structure of sentences, they are beyond the reach of any linguistic experiences a child can have. Since the relations are thus abstract, no matter what concrete interpretation is correlated with them (e.g., actor–action with subject–predicate), the correct association of surface structure and abstract deep structure is also beyond the reach of experience. The gist of the claim that the basic grammatical relations describe children's innate abilities is the following. Two words—for example, one classified as a noun and the other classified as a determiner—*inevitably* comprise a particular constituent—in this case a NP if they interact meaningfully. Conversely, if two words are understood by a child as standing in a particular grammatical relation in adult speech—for example one word modifying the other—one word is *inevitably* classified as a N and the other as Det. Each of the basic grammatical relations thus imposes a rigid constraint on the classification of words whenever a child expresses or comprehends meaning. A hierarchical arrangement of sentences automatically results.

Evidence exists that the basic grammatical relations are honored in children's earliest patterned speech, if not before. One of Brown and Bellugi's (1964) subjects, for example, constructed all his early utterances so as to conform to the basic grammatical relations (McNeill, 1966) even though there was no way to discover these relations in his parents' speech. Similar observations have been made of children exposed to Russian (Slobin, 1966a, in press a) and Japanese (McNeill, 1968). Young children apparently manifest similarities to one another in spite of diverse linguistic experiences, and do so in a part of syntax relevant to the deep structure of sentences. One is led to believe that the similarities exist because the basic grammatical relations reflect innate linguistic abilities, which emerge early and are common to all members of the species [cf., Bruner, Olver, Greenfield, *et al.* (1966) for some discussion of this possibility].

According to the argument proposed here the hierarchical arrangement of speech is inherent in the ability of children to comprehend and express meaning. Of somewhat greater obscurity, however, is the way in which the categories related by the basic grammatical relations are themselves elaborated in development. We must consider at least two hypotheses—differentiation and feature-assignment—each suggested by different observations of children's early speech. Feature assignment is the more general hypothesis, but both hypotheses are consistent with the preceding discussion of the basic grammatical relations. They differ only in what is supposed to be the origin of the categories related by the basic grammatical relations—a hierarchy of grammatical categories or a set of basic syntactic features.

An instrument in children's development, all children have, at first a simple di- or trichotomization of their vocabulary into grammatical classes. Typically one or two pivot (P) classes are combined with an open (O) class, resulting (for one child) in such sentences as *bandage on, blanket on, fix on*, etc. The distinction between P and O reflects a genuine grammatical invention by a child. Words from the P class rarely stand alone in a child's speech but words from the O class often do so. The constraint on the occurrence of P words indicates that they have been organized in a novel way since before the P–O distinction is drawn all words have the privilege of occurring alone—necessarily, since all utterances at this point consist of single words. The interpretation of the grammatical invention, however, is something less than clear.

On the one hand, there are observations of the following kind. The early sentences of one of Brown and Bellugi's (1964) subjects appeared to be organized around a P class that contained the articles (*a, the*), two demonstratives (*this, that*), two possessives (*my, your*), various adjectives, and the words *other* and *more*. These are the adult categories; for the child, the words were all pivots. The process of development beyond this point was differentiation: first the articles were removed and used in unique contexts, then the demonstratives, then the possessives and finally the adjectives, leaving behind a few words in a residual P class. In five months, five grammatical categories had emerged from a single heterogeneous ancestor class.

In order for development to have followed such a course the original P class must have been "generically appropriate," i.e., based on distinctions that later proved to be correct when differentiation actually took place (McNeill, 1966). Brown and Bellugi's subject, for example, placed both the articles in his P class; he did not have one in the P class and the other in the O class. Similarly, every adjective (about a dozen) then in his vocabulary was classified P, none was classified O. His P class contained every available member of several adult classes, even though these classes were not yet themselves recognized in the child's grammar.

I have suggested elsewhere (McNeill, 1966) that generic classification and the differentiation it supports reflects the existence of a hierarchy of grammatical categories, the more superordinate layers of which are universal, the more subordinate layers of which are the idiosyncratic refinement of the universal categories, for each language. (Such a hierarchy, of course, is not the same as the hierarchy associated with the basic grammatical relations—despite the similarity of terminology.) The existence of a universal hierarchy of categories would explain not only differentiation in the development of grammar but also some aspects of the interpretability of children's speech by adults.

Differentiation based on such a universal hierarchy of categories would result from classifying words into ever more subordinate divisions of the hierarchy. The initial division, for example, might be between modifiers and the words they modify. The outcome would be a P and O class. The next division might be between words that modify count nouns and words that modify all nouns. The outcome would be to remove the indefinite article from the P class. And so forth, further subdivisions being made on a comparable basis. Such an account fits Brown and Bellugi's subject well enough. However, a basically different view, reflecting a basically different conception of the origin of grammatical categories, can be proposed and may be closer to the truth. As noted above, differentiation as a process of development presupposes that a child's initial grammatical categories are generically appropriate. The P class, for example, must contain every current example of the adult grammatical classes later to be formed out of it. However, not all children arrange their vocabulary in this way. According to Slobin (1966b), one of Miller and Ervin's (1964) subjects located adjectives in both the P and O classes, which makes differentiation of the adult class of adjectives impossible. In the case of this child a form of reclassification had to occur instead, since the P-adjectives and the O-adjectives both had to be dislodged in order to develop the adult category of adjectives. One of McNeill's (1965) Japanese subjects showed the same initial arrangement—adjectives in both the P and O classes. The same phenomenon, inconsistent with differentiation as a mechanism of development, but appearing in the speech of children exposed to utterly different languages, suggests that something basic has been missed. We would like to have a hypothesis broad enough to cover children who differentiate primitive grammatical classes as well as children who reclassify them. In fact, such a hypothesis can be developed from the remarks already made about the basic grammatical relations.

Let us take into account a fact not recognized before. Whenever a child places a semantic interpretation on a sentence heard in parental speech, he may in addition assign syntactic features to the words of the sentence—i.e., construct a dictionary entry for some or all of the words, using his understanding of the sentence as a source of information. What features might a child employ? A natural source exists in the categories already organized hierarchically by means of the basic grammatical relations.

Note that it is not important to assume that a child makes an assignment of features on every occasion that he understands a sentence in parental speech, or that he understands all of a sentence when he does make an assignment of features. It is only necessary to assume that when a child does understand part of a sentence, he does so by means of relations among some or all of the categories S, PredP, NP, etc. This assumption is of course fundamental to the entire discussion of child language presented here, so making it again introduces no special complications; on the contrary, doing so provides further motivation for making the assumption in the first place.

How might an assignment of features take place? Syntactic features indicate either the category to which a word belongs or the contexts in which the word can appear (Chomsky, 1965). For example, *boy* is a member of the category N and can appear after a determiner. We can represent its dictionary entry then as [+N, +Det____], the dash indicating the position occupied by *boy*. At some point children must begin to compile dictionary entries like this. My suggestion is that they begin with the basic syntactic categories of the grammar, i.e., N, Det, NP, V, VP, and S. If a child understands *The ball hit the window*, he will necessarily have organized it in terms of the following phrase marker,

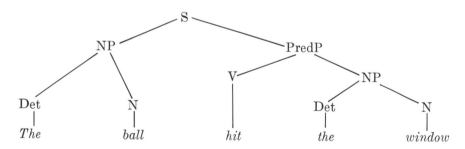

Each word in the sentence could potentially be classified according to the position occupied in this structure. For example, *ball* could receive the feature [+N], that being the category to which it is assigned by its role as the subject of the sentence and it could be given the contextual features [+Det____, +____PredP], these being the environments of *ball* within this phrase marker. In a different sentence, *The man hit the ball*, *ball* could also receive the features [+V____] and [+NP____].

Of the six contextual features made available through elementary phrase markers a particular child at a particular time may use every feature or any subset of them. The most elementary method would be to start with just one feature and classify all appropriate words in terms of it. A slightly more complicated method would be to use two or more features but classify words disjunctively, assigning no more than one feature to any word. A still more complicated method would be to use two or more features and to classify words conjunctively, assigning every appropriate feature to every word. The different methods would correspond to different levels of understanding by a child.

These considerations apply both to the generically appropriate P class of Brown and Bellugi's subject, and to the other children's cross classi-fication of adjectives. Regarded as a devotee of feature assignment, Brown and Bellugi's subject was using the most elementary method mentioned above—classifying words in terms of just one feature set. The feature set was [+Det, +____N] and it automatically led to a generically appropriate classification of articles, adjectives, possessives, demonstratives, and determiners. A classification of P words as [+Det, +____N] also accounts for the adult intuition that the child's sentences at first often involved modification, as it is through the modification re-lation that the feature set [+Det, +____N] becomes available.

Whenever a child employs just one feature as a basis of classification the outcome will be generically appropriate. But when a child employs two or more features, either disjunctively or conjunctively, the outcome will not be generically appropriate. Suppose, for example, that a child disjunctively classifies words in terms of [+____N] and [+NP____], that is, in terms of modification and predication (for convenience we use only the contextual features). Some words can be classified only [+____N]—articles, for example. Others can be classified only [+NP____]—verbs, for example. Adjectives, however, can be classified both ways: [+____N] in *the red ball* and [+NP____] in *the ball's big*. As long as these two features are applied disjunctively, some adjectives will be placed in a category with the articles, possessives, demonstra-tives, and determiners, whereas other adjectives will be placed in a second category with common nouns and verbs. Adjectives will thus be cross classified. From this point of view Ervin and Miller's and McNeill's subjects were classifying disjunctively, using the two features [+____N] and [+NP____]. One observation in support of such an analysis comes from the actual composition of the O class in both cases. Besides adjec-tives the O classes of these children contained nouns and verbs but nothing else. Nouns and verbs, of course, are the other two adult classes that could receive the feature [+NP____] within simple phrase markers.

Eventually children come to classify conjunctively, in the case of adjectives, both [+____N] and [+NP____] are assigned to every word. This step would lead to differentiation for Brown and Bellugi's subject and to reclassification for Ervin and Miller's and McNeill's subjects.

Notice that while the ultimate basis of a correct assignment of features is the correct comprehension of the meaning of parental speech, there is no guarantee from the process here considered that a child's comprehension of adult speech will be correct in all cases, nor even in any cases. Children may well differ in how much they correctly understand. Whatever meaning a child does place on an adult sentence, however, must be organized in terms of the basic grammatical relations—this is the substance of the claim that these relations are a reflection of innate predispositions. Consequently, any misconstrual of parental meaning will lead to an incorrect reconstruction of the order of arrangement of categories in the adult language. For example suppose that a child understands *The man hit the ball* to mean what in adult English would be rendered *The ball hit the man*. An ambiguous extralinguistic situation could lead to this kind of confusion. Given such a misinterpretation a child *must* then organize the total sentence as,

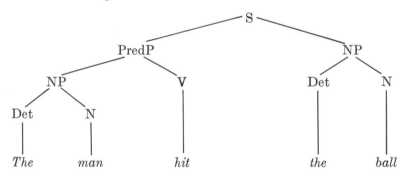

and draw the incorrect conclusion (for English) that predicates precede subjects in sentences. A child who misunderstands parental speech in this way should then utter sentences backwards for a time. Something of the kind appears to have happened to Braine's (1963b) subject described in Slobin's chapter (cf. Table 1).

The P class for Braine's subject contained adjectives (*Big, more, pretty*) and a possessive pronoun (*my*). In these respects, his P class was the same as the P class of Brown and Bellugi's subject, and these words presumably were marked [+____N]. However, the P class of Braine's subject also contained *allgone, byebye, see, night-night,* and *hi*. We cannot tell from Braine's account if these words served as modifiers when combined with words from the O class, and so were also marked [+____N]. However, this function seems quite unlikely for them. A more plausible role, at least for *allgone* and *byebye*, is that of predicate. *Allgone boy* would then correspond to *The boy is allgone*, and *byebye Columbus* to *Columbus is going byebye*. The two P words would be marked [+____NP], the feature for verbs, but the grammatical relation served is predication. So in this instance predicates go *before* subjects. *See* and *night-night* are less clear as to their significance. Expressions like *see car* and *see sock* seem to be verb–object pairs, whereas *see boy* might be either verb–object or predicate–subject. Thus, although *see* is also marked [+____NP], at least some and possibly all of its uses are in relation to objects of verbs, not to subjects of sentences. *Night-night* may be like *allgone*, as in *Night-night mommy*, meaning that mother is going to bed. Or *night-night* may be like *hi*, that is, not a verb at all, but some kind of salute, meaning that the child is going to bed.

Looking only at the reasonably clear cases of *allgone, byebye,* and *see,* we find that two different grammatical relations result in identical featural markings—all are [+____NP] but the first two are related to subjects and the third is related to objects, at least some of the time. Pivot–open sentences thus present an ambiguity in grammatical function. Although we do not know what phrase markers were actually available to Braine's child at the earliest stage, the most elaborate possibility is the following:

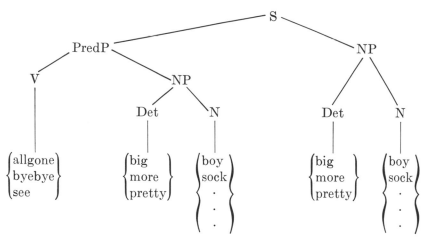

The analysis just given, of course, merely shows how the P class of Braine's subject can be interpreted on the lines established above. It has no independent justification. To support the interpretation, we require information on the child's intended meaning for such expressions as *allgone daddy, see daddy,* and *see sock,* information that is difficult to obtain in general and not available at all in this case.

However, note that in regarding *allgone, byebye,* and *see* as marked [+ NP] but as playing different grammatical roles, we at least make an intelligible claim about the child's linguistic abilities. The opposite interpretation that the child's sentences are derived directly from adult models—ascribes thoroughly mysterious powers to the child, asserting in effect that what he does is beyond explanation. A sentence such as *allgone sock* has no direct model in adult speech, and it must therefore explain the fact that a novelty of some kind has occurred. On the analysis given above the novelty is a misconstrual of the order of constituents in English and arises from the inevitability of expressing meaning, including mistaken meaning, in terms of the basic grammatical relations. The alternative analysis assumes that the child constructed *allgone sock* from superficially homogeneous examples found in parental speech—*Remove the sock* or *Burst the balloon*—and uses it to express a novel meaning. The child has invented either a new word order or a new meaning. The assumption that children have the ability to create esoteric meanings is to abandon hope for explaining linguistic development altogether. It should therefore be the last hypothesis we adopt.

I have considered two distinct hypotheses about the origin and development of children's grammatical classes. One hypothesis is that they arise from a universal hierarchy of grammatical categories, and the other that they arise from syntactic features themselves derived from the basic grammatical relations. On the evidence currently available the second hypothesis is the better supported. It accounts for differentiation and reclassification as the two forms of development so far observed and makes quite specific claims about the interconnection of semantic interpretation with the grammatical forms of child speech. It is advantageous on the double grounds of comprehensiveness and specificity. In addition, it corresponds more closely to the analysis that has been adopted for adult grammatical competence (Chomsky, 1965) and so accounts for the beginnings of the adult system in a natural way.

Apart from the relative merits of these two hypotheses, however, there is a general observation that supports either of them against any weaker hypothesis. The observation is that children's speech is at first semigrammatical in the technical sense of a generative grammar (Chomsky, 1964) and that development consists of a reduction of such semigrammaticalness. The observation is based on the fact that adults can judge which of two telegraphic sentences was earlier in development solely on the grounds of relative grammaticality, just as adults can tell that *Golf played aggressive* is less grammatical than *Golf played John* (McNeill, 1966). Under the differentiation hypothesis a child's development of grammatical classes and an adult's judgments of grammaticality both relate sentences to different levels in a hierarchy of categories. The two kinds of performance come together because they rely on the same hierarchy. Under the feature-assignment hypothesis, adult's judgments of grammaticality and children's development of grammatical classes both depend on the stock of syntactic features. The two kinds of performance come together because they share the same features.

The previous sections have all had to do with one part or another of the deep structure of sentences. We turn next to transformational structure, and to the miniscule amount that can be said of its development.

2. The Emergence of Transformations

It is in this aspect of the acquisition of language that children bring their intrinsic grammar into accord with the grammar of their native language. It is here, accordingly, that the interaction between a child's innate linguistic capacities and the corpus of speech he receives from his parents takes place. Moreover, it is through the acquisition of transformations that children come to produce linguistic abstractions.

There are several reasons, therefore, why the acquisition of transformations provides one of the more interesting aspects of the study of linguistic development. Unfortunately, it is also one of the less well understood. No one really knows how a child formulates transformations, or why he does it, or even when he does it.

In terms of the argument advanced previously, the acquisition of a single transformation, itself possibly a complex of elementary transformations, marks the discovery for each particular sentence type of the relation between deep and surface structure. Since the elementary types of possible relations are limited in number, the simplest course of development would be for a child to acquire transformations in a step-wise manner—first noticing one elementary relation, then another, then a third, and so on, until the entire transformation has been reconstructed. However, more complex lines of development are also possible, and, indeed, may be the rule; the development of negation will be instructive at this point.

First, however, I shall discuss morphological regularizations. Consider a child who says *foots* instead of *feet* or *digged* instead of *dug*: he makes two rather straightforward contributions to psychological theory. One is that the imitation and practice of incorrect surface forms is irrelevant to the acquisition of transformations, at least in these cases

of morphology, and the other is that transformations themselves require
no practice to enter grammatical competence. Let us consider the imitation of surface forms first.

Imitation could play a role in language acquisition by introducing
novel forms into a child's grammar. For example, a child who does
not yet inflect verbs for the progressive aspect might first use -*ing* by
imitating such sentences as *Your nose is dripping, Adam* (once imitated
the relation between -*ing* and base forms could be noticed, perhaps
through trial and error—trying -*ing* first with one deep structure and
then another and checking to see which pairings are well received. The
objection to this account is simple. Rather than absorb novel forms by
imitating them, children reduce imitated forms to the current level of
complication of their grammars (Ervin, 1964). A child not yet producing
the progressive aspect would imitate the relevant part of *Your nose
is dripping, Adam* as *nose drip,* not as *nose dripping.* There are circumstances when imitation is grammatically progressive, but these are special cases and do not reflect a general didactic role for imitation (see
McNeill, 1966, and Slobin, 1967). Thus a child's imitations, if they have
any reinforcing effects, must be reinforcing the wrong things. I conclude
they have no reinforcing effects.

Moreover the successful acquisition of a transformation apparently
requires little or nothing in the way of overt practice. The evidence
for this remark is summarized in Slobin's chapter. In the case of both
the past-tense inflection of verbs and the plural inflection of nouns,
children initially produce the correct strong forms (*dug, feet*), then
adopt the weak forms (*laughed, feets*), while at the same time losing
the strong forms (*digged, feets,* or *foots,* instead of *dug, feet*). The
strong forms, being frequent in adult speech, could be acquired at first
as independent vocabulary. However acquired, they become frequent
in the speech of children also, and so receive a good deal of overt
practice. When the correct strong forms disappear and the incorrect
weak forms emerge we know with certainty that a child's practice with
surface forms has little or no effect on his acquisition of transformations,
a conclusion reached in the preceding paragraph. The converse fact,
that the weak verb and noun inflections appear everywhere after little
or no overt practice, favors the belief that a child does not require
many pairings of abstract base and overt surface forms in order to reconstruct a transformation. Indeed, the establishment of a connection may
be entirely covert, as Ervin (1964) concluded. The evidence, at any
rate, is that surface forms appear in a child's speech only when *already*
related to base forms—i.e., only when already capable of receiving a

semantic interpretation via deep structure. Thus, the possibility of overtly practicing a form depends on having acquired it.

We turn next to the acquisition of negation in English. The events here are complex and rich. Slobin, following Bellugi (1964), traces the development of negation through four stages. Since the four stages reveal different phenomena, they will be discussed somewhat out of chronological order: First, Stage 1, then Stage 4, and finally Stages 2 and 3.

The negative sentences of Stage 1 are all based on the schema NEG + S or its reverse, S + NEG: *No singing song, No sit there, No David fun play, Wear mitten no.* In every case a negative element is affixed to an otherwise affirmative sentence, the internal "structure" of which is left undisturbed.[2] As Slobin notes, these sentences are remote from the available adult models, so we cannot expect to account for them as simple deviations from adult speech; instead, a different principle seems to be operating.

The deep structure of a negative sentence in English is built on the schema NEG NP PredP (Klima, 1964), in which NEG falls outside the boundaries of the rest of the sentence. One hypothesis about this location of NEG is that it reflects an aspect of children's capacities for language—an ability to deny a proposition by attaching a "minus sign" to the proposition denied. On this hypothesis the location of NEG describes an aspect of the linguistic predispositions of children, and should therefore be duplicated in the linguistic descriptions of other languages. It does appear also in Japanese (Kuroda, 1965) and Russian (Slobin, 1966a, in press a).

Assuming that sentence-external NEG is a manifestation of children's capacities, then all children must learn to relate this schema to the particular surface structure taken by negative sentences in their native language. Until these relations have been acquired, however, negation will be directly patterned on the basic schema. Hence, the negative sentences of Stage 1: Stage 1 occurs before any of the transformations involved in English negation have been acquired and sentences necessarily have the form NEG + S or S + NEG. Moreover, negation of this kind persists, despite changes elsewhere, until a child has acquired an order-changing transformation for negation. Such a transformation is acquired, it turns out, in Stage 3, and sentences like *No drop mitten* then disappear. In line with the hypothesis presented in this paper we

---

[2] Recently, Bloom (1970) has challenged this interpretation, giving evidence that such sentences are not negative, but rather are affirmative contradictions of previous adult utterances accompanied by anaphoric negation. It is not yet clear whether this interpretation can be extended to Bellugi's data.

would say that the schema S + NEG has been made abstract. Early
negation in the speech of Japanese children also takes the form of
S + NEG (McNeill & McNeill, 1968), and as Slobin notes, so does
early negation in the speech of Russian children. We have recently
begun observing the speech of a little boy acquiring French and his
negative sentences adhere to this schema also.

In Stage 4 of Bellugi's analysis there are sentences like *He can't have
nothing, I can't go nowhere,* and *I never had no turn.* We find even
I don't do nothing with no string. The double negatives result from
use of various negative indefinite pronouns—pronouns based on *no.* In
Stage 3 a few months before, negative sentences employed affirmative
indefinite pronouns instead and took a form like *You don't want
some supper, I didn't see something,* and *You don't want some bottles.*
Beyond Stage 4 are sentences that use affirmative indefinite pronouns—
pronouns based on *any*—which will be well formed with respect to
pronouns when they appear: *He can't have anything, I can't go any-
where,* and *I never had any turn.* The order of appearance of pronouns
in the development of negation is therefore: *some → no → any.* Why
is this order, rather than any of the five other possible orders, followed?

One interpretation is that in the beginning children do not have special
negative pronouns, but rather achieve negative effects by inserting negative operators, such as *don't* and *can't* [called "negative auxiliaries" by
Klima and Bellugi (1966)], into affirmative sentences. Thus *I want some*
is negated in Stage 3 by *I don't want some.* Such a pattern clearly
shows that the pronoun *some* is itself affirmative in Stage 3. Children
can therefore be led to the hypothesis that in English the sign of the
pronoun matches the sign of the sentence. Such a hypothesis would
make negation in Stage 3 (*I don't want some*) unstable and lead naturally to the negatives of Stage 4. In Stage 4 affirmative pronouns appear
only in affirmative sentences (*I want some*) and negative pronouns in
negative sentences (*I don't want none*). What these children have yet
to learn, and it will take them many months, is that in English the
sign of the pronoun of a negative sentence must mismatch the sign
of the sentence: *I want none* and *I don't want any.* The child's initial
solution misses this fact of English by extending the matching hypothesis
of Stage 3, which applies to affirmative sentences, to negation, thus
ushering in Stage 4 by inventing double negation. The child assumes
English is more orderly (and therefore simpler) than it actually is. He
also follows the principle, which according to Jakobson (1969) is universal, that unmarked forms are simpler than marked forms and therefore
occur earlier in development.

The discussion so far has pictured children changing their grammars as if this were a process not itself in need of explanation. We have taken it for granted that, for example, a child would adopt the sign-matching hypothesis in Stage 3, and so push himself into Stage 4. But it is far from obvious why a child should do this. The necessities of communication do not require it, since the negative sentences of Stage 3 convey the concept of negation quite as well as the negative sentences of Stage 4. Indeed, the primitive negative sentences of Stage 1 convey negation as well as the sentences of any later stage. Nor can a desire to please adults account for linguistic change, not at least in the case of the negative pronouns, for a child adopts a form outside his parents' dialect. We must ask, therefore, what makes a child alter his grammar. The events of Stages 2 and 3 suggest a partial answer to this question, and it is to these events that we now turn [for further discussion, see McNeill (1966)].

In Stage 1 there were two forms of negation—one for assertion and one for questions. Neither involved a transformation. In Stage 2 there was a considerable development of negative forms—six different varieties in all—but again, with the exception of imperatives, none appeared to involve transformations. However, the six different categories of negation in Stage 2, one for each of the different situations in which negative forms appear, present a degree of cumbersomeness that may have led to the developments of Stage 3. Only two additional varieties of negation appear in Stage 3. If the system were still categorical as in Stage 2 these changes could be regarded as a further complication. But as already noted, among the developments of Stage 3 is a complete disappearance of sentences built on the schema NEG + S or S + NEG, suggesting that the schema has become abstract and that the transformations involved in English negation have been acquired. Bellugi (1964) found independent evidence that precisely this development takes place in Stage 3. One explanation for it is that the transformations result from the overabundance of special cases in Stage 2. The transformations greatly simplify the grammar. With these relations taken into account there is just one category of negation, associated in different ways to different surface structures, rather than the seven categories of negation that would otherwise have been involved.

We can take the activities of a grammarian as a metaphor of what a child does to acquire a language. The two, child and grammarian, have goals that are in part the same. Both want to reconstruct the competence of the speakers of a language—the grammarian to describe it, the child to acquire it. Just as a grammarian uses the criterion of overall simplicity to justify the introduction of particular transformational rules, so a child may be guided by considerations of simplicity to devise the same rules. In both cases transformations achieve economy and economy is the guide. The principle of economy was invoked previously in our discussion of the negative pronouns of Stage 4, and before that in our discussion of morphology. Whatever else motivates linguistic change in children this principle would seem to be one major source of change.

3. Additional Remarks

The contributors to this volume show some eagerness to sort one another out. Each author emerges from his discussion as unique. I am not sure what this says about psycholinguistics, but it seems to reveal an ethologically interesting sense of territoriality among psycholinguists. I will pursue the opposite goal and argue that at least some of the alleged differences among us do not exist.

Palermo remarks that in the original symposium from which this book derives he occupied an extreme position; given that there were only two of us, and that we disagreed, that is of course true. However, Palermo also believes[3] that he has now been moved to an intermediate position through the addition of Staats—somewhere to the left (if I may use this orientation) of Staats and to the right of Schlesinger, who is in turn to the right of me. This left-to-right order of psychologists is based on Palermo's conception of what comprises a "psychological" as opposed to a "linguistic" approach to psycholinguistics. One might dispute his definition of these terms [as, for example, does Bever (1968)], and arrive at a different order. However, as Palermo points out, such disputes require comparing scientific paradigms and probably are beyond rational discussion. I will consider instead another basis of comparing the four contributors (McNeill, Palermo, Schlesinger, and Staats), which does not depend on prior agreement as to paradigm.

The comparison involves nativism. On this dimension, as Palermo agrees, Staats is extreme. However, the extremity may be in a direction different from what a casual reading of Staats leads one to expect. Ervin-Tripp and Slobin (1966) and Palermo (this volume) have pointed out that Staats' (1963) proposals lead to the wrong kind of structure for language. Staats however now emphatically denies the criticism. He tells a story of how someone might utter *The end with the torn shirt runs downfield* to illustrate how embedded sentences are consistent with his proposals. At first glance this is astonishing. Staats offers us what appears to be a contradiction: a finite-state grammar that copes with embedded sentences.

---

[3] As of the time of writing—Editor.

However, there is an explanation, and it is that Staats is a nativist! In fact, he is the outstanding nativist here represented.

Interpreting Staats as a nativist is the only way to understand him. Since Staats presumably does not expect anyone to say *The end with the runs torn downfield shirt,* where a visual stimulus interacts in a slightly different phase relation with an unfolding sentence, it is plain that Staats is arguing that something more abstract than a finite-state grammar can be acquired through the process he describes. If we do suppose that Staats has in mind the acquisition of something abstract enough to account for sentence embedding, then the following quotation can only mean that the set of all possible sentence embeddings is innate and that language acquisition merely is a matter of selecting the member of this set that happens to be used locally:

> It would seem that certain word responses come to follow other word responses because in the spoken and written customs of a language community those words as stimuli occur in that order [Staats, 1963, p. 169].

A child spontaneously produces "verbal behavior" according to this theory, and behavior of the right kind is selected by reinforcement. Since the right kind of behavior has underlying it more than the strings of words a child actually produces, as Staats apparently admits in the case of embedded sentences, it is clear that reinforcement selects a grammar that contains more abstract information than is actually present in the reinforced speech of a child. If we take the structure thus selected to be a transformational grammar, Staats' proposal comes close to and possibly surpasses the "idealization" of language acquisition described by Chomsky (1965):

> A language acquisition device . . . must search through the set of possible hypotheses G_1, G_2, . . . , which are available to it . . . and must select grammars that are compatible with the primary linguistic data [p. 32].

Chomsky does not speculate on the actual method of selecting a grammar. However, Staats does: it is reinforcement. Whenever a sentence has been embedded in accordance with the locally correct innate possibility, the child is rewarded in some way.[4]

On the dimension of nativism, therefore, Palermo remains extreme in the empiricist direction. I judge myself and Schlesinger to be intermediate in this respect, and Staats to be extreme in the direction of

---

[4] Alternatively, Staats believes in preestablished harmony—i.e., nativism on a cosmic scale. It just happens that external events are noticed always exactly at embedding points in sentences. Since such points differ in different languages, Fate would have to control the language community into which each of us is born and the second languages we can learn, as well as the sentences we utter.

nativism. The ordering assumes, of course, that Staats means what he says about finite-state grammars, sentence embedding, and the like.

Faced with the prospect of crediting children with a large balance of a priori structure, a number of psycholinguists have felt an urge to explain it. Explanation is of course commendable, it is the ultimate goal for all of us. However, certain basic distinctions cannot be overlooked if true explanations are to be found and false explanations avoided. Two scholars, in particular, have issued a strong call for limiting explanations to a certain kind, a limitation that makes it impossible to say if the explanations are true or false. It is worthwhile examining the situation closely. According to Schlesinger's chapter the underlying structures of sentences, which in his theory are called input-markers, . . . are determined by the innate cognitive capacity of the child," and he goes on to say, "There is nothing specifically linguistic about this capacity." Sinclair-deZwart (1968) has similarly written that, "Linguistic universals exist precisely because thought structures are universal." Schlesinger and Sinclair-deZwart do not have the same point of view toward language, but with respect to the explanation of linguistic ability their arguments are the same. Both are discussing abstract linguistic structures. The influence of thought in their view is visible in this nether region—in the universal underlying structure of language—and the question raised has only to do with this abstract and universal aspect of language. The question is not whether the structure of thought influences the grammatical forms in a *particular* language [as Sinclair-deZwart (1967) has shown in French], nor of whether there exists an association of linguistic and nonlinguistic abilities in various kinds of deficit [as discussed by Furth (1966), negatively, regarding deafness].

Contrary to the claims just quoted, the abstract structure of sentences cannot be uniformly explained as a reflection of thought in language. They may equally reflect specific linguistic abilities. A distinction must be drawn between at least these two kinds of linguistic universal. It is possible that further divisions will prove useful, which would move us even further from the monolithic situation implied by Schlesinger and Sinclair-deZwart in the statements quoted before. The following distinction will serve as a beginning:

1. *Weak linguistic universals* have as a necessary and sufficient cause one or more universals of cognition or perception.

2. *Strong linguistic universals* may have universals of cognition or perception as a necessary cause, but because a strictly linguistic ability also is necessary cognition is not a sufficient cause.

The empirical content of this distinction is purely psychological. Linguistics has nothing to do with it. Linguistic theory, wherein it is postulated what is universal in language, gives no hint of the causes of linguistic universals. Consider the grammatical categories of nouns and verbs. They appear universally in the underlying structure of language because linguistic descriptions of a transformational type are universally impossible without them. According to the theory of language acquisition described earlier in this paper, linguistic descriptions always contain nouns and verbs because children spontaneously organize sentences in terms of noun and verb categories. As we saw before, there is evidence for this. Now, in addition, we wish to explain this activity of children. If nouns and verbs are weak linguistic universals they have a necessary and sufficient cause in cognitive development. It is not too difficult to imagine how this could come about, at least in general terms. Most theories of cognition provide room for something like the notions of actor, action, and recipient of action, as categories of intellectual functioning available to young children. We might argue that nouns and verbs, if they are weak universals, are the automatic reflection in language of these universal cognitive categories. Because of the need to talk about objects and actions, nouns and verbs appear in a child's grammar. Further syntactic operations, such as concord, are then defined for this distinction. However, if nouns and verbs are strong universals an additional linguistic ability is necessary besides the cognitive categories of actor, action, and recipient of action. The cognitive universals might be necessary but they are definitely not sufficient to cause the appearance of nouns and verbs in child grammar.

The essence of the strong–weak distinction is the psychological status of linguistic notation. Do the linguistic terms "noun" and "verb" refer to universal processes of cognition, which are given special names in the case of language, or do "noun" and "verb" refer also to specific linguistic processes, with an independent ontogenesis? Does cognition automatically lead to expression or does it require the boost of a specific linguistic ability? No way exists to prejudge this question; there is no consistent answer. The question of whether the structure of thought influences the structure of language therefore necessarily remains open. It never can be closed. The only way to proceed is to raise the question for each linguistic universal in turn. Moreover, there is no reason to suppose that a proper investigation will always lead to the same answer with every universal. It is not inconceivable that language is a mixture of weak and strong universals. In fact, I believe the structure of language is spotty in just this way, for the following reason.

As an example of how the distinction between weak and strong universals can be approached, consider an observation recently reported by Braine (1971). He taught his two-and-a-half year old daughter two made-up words, the name of a kitchen utensil ('niss') and the name of walking with the fingers (seb). The child had no word for either the object or the action before she was taught niss and seb. Neither word was used in a grammatical context by an adult, but the child used both in the appropriate places. There were sentences with niss as a noun, such as *that niss* and *there niss*, and sentences with seb as a verb, such as *more seb* and *seb Teddy*. More important in the present context there were sentences also with niss as a noun, *that niss* and *there niss*, but none with niss as a verb. The asymmetry suggests that verbs are weak universals and nouns strong. Association with an action is necessary and sufficient for a word to be a verb but some additional *linguistic* property can make a word into a noun. Association with an action does not block the classification. The situation is not as neat as we might like, however, for association with an object also is sufficient for a word to become a noun. We should further subdivide linguistic universals into weak, strong, and "erratic" types. An erratic universal is one in which the linguistic universal has two sufficient causes and therefore no necessary ones. Both the cognitive category of an object and a linguistic ability can cause a word to become a noun.

It is worth pointing out in passing that by distinguishing among linguistic universals according to causes we narrow the range of speculation over the origins of language. Only strong and erratic universals are the result of the evolution of linguistic abilities. Weak universals have a different history.

To conclude, I would argue that no progress can be made in the explanation of linguistic universals unless we observe these basic distinctions among types of universals. Attending to them opens the way to understanding man's biological endowment for language. But sweeping remarks, that all universals of language are in reality universals of cognition, cross the line separating science and dogma.

On Learning to Talk: Are Principles Derived from the Learning Laboratory Applicable?*

DAVID S. PALERMO

Pennsylvania State University
University Park, Pennsylvania

Let me begin by confessing that I feel a little bit like the monk in the monastery attempting to determine the number of teeth in the mouth of a horse without ever having seen a horse. While the research in which I have been engaged for the past several years has involved the study of children dealing with problems involving words, none of the work which I have been doing would be considered a study of language acquisition. As a matter of fact, all of the research which I have published has involved children who have long since acquired the basic grammar of the language and only recently have I begun to work with children below the fourth grade. Thus, the things which I have to say will be based, for the most part, upon principles which have more or less substantial evidence from laboratory work which, it is assumed, may have some relevance to the topic at hand while never directly tested in connection with that problem. I am highly likely to behave as the child and overgeneralize where it is inappropriate but, as in the case of the child, I expect that additional data will quickly correct me.[1]

* The writing of this paper was supported by a Public Health Service research career program award HD-28, 120 from the National Institute of Child Health and Human Development. The paper was written in connection with research supported by Grant GB 2568 from the National Science Foundation. The constructive suggestions of Charles N. Cofer are gratefully acknowledged.

[1] In light of additional research evidence as well as arguments presented in this volume and elsewhere, the author has changed his theoretical position from that which he held in 1965 and which is presented here. The reasons for changing as well as the author's present orientation are presented in D. S. Palermo, Research on language acquisition: Do we know where we are going? In L. R. Goulet and P. B. Baltes (Eds.), *Life-Span Developmental Psychology: Research and Theory.* New York: Academic Press, 1970.

I take comfort from two facts: first, I was invited to make this fanciful theoretical flight by those who have studied language acquisition *per se* and second, the data are meager. In fact, ten years ago a book such as this would have been ridiculous because the monumental efforts of collecting language acquisition data from very young children by the discussant, Ervin-Tripp and her colleagues (Miller & Ervin, 1964), Brown and his colleagues (Brown & Fraser, 1963) and Braine (1963b) were not available until quite recently. Furthermore, the linguistic theory advanced by Chomsky (1957), which has acted as an accelerating catalyst to the work in this area, was equally unavailable. The systematic data collection efforts of these persons has advanced us a long way, but it is clear that we must move ahead with caution when we consider that we have extensive data on but a handful of children most of whom come from relatively rich linguistic environments. It is trite but true that we have progressed considerably from the anecdotal data to which we were limited less than ten years ago, but we have a great deal to do before we can have much confidence in statements which we make about language acquisition.

Nevertheless, it is apparent that the data in hand show some remarkable regularities across children. Slobin, in the initial chapter in this volume, has pointed out but a few of these regularities. There is no one who would argue that there is no system to the language which we use, although most of us can not verbalize many aspects of the system, but I am sure that most persons are surprised at the regularities which have been found in the initial efforts of the child to acquire the system regularly presented to him by the various sources of language input available to him. It is certainly true that all of the utterances of the child do not show discoverable regularities, but the fact that large portions of the language of a small group of children can be shown to follow similar patterns is a finding of considerable importance and demands some theoretical accounting.

Before attempting to advance some theoretical guesses, and they can be no more than guesses for that is as close as we can get to explaining descriptive data without any experimental manipulation of the variables considered important, I would like to take a few pages to present some background relevant to the hypotheses which I want to apply to the data that have been presented.

While the study of language acquisition, or learning, has a pitifully short scientific history, the laboratory study of verbal learning and verbal behavior has been productive over a considerably longer period of time. It seems to me that some of the experimental findings derived from this work, while far from providing a comprehensive account of language acquisition, may have a bearing upon, and provide some clues to, the understanding of how a child learns to talk.

The major efforts of those working in this area have been devoted to the examination of variables which influence paired-associate learning. While the study of serial learning and other verbal learning problems devised to examine specific phenomena have been employed, much of what we can say about verbal learning comes from the paired-associates problem. In this learning problem, the subject is faced with the task of associating a set of stimulus–response pairs generally composed of word, or word-like items. He is presented, one at a time, with a series of verbal stimuli arranged in a number of random orders, to each of which he is to learn to give verbal responses arbitrarily paired by the experimenter with the stimuli. In most cases, the subject has had no previous experience with the items as pairs. Thus, paired-associate learning, by the contiguous presentation of stimulus and response, involves the establishment of associative relationships between two previously unassociated items such that the functional aspects of the stimuli come to call out, elicit or lead to the responses paired with them. Characteristically the subject learns the list over a series of trials without making many overt errors, i.e., the subject tends not to respond at all until he is at a point of being reasonably sure that when he makes an overt response it will be the correct one.

It is clear from several studies (e.g., Underwood, 1963; Jenkins, 1963; Jenkins & Bailey, 1964) that it is necessary to point out that the associative relationship acquired is between the functional stimulus and the response. The subject does not necessarily use the stimulus that the experimenter presents, at least not all of it. This, of course, relates to an old problem for psychologists concerning the definition of the stimulus (Spence, 1956). In any case, it is the most salient or meaningful characteristics of the environmentally presented, or potential, stimulus which will be the functional, or effective, stimulus for the subject, if those characteristics will allow learning. Thus, the subject selects from his environment specific stimuli to which he responds. The less salient or meaningful the stimuli for the subject, the more difficulty he is likely to have in learning the associations required.

Turning to the response side of the paired-associate task, we find that, here too, performance is affected by the characteristics of the material presented to the subject. The rate of acquisition is clearly a function of the amount of past experience with, or meaningfulness of the responses (e.g., Noble, Stockwell & Pryer, 1957; Palermo, Flamer, & Jenkins, 1964). In fact, the data would suggest that response meaningfulness is more potent in terms of its influence upon rate of learning than

stimulus meaningfulness (Mandler & Campbell, 1957). It should be
pointed out, in addition, that Underwood and Schulz (1960) have suggested, and the data seem to bear them out, that there are two phases
in the learning process: a response learning phase and an associative
phase. The subject must first discover the pool of items to be acquired
and be able to recall these items, and then he can proceed to the task
of associating a particular response with a particular stimulus. Furthermore, it should be noted that there is considerable evidence to support
the contention that when a subject is required to learn to make a response to a stimulus, he is learning, at the same time, what the stimulus
is for that response, i.e., the establishment of the traditional S-R associative connection involves learning an R-S connection as well (Murdock, 1956; Palermo, 1961).

The study of paired-associate learning, however, is not limited to single
list learning and the studies of multiple list learning in which associative
relationships are established among multiple stimuli and response across
lists are of greater relevance to this discussion (Jenkins & Palermo 1964).
I am referring to the relatively recent, and rapidly expanding, literature
dealing with mediation phenomena. Three basic paradigms have been
used to demonstrate the mediation effect within the paired-associate
situation.

The first paradigm has been referred to as the chaining model. The
subject is required to learn a series of lists of paired words in which
each successive list has as its stimuli the responses of the previous list
and the final list, which is the test for mediation, is composed of the
stimuli of the first list and the responses of the last preceeding list.
Thus, in the three stage paradigm, the subject learns A–B followed
by B–C and mediation is tested on the last list composed of A–C pairs.
It is assumed that learning of the A–C pairs in the final list is influenced
by the mediating B term which links the A and C terms as a function
of learning the previous lists. Thus, the subject learning A–C has acquired a sequential chain of associations from A to B to C. For example,
if the subject first learns to respond to the word "other" with the word
"man" in List 1 and then learns to respond to the word "man" with
the word "car" in List 2, he should have no difficulty in responding
to the word "other" with the word "car" in List 3. It will be noted
that the words "other" and "car" in this example have never occurred
together but, as a function of the implicit or explicit occurrence of the
mediating word "man," there is a chain of associations forming a sequence "other," "man," "car."

The second type of design has been referred to as the response equivalence paradigm. In this case, the subject may be required to learn several

different responses to the same stimulus and, as a result, these responses come to have equivalence in the sense that presenting one as a stimulus will tend to elicit the others as responses. Thus, in the three stage paradigm, the subject learns B–A followed by B–C and then mediation is tested in an A–C list. Again it is assumed that learning the A–C pairs in the final list is influenced by the mediating B term which is associated with both the A and C terms as a function of previous list learning. An example of this paradigm might include the learning of "big"–"boy," followed by learning "big"–"boat" with an expectation that in a third list "boy" and "boat" would be easily associated because, as a function of having learned "big"–"boy" in list 1, "boy" occurs as an implicit response to "big" in List 2 forming a chain from "big" to "boy" to the new response in List 2, "boat." As a function of this chain, established in List 2, the subject has no trouble acquiring something he has already learned despite the fact that "boy" and "boat" have never before explicitly occurred together in the experiment.

Finally, the third type of design is known as the stimulus equivalence paradigm. Here the subject may be required to learn the same response to several different stimuli, i.e., it is quite similar to the response equivalence design except the equivalence is developed on the stimulus side. The stimuli come to have equivalence in the sense that presenting one as a stimulus will tend to elicit the others as responses. In the three stage paradigm, the subject may learn A–B followed by C–B and, as in the previous paradigms, he is tested for mediation on an A–C list. Once again, it is assumed that the B term acts as a mediator. In this case, the occurrence of mediation requires R–S as well as S–R associations during learning of the previous lists. When the A term is presented in the third list it is assumed to lead to the overt or convert occurrence of B as a function of first list learning and the B term will elicit the correct C term because during List 2 learning, backward as well as forward associations were established.

All of these three stage paradigms have received strong experimental support both with adults and with grade school children (e.g., Horton & Kjeldergaard, 1961; Nikkel & Palermo, 1965; Palermo, 1966). Some of the results with children are more impressive than those obtained with adults. In addition, there is evidence to support the mediation interpretation when larger numbers of associative links play a part prior to the mediation test (Russell & Storms, 1955; McGehee & Schulz, 1961). The materials used in these experiments have included words of high and low frequency, trigrams and combinations of these. In many cases the first link in a paradigm has been assumed from word association norms with equally impressive results. Finally, it is clear that the results are not limited to the usual paired-associates task but may be extended to such things as mediation of attitudes, for example (Eisman, 1955).

While the chaining paradigm involves the sequential linking of items, the stimulus and response equivalence paradigms involve a kind of stimulus and response concept formation. In the chaining case, the responses of the first list become associated with the stimuli of that list and are then used as stimuli for a subsequent set of responses which, in turn, may be used as a stimuli for other responses and so on. Breaking into any part of the sequence should allow associations to run off from that point to the end of the chain although the evidence for R–S as well as S–R learning would suggest that associations in either direction might occur. In the case of the stimulus and response equivalence para- digms, however, classes, or conceptual groupings, of stimuli and re- sponses may be developed as a function of the fact that members of the classes have the same privileges of occurrence during acquisition, i.e., in the response equivalence paradigm, for example, a number of different responses become associatively related in a conceptual class because they are all made in the presence of a particular stimulus or set of stimulus conditions. While little is known about the manner in which the subject is able to identify classes of stimuli and responses in such paired-associate tasks, it is clear that some sort of selector mechanism, as Underwood and Schulz (1960, p. 143 ff.) have called it, does operate to delimit the groups of items acquired in such a way that they are not confused with other responses or classes of responses.

In summary then, if we assume that language acquisition is not basi- cally different from any other acquisition task faced by the human orga- nism, and I would be willing to make that assumption at this point, these laboratory derived data would suggest that we need to consider a variety of variables when we look at what may be influencing the behavior exhibited by the child as he approaches the performance cri- terion of adult language patterns. We shall certainly wish to examine the characteristics of the stimulus situation, both in terms of contextual cues and linguistic cues, in order to determine the relationships between the functional stimuli among the many potential stimuli available, and the language or verbal behavior observed. We will be interested in the amount of exposure to aspects of the language as it relates to re- sponse integration and meaningfulness prior to the occurrence of overt responses which may or may not be judged as linguistically acceptable. We will wish to determine what are meaningful characteristics of the environmental situation from the child's point of view. We will want to know what the functional stimuli are. We shall be interested in the opportunities for, and evidence of sequential relationships and class or concept formations in the child's behavior since this appears to be a characteristic of language. If these were the only variables of importance it would be most surprising but these may give a start to the analysis and provide the impetus to experimental, as well as descriptive, research on child language acquisition.

Let's look now at the child's acquisition of language and see if these principles can account for any of the observations which have been made. We need, however, to make a few basic assumptions about the child. I will assume that the child is capable of learning relationships between stimuli and responses, i.e., that he can learn. Second, I assume that he can make conceptual generalizations when the stimuli or responses can be grouped on some sort of dimensional or mediational basis. Further, I assume that the generalizations, or concepts, can be subdivided in an hierarchical arrangement and, thus, continually refined. This latter assumption is one for which there are no experimental data of which I am aware, i.e., no one has taken the response equivalence paradigm, for example, and having established equivalence among a number of responses, subsequently arbitrarily divided them into subgroups such that some of the responses are appropriate when the stimuli are presented in one context and others are appropriate when the stimuli are presented in another context. I certainly believe, however, that this is experimentally demonstrable and that the conditions under which varying amounts of interference would occur could be specified. It has been demonstrated, incidentally, that pigeons can learn to make one response to a colored key when the context includes lights on and a different response to that key when the context includes lights off. One final assumption about the child is that he is highly motivated to learn to use the language. Certainly he has far more motivation than the college sophomore working as a subject in the laboratory.

Now let me further assume that when the child does say something, as different as it may be from the adult language, it is accepted by, and frequently communicates to, the adult to whom it may be spoken. I believe that the acquisition of language may be much like the process which Skinner has called shaping, in the sense that initially the parent will accept any efforts the child makes and, as the child shows progress, the requirements for communication become more and more stringent. The motivated child wishes to communicate more precisely and the parent wishes him to do so. It is not a matter of the adult dropping pellets for each correct utterance, but is a matter of achieving a goal of mutual intelligibility.[2] Clearly many of the linguistic exchanges between the parent and child require interpretations on both sides and these interpretations become less and less necessary, or dependent upon contextual cues, as the child approaches the criterion.

Now when the child acquires his first words he probably does so as a function of simple conditioning or paired associate learning. The parent places objects, including himself, before the child and labels them; he frequently indicates observable characteristics of those objects in adjective and verb forms; and he may even do such things as wave the child's hand and say "by-by." Thus, the single word utterances of the child tend to be content words such as "ball," "dolly," "mommy," "big," "go," "allgone," and so on. These are labels and descriptions of objects and events which have clearly observable correlates. Generally the child emits his first word at about the age of twelve months and for six months or so he uses only single word utterances as he torturously builds a small vocabulary. But the objects in the child's environment do things, objects he wants are not always available to him, and he does not always have success with one word in communicating these ideas to those about him. One-word utterances are not enough!

Some of the single word utterances of the child may, however, occur under the same or similar, stimulus conditions. For example, conceive of the environmental conditions in which the child's ball is on a shelf in sight, but out of reach. The child may obtain the ball on the shelf by saying "want," and perhaps pointing, or he may obtain the ball by saying "ball." Sometimes he says "want" and sometimes he says "ball" and both utterances may bring about the desired result, i.e., both are correct responses for the same stimulus situation. We have then the simplest case of response equivalence and the occasion for the occurrence of "want" to elicit "ball" and, thus, the two-word utterance is possible. But "want" may have been used interchangeably with "truck," and "dolly," and "horsie" in which case we have a class of words which go with "want." We have a pivot word "want" and an open class of items which a child may want at one time or another. Thus, the pivot-word–open-class construction may come from the response equivalence paradigm. Once the open class equivalences are established, the child

---

[2] Thus, the child learns that when he says "that flower" it is sometimes misinterpreted, but "that a blue flower" is more frequently responded to appropriately, and when additional syntactic details are added communication is more efficient. The child is not necessarily told (given verbal pellets) that a particular utterance is correct or incorrect. He discovers the syntactic details which allow more precise communication by attaining his desires more frequently and rapidly as he meets more of the criterial requirements.

is capable of generating all kinds of new utterances which he has never heard. Similarly we can imagine the occurrence of many situations, or stimulus conditions, which elicit the same response. For example, when daddy leaves the house, he is "allgone," when the milk leaves the cup it is "allgone," and when the truck disappears under the bed, it is "allgone." A construction of the open class followed by the pivot word may be conceived as derived from the stimulus equivalence paradigm. Again, the child has productive language capabilities because of the equivalences established.[3]

The less frequent open–open class two word construction may arise in much the same manner. The child may see two objects contiguously in the environment and respond by naming as in the two word utterances "man car" or "milk cup," for example. The contiguous occurrence of two objects in the environment would, thus, lead to the occurrence of two-word utterances of the open–open class type. I suspect, however, that the pivot–open and open–pivot constructions of the child are the earliest two-word utterances and that the open–open type of construction comes slightly later as a precursor of three- and four-word utterances.[4] The open–open construction generally involves the omission of the pivot word necessary for communication. Thus, in the construction "man car" the pivot word "in" may be missing, and in the construction "car bridge" the pivot word "under" may be missing if the interpretations assigned to these utterances are correct. The utterance is possible through chaining from open to pivot to open word classes. The difficulty with this interpretation is that for the chain to be established we must assume that the class of pivots acts as the mediator rather than specific words since the pivot words tend to have fixed positions. If we assume that position of a word in an utterance is also a cue, or functional stimulus,

---

[3] It should be pointed out in this context that the theory has little to say about order in the stimulus equivalence and response equivalence paradigms. There is no basis for predicting that "want ball" is any more likely than "ball want" or that "allgone milk" is more likely than "milk allgone." It would be necessary to postulate that the most frequent order apparent in parental utterances such as, "Do you want the ball?" or "The milk is all gone," would increase the probability of "want ball" and "milk allgone." While this hypothesis for the determinant of word order seems to fit this author's best guesses about the frequency of word order in parental utterances and the word order in most of the available examples of children's P–O and O–P constructions, it does not fit the constructions which Braine (1963b) reports for Gregory who used "allgone" as a pivot word in the first position.

[4] Since this paper was written, Braine (1971) has also argued that the open–open construction is a later development and represents a more complicated structure than the P–O and O–P construction.

then the chain from open class first position—pivot class second position to pivot class first position–open class second position allows a chain from open class to open class with the mediating pivotal word position omitted, but implied, in the utterance. Some of the utterances of Steven in Braine's work suggest that the pivot is not completely dropped. Parts of what might be pivot words are uttered by Steven but not in a way which is interpretable (Braine, 1963b).

Before proceeding with an analysis of the three-word utterance, it must be remembered that the child is not developing all of those constructions independently. His parents provide him with a great variety of other linguistic utterances, in addition to the specific lessons about labels, which are correlated with events in the child's environment. Thus, there is a great deal of linguistic stimulation presented to the child (at least in the environment of the children on which we have data.) Looking at it from the child's point of view, there may be a number of salient cues associated with the complex stimulus pattern presented. There are, for example, meaningful lexical items scattered throughout the stimulus pattern, some aspects of the pattern are stressed relative to other aspects, some of the meaningful and stressed items tend to have positional patterns in the utterances, and many of the utterances are correlated with other environmental events. All of these characteristics, and undoubtedly more, surely play a part in determining what the functional stimuli for the child will be and, therefore, which stimuli will influence his linguistic behavior.

The three-word utterance generally seems to take the form of pivot-open–open; open–pivot–open; or open–open–pivot. I think we can assume in each of these cases that initially the child is chaining together sets of words which occurred earlier as pairs of words and as single word utterances. Thus, the child may have uttered "other man" and "man car" which is the arrangement in the three stage chaining paradigm which would allow for the utterance of "other man car" with the mediator "man" overtly present in the utterance. This is a sentence of the type pivot–open–open, but there is no reason to assume that constructions of the type open–pivot–open or open–open–pivot would not be constructed in a similar manner.[5] Furthermore, there is no reason

[5] For example, if "man car" and "other car" are utterances of the child, then "man" and "other" acquire stimulus equivalence making them capable of eliciting each other as well as eliciting "car" and the construction "man other car" is possible. As noted earlier, however, such an explanation alone does not account for the problem of order and, thus, must predict that "other man car" is as likely a "man other car," other things being equal.

to assume that this is a construction with no depth. It may be assumed that the chain of two sets of two-word constructions may be responded to as one pair construction superimposed upon another. If the child could be induced to break the sentence in the "other man car" example into two parts, it would be predicted that he would break it into "other man" and "car" on the assumption that the pivot–open class construction is learned as a unit, and "car" is either a single word utterance or comes from an open–open class construction which is assumed to be a three-word utterance with the pivot word omitted. It is clear that with such constructions and the open class equivalences, all kinds of new words may be inserted into the open class slots to construct new utterances never before heard. The child needs only three open class words and two pivot words to construct 36 three-word utterances, none of which he may have heard as such, although a few of them may have been heard in an expanded version.

Now the child also adds other kinds of lexical items to his utterances. For the most part, the words he uses in his early constructions are labels specifically taught and descriptive words about those labels (adjectives and verbs). These are the stressed words in the adult language which he hears. There are, however, other aspects of the complex linguistic stimuli to which he is exposed and these, too, make a difference in communication, e.g., words such as "a" and "the," descriptive words such as "cowboy" in relation to hat, "blue" in connection with flower and so on. When these words do make a difference, and communication breaks down because they are not attended to, then these words are also stressed in speech. If I say to one of my children "You may have a piece of candy," and he takes a handful, I repeat the sentence putting a different stress on the words involved, "You may have *a* piece of candy." Assuming that these events occur, and we have little basis on which to judge, such experiences will call to the attention of the child the importance of the unstressed words as well as the stressed ones. Furthermore, attention to these items will lead to their appearance in utterances of the child and they will appear according to the rules the child develops through the associative consistencies with classes of words he has already developed. For example, the child may have acquired a stimulus or response equivalence class of words we might label loosely as nouns which he has not as yet differentiated with respect to singular and plural or mass nouns and count nouns. He observes that his parents say "a car," "a toy," and "a dog," all of which are members of his class which we have called nouns. He therefore feels free, at this time, to substitute for "car," "toy," and "dog" other members of his noun class.

Most of the time he will be correct, and even when he says "a busses" or "a milk" I suspect that it is frequently accepted without correction[6] and, on occasion, overtly rewarded because it sounds cute to the adult. This kind of situation is not much different from the difficulty the child has with inflections of verbs for past tense and nouns for plural and possessive. We need only consider the case of the inflection of verbs for past tense since that is the case in which there is the peculiarity of the correct inflection of the past tense of irregular verbs first, followed by incorrect generalization of the regular verb form inflection to the previously correctly formed irregular verbs. In the case of the strong verbs such as "come," "do," and "break," It is clear that these are learned early and I would assume that the past tense form is learned by simple rote. They are frequently used by adult and child making the possibilities for rote-learning feasible. As the child acquires a vocabulary, however, a large number of different words of the verb form are acquired. Once the child attends to the tense markers, we have a stimulus equivalence paradigm arrangement in which the stimuli, the base forms of the verbs, acquire equivalence because the same inflection is used to form the past tense. (There may be other bases for forming such equivalences, semantic ones for example.) Thus, experience with a few members of the regular verbs will lead to generalization of the inflection for all members of the class of which both strong and weak verbs form a part. Again, the fact that the generalization is incorrect part of the time does not seriously impair communication and, thus, is not quickly corrected.[7]

How now does the child learn to negate some of the utterances he may wish to make? The word "no" comes into the child's vocabulary at a fairly early age. He may be taught a meaning of the word very early, long before he utters any words, through straightforward classical conditioning. My sample is small, although not small relative to the numbers of children we are considering here, but all four of our children learned when they were crawling that the word "no" emitted by their parents meant, "Stop what you are doing or about to do." It was taught by the simple method of presenting the conditioned stimulus "no," in the appropriate context, followed very quickly by a noxious unconditioned stimulus such as slap on the hand. Children can, and did, learn

---

[6] Brown (Brown, Cazden, & Bellugi, 1969) reports that parents are not particularly inclined to correct the grammatical errors of the child but rather they are more likely to focus upon the truth value of the child's utterances.

[7] See the Additional Remarks at the end of this chapter for the report of an experimental analogy to this natural observation about the development of inflections (Palermo & Eberhart, 1969; Appendix to this volume).

the meaning of the word quickly and, at later ages, often may be observed using it to direct their own actions as in the case of the child who walks around the bowl of candy on the coffee table saying to himself, "No, no." I am surprised that "no" is not more frequently a pivot word than appears to be the case in the protocols available.[8]

The initial negatives the child learns may be learned by rote as in the case of "no more"; or they may be a case of paired-associate learning of "no" plus one or more word affirmative utterances or an affirmative utterance plus "no" at the end; or it may be a case of "no" being a pivot word with an open class of single or multiple word utterances which may occur before or after it. In the latter alternative, we may have a special case of the pivot–open or open–pivot class utterance in which the word denoting negative is a pivot and the affirmative or declarative type of utterance, regardless of the number of words, composes the open class.

Once the child begins to negate his sentences then both he and his parents may begin to attend to the stimuli which are functional to the communication of negative forms. The parent may have been trying to teach the child this form for some time before the child begins to be concerned with it. The child, for example, says "Candy" (with or without rising intonation) and the parent responds, "You can't have any candy until after supper." If the child then reaches for the candy, the parent is likely to say, "No, you *can't* have any candy." The parent has presented a stimulus–response pair, i.e. "no" plus sentence, for paired-associate learning or the parent has presented the "no" pivot plus open class frame. In addition, however, the parent has placed additional stress on part of the negative sentence to call the child's attention to the fact that "can" plus "'t," or "not" as the case may be, is important and makes this sentence different from the affirmative form. Since the child apparently does not use auxiliaries at this point, the child may be learning that the auxiliary with "'t," or "not," is the important aspect of creating a negative. He is not learning "can *plus* not" but rather, he is learning that a single unit "can't" makes the negative and only later does he learn that there are two, not one, units involved in the utterance. This would be a case of response integration which is inappropriate and, subsequently, the child will have to learn to break the integrated unit into its component parts.

[8] Perhaps the permissive child rearing practices which are currently in vogue have reduced the frequency of "no" as an utterance directed toward children by parents. It might be of interest to determine whether different child rearing practices might influence the use of this word by children and the development of negative transformations in general.

Once the auxiliary negative unit has been recognized as an important feature, or functional stimulus, in the class of negative utterances, it will be used as such. Once again, there are situations in which the child will be correct in his constructions and occasions in which he will not be correct. For example, "No, I can't see you" and "Don't leave me" are grammatically correct utterances, while "I don't sit on Jack coffee" and "Why not cracker can't talk?" communicate but they are not grammatically correct. In the sentence beginning "I don't sit . . ." the child has not acquired the complicated special case, "I am not sitting   " and has overgeneralized from the classes of lexical items he has available to him. In the case, "Why not cracker can't talk?" he has taken a grammatically correct question form, "Why not?" and put it together with a grammatically correct negative-declarative "cracker can't talk" and formed a grammatically incorrect double negative question. While redundancy is clearly a part of the language, this particular case is not acceptable in the criterion language. Thus, we find in the next stage of the child's acquisition of the negative question form that the redundant "not" drops out of the sequence and we get the more grammatically correct "Why cracker can't talk?" He still must learn, of course, the inversion of auxiliary and noun phrase to make this completely correct in terms of the criterion language, ignoring the missing article.

The third phase of the development of the negative appears to be primarily a function of learning which is not specific to the negative. He is now learning intonation contours for sentences and these are applied to negatives as well as other sentence forms. He has now separated the auxiliary from the negative so that he might be predicted to begin to say "can not" now when he only said "can't" prior to this. Indefinite determiners are coming into his language as lexical items and are used in negative sentences as well as in simple declarative sentences. He must learn that with the negative form sentence there are special rules which apply to this class of words, i.e., this is a case of breaking down a response equivalence class which has been overgeneralized so that under the conditions of the negative case another equivalence or subclass equivalence is correct.

The rapidity with which all of these linguistic events which we have been discussing occur has been noted as surprising. I do not agree that it is unusually rapid learning, for I think we frequently underestimate the learning capabilities of a child who is interested in learning. In addition to the high level of motivation, there is a great amount of linguistic stimulation on all sides of the child especially since the advent of TV. Finally, there is a tremendous amount of practice every day in the child's life. I am not particularly impressed that learning of language grammar is achieved in a matter of three or four years.

I have not attempted to analyze each individual instance which has been presented, but I will leave the data at this point and attempt to summarize. We are faced with an array of utterances made by a group of children. Distributional analyses of the arrays of each child show that there are regularities in those data. As with any other array of data in which there are consistencies there are also inconsistencies. We need to account for them all, but our task here has been to see what we can do with the consistencies first and hope that as we do so the apparent inconsistencies will either be revealed as consistent with the theoretical analysis once constructed, or, require modification in the theory.

The theory which I have attempted to apply here is one developed to account for the learning of a variety of behaviors exhibited by the human organism. The emphasis has been upon the concepts of mediation, with particular attention to the development of sequences through chaining and classes through equivalences when consideration is given to the characteristics of the stimulus complex presented to the child and the aspects of that complex which may act as the functional stimuli for him. I have assumed that language learning is not basically different from any other kind of learning except in the complexity of the stimuli presented and responses to be learned. There is little question that the theory is incomplete in its ability to handle the phenomena associated with paired-associate learning for which it was devised. That the theory will not account for all of the data which we are considering here is not surprising, but the fact that it does account for as much as I believe it does is more surprising. But whether the theory adequately handles the data or not is less important, at this point, than the stimulus value it may have for experimental research with both natural language and artificially developed languages. It is in such research that we will find the answers and the basis for reducing the speculative nature of our accounts of how a child learns to talk.

One final point may be relevant. Both the linguist and the psychologist are concerned with the problems of language to which we are directing our attention, but the two disciplines do not have the same goals in mind. A failure to recognize the difference in the directions of the two efforts may lead to confusions which are unnecessary and irrelevant to the goals of either. The linguist, at least the linguist of the generative grammar group, has set as his goal the formulation of a set of rules which will allow the generation, or prediction, of all possible grammatically correct utterances which a native speaker of a language might conceive but no utterances which would be considered grammatically incorrect by a native speaker of the language. Thus, analysis of the language is the primary goal of the linguist with the specified behavior of the native speaker as a check upon the adequacy of the linguistic analysis. From the psychologist's point of view, this is an acceptable, though limited behavioral problem in which the characteristics of a language are analyzed for the purposes of predicting responses of grammatical acceptance of language utterances by a particular population of people.

The psychologist, however, is interested in developing a theory to account for the verbal behavior, among other behaviors, of organisms regardless of the grammaticality of the verbal behavior. The explanation and prediction of all behavior is the primary goal of the psychologist. The grammatical characteristics of the language are of secondary importance in the sense that they may be used primarily as a guide to understanding aspects of the structure of the behavior being observed. The structure which the linguist attributes to the language for the purposes which he has in mind may or may not have any direct bearing on what the organism is doing either when he acquires the language or after having acquired the language, when he utters a statement which may or may not be grammatically correct.

We are attempting here to account for how the child learns to talk. We have been helped considerably in understanding the problem by the linguistic analyses of the rules of the grammar but those rules do not necessarily help us to understand the variables which account for the behavior exhibited by the child. They are rules about language. The rules about behavior may be of quite different sorts.

Additional Remarks

If it is assumed that the position presented by the transformational grammarians represents a new paradigm for psychology, in the sense in which Kuhn (1962) has used the term paradigm in connection with scientific revolutions, then there is little point in persuasive discussion which attempts to argue logically from the orientation of one or another paradigm. Two different paradigms have two different theoretical orientations, two different notions of what are relevant problems for investigation, two different methods of obtaining answers—and there is no continuation from one to the other. Shifting paradigms is, in Kuhn's opinion, a discontinuous process which is afactual in nature and based more upon the *promise* of the new paradigm for the problems poorly handled by the old than upon the adequacy of the new paradigm for all problems of interest. Thus, to argue the adequacies of one paradigm to a person operating within the other paradigm is to present a logical argument which is irrelevant.

Despite this view of the history of science, there appears in the chapters presented here a continuum from a staunch "new" paradigm position represented by McNeill through an intermediate position represented by Schlesinger to an equally vigorous stand in support of the "old" paradigm by Staats. In addition, there appears to be a dimension, which for lack of a better description, seems to relate to the stress placed upon the first two as opposed to the last three syllables in the word psycholinguistic. While it is not necessary for the two dimensions to be correlated, it would appear that McNeill focuses more upon the linguistic while Staats focuses primarily upon the psychological and, again, Schlesinger is in an intermediate position. While the present author was asked to represent an extreme position in the original symposium out of which this book grew, I would like to conceive of myself in an intermediary position on both dimensions: closer, perhaps, than Schlesinger to Staats on the psychology dimension but congruent with Schlesinger with respect to paradigm.

I would like to examine some of the problems associated with the two anchor positions of McNeill and Staats recognizing that in so doing I may speak irrelevancies to both from the orientation toward scientific history taken by Kuhn.

It seems to me that the form of the analysis of language presented by Chomsky and his colleagues (e.g., Chomsky, 1957, 1965; Halle, 1964; Katz & Fodor, 1963) is clearly a great contribution to psychology as well as to linguistics. It has provided psychologists with a handle on the problem of language long pushed to one side for reasons which are historical to psychology as well as to reasons related to the adequacies of previous linguistic analyses for psychology. The problem is to establish how a theory developed in the field of linguistics is relevant to the field of psychology. To reiterate the last point made in my previous comments, linguistic theory is developed to satisfy the criteria of the science of linguistics and not those of psychology. The goals of the two disciplines are not the same and there is no reason to assume that a theory devised for one should be adequate for the other. Thus, it is very surprising, for example, that McNeill should be concerned that the order of emergence of indeterminate pronouns in the child's language acquisition is not the same as the order of derivation of intermediate pronouns in the grammar of English. There is no reason why the linguist's analysis of language should correlate with the child's acquisition of

language. Such assumptions confuse linguistic theory with psychological
phenomena. McNeill seems to make this kind of error in another context
when he states that " . . . the hierarchical arrangement of speech is inherent in the ability of children to comprehend and express meaning . . . ."
To say that sentences are hierarchical is to say that one way of analyzing
them linguistically is hierarchically, but that may not be the way the
organism operates. The three-word utterances of children are hierarchical
because that is the way we analyze them for linguistic purposes but not
necessarily because that is the way the child organizes his behavior. There
is no counter evidence at this point to the notion that advances that
these are merely strings of three words. Two theories lead to two ways of
conceptualization and data alone will give the answers as to which conceptualization is most fruitful. It might be pointed out here that McNeill's
syntactic features analyses of the development of the pivot–open constructions apparent in the initial utterances of children is amazingly reminiscent
of my own discussion in terms of mediation, as well as Braine's theory
of contextual generalization (1963a). The terminology varies as do some
of the derivations but the theory seems little different stripped of the
surface elements. In any case, McNeill seems to have accepted a new
paradigm and his confidence in the theory leads to occasional overstate-
ments [as in the case of indicating that syntax is complete by age four
when Menyuk's data (1963) suggest that even in the first grade at
least syntactic performance, if not competence, is still unstable] and
the occasional confusion of fact with theory in the absence of data.
While aspects of the theory have a great deal of appeal, little is to
be gained by attempting to establish its usefulness in this manner. It
is experimental research on which the theory will be honed.

On the other hand, at the other extreme, Staats does not seem to
come to grips with the complexities of language. He seems to accept
the Markov chain model of sentence formation without responding to
the strong argument which Chomsky (1957) has forcefully presented
against such a model. The arguments for some higher order organization
of language behavior, even if only at the level of rules [less easily con-
ceptualized in S–R terms, see Jenkins & Palermo's (1964) analysis of
the Esper experiments], is rather convincing. In general, the eleven
aspects of language presented by Staats are of concern, but they do
not deal with acquisition or with some of the other problems (e.g.,
ambiguities of semantics and syntax and equivalent meanings of active
and passive sentences) which must be faced by psychologists. Further,
Staats' examples of how learning theory can handle various observations
of child language do not seem entirely convincing. His analysis of "Bread
please" is reasonable within a learning framework but does not appear

equally convincing when examples of actual child utterances are considered. Thus, there is little similarity in his description of the acquisition of this phrase and the utterance "Allgone outside." The theoretical learning analysis necessary to get from parental speech to the child's speech, as Staats presents it, is formidable. The complexity of the problem must be admitted before the principles of learning which may be involved can be developed and applied. His treatment of the negative sentence appears to be another case of oversimplification and convenient ignoring of some of the data, e.g., the double and triple negative in the fourth stage of development. Again, the treatment of the learning of concrete words may be reasonable within a learning framework but application of a similar approach to abstract words such as "fun," "right," and "pretend," or the function words, does not seem as convincing.

In addition, Staats implies that memory span is merely a function of training and that, in principle, a child could be trained to imitate an infinitely long sentence if the associative bonds from word to word had been trained in. While such an argument could be tested, it seems that Staats is using such arguments because he is unwilling to agree that the concept of maturation (or for that matter genetics and/or biology) are relevant to considerations of language. He does pay tribute to the biology of the organism but continually attempts to provide other kinds of explanations to avoid the biological. It seems inconceivable that genetics could have relevance to height, weight, eye color, resistance to disease, and not to behavior. The influences may not be as direct but surely they are there and may be used as a part of a theory of learning without diminishing the effectiveness of the learning theory.

Finally, Staats also oversimplifies the problem of imitation, ignoring some of the linguistically important variables and focusing upon the importance of instructional procedures which parents only occasionally use. It seems reasonably clear that parents do not spend a great deal of time giving instructions in language in any organized fashion such as "Can you say . . . " as Staats argues. In fact, the analyses of Brown (Brown, Cazden, & Bellugi, 1969) suggest that the parent concerns himself more with the truth value of the child's utterances than with the grammatical form which the utterances take. If syntax is learned in the simple manner Staats presents, the child is certainly learning very quickly under adverse learning conditions.

On the other side of the ledger, however, the arguments of a learning psychologist cannot be ignored completely because there are numerous aspects of the data which support a learning interpretation. As Staats points out, there is a variety of learning theories and most are more sophisticated than the Watsonian brand of learning theory which seems too often what the critics have in mind when they attack S-R theory. None of the S-R theories, at the present stage of development, is capable of handling all of the data but some are capable of handling parts of the data. To say that learning has little to do with language acquisition is to ignore the findings that, for example, the syntax of passive sentences is late to be acquired, the acquisition of morphophonemic rules is directly related to the frequency with which the rules appear in the language (Berko, 1958), and additions are made to the lexicon throughout life. In addition, some of the predictions made by Staats from his learning theory can be verified. For example, our data on word associations to the stimulus word "he" support the prediction of Staats that irregular verb responses are more likely and more frequent than regular verbs for children in grades one through four (Palermo & Jenkins, 1966).

Such facts lend support to a learning analysis of language and suggest that to discard learning theory as irrelevant is to "throw the baby out with the bath." Arguments which indicate that the child cannot possibly discover rules from parental input merely admit to ignorance of the relationship between parental language and child language and are not statements of fact. It is certainly not clear what aspects of parental speech are relevant to the child as he attempts to acquire the complexities of the language. It is better to admit ignorance than to push the explanation into an unexplorable pigeonhole and close the door to other possibilities. Certainly there is some relation between input and output, but what that relationship is remains to be discovered by any means feasible.

The rejection of S-R learning theory is peculiar in another sense if one includes the concept formation and mediation literature. In the latter case, I refer to the literature demonstrating mediation in the paired-associate learning task rather than that advanced by Osgood to account for meaning. I do not believe the arguments rejecting the mediation account of meaning have any relevance for mediation in the paired-associate task and it is a mistake to reject all mediation literature on the basis of the presumed inadequacies of one form of mediation theory (McNeill, this volume). In any case, the rejection of this literature seems to be a rejection of the very kind of experimental evidence relevant to understanding language acquisition. It is this literature which deals with the acquisition of rules and the development of abstract categories and examines the influence of rules and categories on other behaviors. The rules studied in past research may not be directly analogous to language but they certainly could be constructed in a manner which would make them so. The present writer (Palermo & Eberhart, 1968) has, for example, used the Esper paradigm (1925) to set up a series of experiments which are analogous to the learning of past tense verb inflection in children.[9] Three experiments were conducted using modifications of the Esper paradigm. Using the study–test procedure, subjects learned 16 paired-associates in which the stimuli were 2-digit numbers and the responses were 2-letter pairs. Each single digit was associated with a letter to form a four-by-four matrix of 2-digit–2-letter stimulus–response pairs. On the study trials the subjects were presented 12 of the 16 pairs in Experiment I, 12 of the 16 pairs plus 4 irregular pairs in Experiment II, and 12 of the 16 pairs plus 2 irregular pairs in Experiment III. In each experiment all 16 stimuli were presented on the test trials. The irregular pairs were presented two or three times as often as the regular pairs in the study trials. The results indicated that the omitted pairs were learned quickly after the rules or regularities of the presented pairs were learned, i.e., the rules were generalized to new instances. The irregular pairs were learned more rapidly than the regular pairs, i.e., the more frequently presented irregular forms were learned first and subsequently the pairs involving a regular rule were learned. Finally, when the regularized rule was learned, after performance on the irregular forms was perfect, it was observed that errors appeared on the irregular pairs and the errors consisted of regularizing the irregular forms. Thus, the performance of college students in this task showed exactly the same characteristics observed by Ervin (1964) in the natural language utterances of children in the acquisition of past tense inflection of verbs.

Whether one wishes to label this research as related to S–R theory or not makes little difference. The point is that it is a start in the direction of understanding rule learning in a laboratory situation with all the controls so impossible in the natural language situation from which we have gleaned so many interesting hypotheses which have spawned theories both S–R and otherwise. It is more comfortable for this researcher to think of these results within a learning framework than in a framework which attributes performance in this task to some innate characteristics of the organism based upon deep structures transformed into surface structures. But this is a personal preference which has little to do with the data and their relation to language acquisition.

No one questions the innate structural differences between the human animal and the rest of the phylogenetic continuum. The central concern is more with the relative importance one wishes to place upon the structure of the organism and the experiences of that organism upon the behavior it exhibits. The fact that S–R theory has had a history of ignor-

---

[9] This research is discussed in greater detail in the Appendix to this volume.

ing the genetic and biological character of the organism is no reason for those who would wish to emphasize those aspects of the organism in the explanation of behavior to cast aside the contributions which S-R theory has made and can make to the understanding of language acquisition. It may well be that language is species-specific, as Lenneberg (1967) has so forcefully argued, but that merely eliminates the possibility that other animals may acquire a language and says little about the learning of language in the human.

Let me close by emphasizing the point that S–R learning theorists of the past have been just as much interested in the mind as any other theoretically oriented psychologist by quoting from an unpublished paper by Spence in which he provided the following definition of psychology:

Psychology is concerned with a certain portion of human experience. From this experience the psychologist constructs what he terms the mind (or covert psychological processes)—a concept or concepts which arise from a peculiar combination of observed facts and the reasoning provoked by their perception.[10]

[10] Although not so explicitly, Spence has made the same point in a number of other places (Spence, 1948, 1956).

Production of Utterances and Language Acquisition

I. M. SCHLESINGER

Hebrew University
and
Israel Institute of Applied Social Research
Jerusalem, Israel

The approach to the explanation of language acquisition which is presented here has been developed on the basis of considerations as to the general nature of a performance model. Accordingly, we shall first attempt to show how the speaker goes about producing an utterance, and only then will an explanation be suggested as to how the child learns to speak in this way.

1. On "Incorporating a Generative Grammar"

Pyschological studies of grammar carried out in the past few years have been instigated by a suggestion which has been repeatedly made by N. Chomsky (e.g., 1965, p. 9), that the speaker–listener "incorporates" a generative grammar. The fruitfulness of this suggestion has not suffered from the fact that (probably intentionally) it is a very vague one. All it does say about a performance model is that one of its components, albeit a very important one, is a generative grammar. The question remains how this component operates.

"Incorporating a grammar" might be taken as a description of linguistic performance. According to this view, there exists an analogy between the psychological processes of the speaker-listener and a generative grammar. The processes by which the speaker produces an utterance are in some way isomorphic to the rules by which the grammar generates the corresponding sentence.[1] The listener, likewise, construes what he hears by producing an utterance which matches with the input. This

---

[1] Following Bar-Hillel (1966), the term "utterance" will be used for the linguistic output of human speakers, whereas the term "sentence" will denote the abstract structures described by grammar, of which utterances may be a realization.

may be taken as the strongest version of Chomsky's statement,[2] and there may be several weaker ones. For instance, the listener might be said to interpret an utterance by means of processes which are analogous to working "from bottom-to-top" of a phrase structure tree. This is in itself rather unlikely, but it is a possible explication of "incorporating a grammar". The "machinery" provided by the generative grammar is there, but it is put to use in a different way.

There is an important difference to which enough attention has not been paid—between the way a grammar generates a sentence and the way a speaker produces an utterance. According to the current conception of generative grammarians, a grammar is a device that starts from the symbol S, for "sentence," and by using rewriting rules and transformation rules ends up with an output string of words (To be exact, phonological rules must also be applied, but this can be ignored in the context of the present discussion.) Suppose now that a speaker is "programmed" in such a manner that he operates by the same rules. When presented with the input symbol S—corresponding, perhaps, to the instruction to make an utterance—he will eventually produce an utterance of one of the sentences of the language. But obviously this is not a sufficient description of what the speaker does. A speaker does not produce just *any* utterance, but an utterance which he finds appropriate in view of the situation at hand, his state of mind, etc. In short, the speaker has certain *intentions* which he realizes in his speech. An admirable phenomenological account of these was given by William James (1892, p. 164)[3]:

> And has the reader never asked himself what kind of a mental fact is his *intention of saying a thing* before he has said it? It is an entirely definite intention, distinct from all other intentions, an absolutely distinct state of consciousness, therefore; and yet how much of it consists of definite sensorial images, either of words, or of things? Hardly anything! Linger, and the words and things come into the mind; the anticipatory intention, the divination is there no more. But as the words that replace it arrive, it welcomes them successively and calls them right if they agree with it, it rejects them and calls them wrong if they do not. The intention *to-say-so-and-so* is the only name it can receive. One may admit that a good third of our psychic life consists in these rapid premonitory perspective views of schemes of thought not yet articulate.

There is no place for intentions in a grammar, but any theory of performance which fails to take intentions into account must be considered inadequate. The model of a human speaker must, of course,

---

[2] Chomsky himself has rejected such an interpretation (Chomsky, 1965, pp. 139–140; 1967a).

[3] Quoted with permission of Holt, Rinehart and Winston Co.

contain certain rules that determine the grammatical structure of the output. These rules, however, must be assumed to operate on an input which represents the speaker's intentions.

If it were to contain only a mechanism operating along the lines of a grammar, the performance model would produce utterances of grammatical strings. Yet these utterances would bear no systematic relationship to the environment. To function properly, the model must specify how this relationship is established. A possible solution might be somewhat as follows: The model "incorporates a grammar" and proceeds by the following steps:

1. The "Grammar Mechanism" produces a candidate for an utterance (i.e., a construct, which the speaker is not necessarily conscious of, and which represents the last step before the utterance is realized in speech).

2. This candidate-for-an-utterance is compared with the speaker's intentions.

3. If the match is not good enough, the information for this comparison is used to arrive at a satisfactory utterance by a series of successive approximations.[4]

To the extent that it proves feasible, the speaker's intentions should be assumed to guide this "grammar mechanism" already at the first step of operation; this might enable the speaker to arrive at the desired output after a smaller number of steps. In the following, some suggestions will be made concerning the performance model. First, we consider the nature of the intentions which must be taken to be the input to the model.

2. Intentions and Input-Markers

The term "intention" has been used here in a rather loose fashion. Clearly, not everything the speaker intends to say finds its expression in his linguistic output. Usually, he distils something from the experience he wants to convey and expresses this in his utterance. What concerns us here is only that part of the speaker's intentions which is ultimately converted into the output sentence; the part, that is, which serves as input to the utterance-producing mechanism. Let us use the term *input marker*, or *I marker*, for the formalized representation of those of the speaker's intentions which are expressed in the linguistic output.

[4] For a description of the general form of such a mechanism, which operates by successive approximations, see Miller, Galanter, and Pribram (1960).

What kind of information is contained in the I marker of an utterance?
Let us take a concrete example. Someone says:

(1)   John catches a red ball

What are the intentions that go into the making of this utterance? It
is obvious that the speaker intended to say something about John and
about catching and about a ball, and it is equally obvious that it is
not only the words in this utterance which must appear in some form
or another in the I marker. If the I marker were to contain just "John,"
"catch," "ball," and "red," and nothing else, it would follow that utterances like (2) and (3) are taken to express this speaker's intentions;
and this is clearly not the case.

(2)   The red ball catches John.

(3)   Red John catches the ball.

Utterances (1), (2), and (3) illustrate the well-known fact that English word order reflects meaning. Now, it cannot be claimed that the
I marker contains information about word order: word order is imposed
on the utterances as a result of the speaker expressing his intentions,
but is is not part of these intentions. What the speaker intends to convey
to the listener is, that it is John who does the catching (and not the
ball), that it is the ball that is red (and not John), etc. In other words,
the I marker must be assumed to contain the information that "John"
is the agent of "catch," that "ball" is the direct object of "catch," that
"red" modifies "ball" (and several other things besides, e.g., that the
"ball" he talks about is one and not many). It is these *relations* between
elements which are included in the I marker. In Section 5 the nature
of the elements appearing in the I marker will be discussed, and in
Section 12 a more formal description of I markers will be attempted.
Here we shall continue with our discussion of a performance model.

How do our I markers differ from underlying P markers (phrase markers)? The latter are the "deep structures" discussed by McNeill (this
volume), and contain grammatical categories such as: verb, verb phrase,
noun, and noun phrase. It is well known that there is no one-to-one
correspondence between these grammatical categories and semantic categories: not all nouns designate "things" and not all verbs designate actions. Hence, the I marker should not be taken to specify such categories
explicitly. This point will be taken up again in Section 5, where the
question is discussed what elements are contained in the I marker.

Further, P markers contain information about order of words (or, more precisely, order of morphemes), which in some cases may be of no semantic relevance. Note that word order is not invariable over languages. Thus, the verb precedes the subject in declarative sentences with nominative subject and object in some languages, and in others, the subject precedes the verb (Greenberg, 1963, p. 77. *et passim*). Relations like agent–action, action–direct object, on the other hand, may be taken to be universal; presumably, it is in this way that humans conceive of their environment (see also Section 4 below). I markers are therefore less language specific than P markers.[5]

The semantic relations obtained in the I marker can also be extracted from the P marker. This follows from the current conceptions of underlying P markers (Katz & Postal, 1964; Chomsky, 1965), according to which no change of meaning is introduced by transformations. The P marker of a given sentence must, therefore, contain all the semantically relevant information of this sentence.

3. Realization Rules

The above comparison between I markers and P markers suggests a possible utterance-producing mechanism which incorporates a generative grammar. This mechanism may be assumed to retrieve from the given I marker an underlying P marker that corresponds to it (i.e., that renders the same semantic information).[6] Since it already contains much of the information of the P marker, the I marker imposes a great deal of constraint on the operations which produce the P marker; only the excess information in the P marker must be retrieved by the mechanism. This may be assumed to be done by a "grammar mechanism" (see Section 1) and would presumably require a relatively small number of iterative steps. After a P marker has been found which corresponds to the I marker, the mechanism applies operations which are analogous to the transformations specified by grammarians, and thus produces the output utterance.

One way of viewing a performance model, then, is that of a mechanism which takes the speaker's intentions as input, in the form of I markers, and converts these into utterances via P markers. This is done by opera-

[5] Since this was written, it has been argued by Staal (1967) on linguistic grounds that the deep structure should not contain order of morphemes.

[6] Of course, a P marker is not a psychological but a linguistic construct. But it is possible to posit psychological constructs that are isomorphic to P markers.

tions analogous to the rules of a generative grammar. I suggest, however, that there is no need for such a roundabout route. It is much simpler to assume that the mechanism arrives at the utterance by applying operations directly to the I marker, instead of first constructing an appropriate P marker. This implies, of course, taking a step away from current conceptions of generative grammar, according to which transformations apply to underlying P markers. It requires a reformulation of transformation rules so that they can be applied to T markers in the performance model.

This reformulation of transformation rules can be quite straightforward. Consider, that to any P marker there corresponds some I marker. Given any transformation rule that converts this P marker into an output sentence, another rule can be formulated which converts the corresponding I marker into an utterance of the same sentence. Note that this does not presuppose a one-to-one relationship between P markers and I markers. There may be more than one P marker corresponding to the same I marker. In this case—since I markers, by definition, contain all the semantically relevant information of the utterance—a transformation rule which is applicable to any one of these P markers may be applied (after the necessary reformulation) to the I marker corresponding to them. The result will be an utterance reflecting the speaker's intentions.

The term *realization rule* will be used for the rules which turn I markers into utterances. Realization rules may really be viewed as transformation rules. The term is introduced only to indicate that the form of the rule applied to the I marker differs from that of the corresponding transformation rule applied to a P marker.

It should be immediately obvious why it is preferable to have realization rules that apply directly to I markers instead of having the model first arrive at P markers. If the phrase structure subcomponent can be shown to be superfluous in the performance model, it will be wasteful to retain it, and the introduction of I markers makes it superfluous. At the same time the present proposal obviates the need of successive approximations. Instead, utterances are produced directly from the I marker by one or more realization rules.

Not only is the description of the speaker's task simplified; the same holds for the listener's task. The listener may be assumed to apply to the input a realization rule in reverse, and thus to arrive at an I marker. (This will be discussed in more detail in Section 12.) Occasionally there will be two possible outcomes of this process. For instance

(4)   Visiting relatives can be a nuisance.

can be construed in two different ways. In this case, the listener may first apply one realization rule, and when this results in an I marker which appears to be semantically anomalous or pragmatically unlikely, he resorts to a different realization rule and arrives at a different I marker. In summary, we propose a performance model consisting of I markers, representing universal semantic relations, and realization rules, which are language specific and convert these I markers into utterances. A more formal presentation of the way realization rules may be assumed to operate is given in Section 12.

4. Implications for Language Learning

The exclusion of P markers from the performance model is motivated by considerations of simplicity, and also, in part, by certain considerations about language acquisition. The crucial problem in current thinking on language learning seems to be how to account for the fact that a child acquires the underlying P markers which are posited by generative grammar. Some theories of language acquisition have been criticized for being unable to explain how the child learns these deep structures which, by definition, are not exhibited in the speech of the environment. (Bever, Fodor, & Weksel, 1965b). It has even been claimed that such an explanation is in principle beyond the capacity of learning theory (Katz & Postal, 1964; Bever *et al.*, 1965b). Some recent theorizing about language learning has revolved around this difficulty (McNeill, 1966, and this volume; Fodor, 1966). The only way out of the difficulty is believed by these theorists to lie in the assumption of an innate propensity for arriving at these underlying structures. Discussions in a recent symposium on language acquisition (Smith & Miller, 1966) evidence an awareness of the methodological problems created by this rejection of Lockean empiricism.

Now, if our above reasoning is correct, this difficulty vanishes. No underlying P markers have to be learned. Utterances are produced directly from the I markers which represent the intentions of the child in a given situation, and which therefore do not have to be learned. Let us elaborate on this point. What the child has to learn are the correspondences between I markers and the utterances of persons in his environment. The I marker is inferred from situational cues. When the mother points to a ball and says: "Give me the ball," the task of the child consists in learning to associate the I marker representing the situation, with the utterance he hears. This is tantamount to learning a realization rule. Language learning still remains a fairly complicated task, of course, but it is one which does not pose insurmountable diffi culties for an explanation in terms of learning theory.

The relations represented in I markers may be taken to be linguistic universals. In (1) the relation between catching and a ball is given in the situation and not imposed by a language. No speaker of any language whatsoever will conceive of the action–object relation as holding, say, between catching and John. It is these relations which are incorporated in the I marker, and this justifies the statement that I markers are not learned, at least not in the way underlying P markers would have to be learned.

Instead, I markers are determined by the innate *cognitive capacity* of the child. There is nothing specifically linguistic about this capacity, and in this it is unlike the innate propensity postulated by McNeill (1000 and this volume). It is just the way the child views the world, and will be the same whether he learns to speak, or fails to learn to speak due to some organic or environmental handicap.

This does not imply that I markers are not affected by experience. On the contrary, later stages of their development presumably result from experience, in particular from experience with language. Thus, the English-speaking child must learn that "± count" is a feature which must be incorporated into the I marker, whereas children speaking certain other languages will not maintain this distinction. The problem of how I markers develop can only be raised here; much further study will be needed before an answer can be attempted.

5. The Elements of I Markers

So far the relations represented in the I marker have been discussed. Let us turn now to the question, what are the elements among which these relations hold. If it be assumed that I markers contain words, there arises the following difficulty in producing utterances. Suppose an I marker contains the words:

John, eat, good

The I marker represents, further, the relations holding between these words: "John" is the agent of "eat" and "good" modifies "eat." An utterance expressing these will be (5), while (6) would be ungrammatical:

(5) John eats well.

(6) *John eats good.

Now, the choice between "well" and "good" is not dictated by the speaker's intentions but by the grammar of English. We propose, therefore, that the I marker contains only concepts that are unspecified as to grammatical category, and the realization rule determines the category in which the concept appears in the utterance. Such a "concept" may be looked upon as a set of words differing from each other only in their syntactic markers, e.g., good (adjective), well (adverb), goodness (noun).

In applying a realization rule, it may turn out that this set does not contain a word with the appropriate syntactic marker. For instance, if John has become tired after swimming, the I marker of a speaker intending to report this may contain, *inter alia,* the concept "swim": swim (verb, transitive), swim (verb, intransitive), swim (noun). Applying a realization rule, (7) might be obtained:

(7)   The swim tired John.

If, however, after eating well, and as a consequence, John has become tired, the same rules cannot be applied because the concept "eat" does not contain a noun, and (8) would be ungrammatical:

(8)   *The eat tired John.

In this case, the speaker will try another realization rule, e.g., one involving a nominalization:

(9)   Eating tired John.

Occasionally, a neologism may be indulged in. Thus, under the appropriate circumstances (8) may be understood correctly. Still another way would be to reformulate the I marker so as to produce a sentence which comes closest to the speaker's original intention. For instance, (10) would be a perfect substitute in most cases:

(10)   The meal tired John.

The latter solution raises the question whether these "concepts" should not be conceived of as being somewhat broader, including synonyms and near synonyms; for instance: eat (verb), edible (adjective), feed (verb), meal (noun), etc. Needless to say, these words will not invariably fit the same context. Thus we may have

(11)   He was fed intravenously.

but hardly

(12)   *He ate intravenously.

(13)   *He had an intravenous meal.

In connection with this question about the scope of the "concepts" in the I markers, there arises the problem of their universality. Is the way we divide our experience into "concepts" innate? To the extent that it is not, how is it learned? These questions need to be further investigated before anything definite can be stated.

6. The Development of Realization Rules

In the following, I shall attempt to show how the child's learning the grammar of his language can be handled within the theoretical framework developed so far. According to our model, I markers are converted into utterances by realization rules. Hence, the theory of language acquisition must explain how the child comes to convert the relations represented in the I marker into his linguistic output; in other words, it must be shown how realization rules are acquired. The problem then, is conceived here in a way which differs from that of most workers (e.g., Braine, 1963b; Brown & Fraser, 1963; Miller & Ervin, 1964; and in the present volume, the chapters by Palermo and Staats). The latter have set out to explain how the child learns to insert words belonging to certain grammatical categories into the correct positions in the utterance. Suppose now that one were able to explain satisfactorily how the child learns to produce grammatical utterances. There still remains the problem of how these linguistic structures become related to the environment (see Section 1). It is this problem of semantics where current theories leave off, and it is here that the present theory begins.

The following sections will show how one might infer from the child's utterances which realization rules he has acquired. Two kinds of realization rules that account for primitive utterances will be taken up first: *position rules*, which accord to each word—or, rather, "concept"—in the I marker its position in the utterance, and *category rules*, which determine the grammatical category that is appropriate in a given position.

A theory of the development of grammar will ultimately have to be interrelated to the general theory of performance which accounts for the language of adults as well as for that of children. Proposals for such a model in Section 12 are of a preliminary nature, and likewise, the attempt made in the next section must be regarded as highly tentative.

7. Position Rules in Two-Word Utterances

Much of the previous work has been based on the assumption that the child learns, for various words in his vocabulary, in which position of the two-word utterance it can occur. This approach, which is based on single words, is abandoned here. Instead, we ask for every *pair* of words what is their relative position in the utterance in view of the relations holding between them.

As shown in the following, there are about eight different relations expressed by English two-word utterances in the published data.

7.1 Agent and Action

The position rule results in:

(14)   (i)   **agent + action**

Examples:

    (ii)   Bambi go   (quoted in McNeill, 1966)

    (iii)   mail come   (Braine, 1963b)

    (iv)   airplane by   (Braine, 1963b)

The last example is of particular interest, because the action is not expressed by a verb. Braine has a note explaining that "is flying past" was intended. In this case, then, the relation between agent and action is expressed by the same position rule as in adult language, but the choice of grammatical category is different. This point will be taken up again in the discussion of category rules (Section 8).

7.2 Action and Object

The position rule is:

(15)   (i)   **action + direct object**

Examples:

(ii)   see sock   (Braine, 1963b)

(iii)   want more   (Braine, 1963b)

(iv)   pick glove   [pick glove up
                          (Brown & Bellugi, 1964)]

7.3 AGENT AND OBJECT

Examples of this position rule are few in the published English data.

(16)   (i)   **agent + direct object**

Examples:

(ii)   Eve lunch   [= Eve is having lunch;
                              (Brown & Bellugi, 1964)]
(iii)   Mommy sandwich   [= Mommy will have a
                              sandwich; (Brown &
                              Bellugi, 1964)]
(iv)   Betty cinna toast   [= Betty is to have some
                              cinnamon toast; (Braine
                              1971, Section 2.22, Table 2)]

This construction was quite frequent in the speech of a Hebrew speaking girl, 20–22 months old. The usual Hebrew word order for active sentences is, as in English: agent + action + direct object. See also Braine (1971, Section 2.26) on construction (16)(i) in Russian in Gvozdev's child.

It appears from the position rules discussed so far that the familiar sequence in the adult sentence occurs in the child's speech in a shorter form, containing only two of the three elements (agent, action, direct object), but those that do occur appear in their correct relative position. Thus we have the following three position rules [(14)–(16)]:

agent + action
action + direct object
agent   + direct object

7.4 MODIFIERS

When one word of the utterance modifies the other, it precedes it. This position rule of child language creates the following structure:

(17)   (i)   **modifier + head**

Examples:

(ii)   pretty boat   (Braine, 1963b)

(iii)   big boat   (Brown & Bellugi, 1964)

(iv)   more nut   (Brown & Bellugi, 1964)

(v)   my stool   (Brown & Bellugi, 1964)

(vi)   baby book   (Miller & Ervin, 1964)

(vii)   baby car   (Miller & Ervin, 1964)

This list contains both attributes and possessives. Ultimately, of course, the child must learn to distinguish between these two and learn the appropriate realization rules. For instance, he must learn to say "my big boat" and not "big my boat." It seems plausible, however, that at the beginning of learning grammar this distinction is not yet made and instead a global class of modifiers is all that is needed for the child to communicate.[7]

Note also that the class of modifiers in the above list is a mixed bag, containing nouns, pronouns, and adjectives. In all cases, however, the order of words is like that of adult speech, which presumably has served the child as a model.

[7] Braine (personal communication) has suggested that the modifier–head relation might be viewed as " . . . a very general semantic relation in which the modifier merely adds information or detail to the concept expressed by the lexical item; then this general relation would be additionally specified by stating its subtype (i.e., the various ways in which a modifier can add information)." According to the currently prevailing view in transformational grammar, adjectives which are noun modifiers are introduced by a generalized phrase marker (Chomsky, 1965, p. 134). But Braine (1971, Section 2.23) states that these adjectives do not appear as predicators in early speech, and concludes from this that adjectival modifiers are not due to transformations. See also Bolinger (1967).

But there are a number of counterexamples, as in Brown and Fraser (1963):

(18)　(i)　doggy tired

　　　(ii)　chair fall down

　　　(iii)　carriage broken

　　　(iv)　that dirty

One way of viewing these would be simply as exceptions to (17)(i), produced at a time this rule has not yet been well enough established. On the other hand, it may be that these are already instances of the operation of a realization rule that accords the correct position to the subject and the term describing its state, as in the adult "Doggy is tired," "The chair fell down," etc. An examination of extensive transcripts of a child's speech may be required to decide which of these explanations applies in each case.

7.5 NEGATION

Unlike the relations discussed above, negation does not hold between two elements, but "operates" on one element. The position rule specifies the order.

(19)　(i)　**negation + X**

　　Examples:

　　　(ii)　no wash　　（Bellugi, 1964）

　　　(iii)　no water　　（Braine, 1963b）

　　　(iv)　no wet　　[= I am not wet; (Braine, 1963b)]

　　　(v)　no down　　[= don't push me down; (Braine, 1963b)]

　　　(vi)　no mama　　[= I don't want to go to mama; (Braine, 1963b)]

Note again the heterogeneous collection of words (and referents) which appear in the second position.

Usually, negation is expressed by "no," but in the speech of at least one child, it appeared as "isn't" (Miller & Ervin, 1964) although the examples given are of utterances more than two words in length.

The word "allgone" may perhaps be looked upon as a negation. This would explain utterances that are not built according to the adult model, such as

(20) allgone shoe   (Braine, 1963b)

7.6 DATIVES

The word indicating to whom something is given, thrown, said, etc., is the dative. So far, I have found only one example:

(21) (i)   X + dative

Example:

    (ii)   throw Daddy   [= throw it to Daddy;
                           (Brown & Bellugi, 1964)]

7.7 OSTENSION

Braine (1971, Section 2.22) has suggested the term *ostensive sentence* for utterances used to identify names, objects, etc. [Miller and Ervin (1964) use the term *demonstrative sentences*.] When these utterances are more fully structured, they begin with an *introducer* like "that," "here," "there," or "it." The term *ostension* may be used for the operation in question; like "negation," it is not a relation holding between two elements. Examples of ostension are numerous. Braine (*loc. cit.*) looks upon "here," "there," "see," and "'s" as introducers.

The position rule is:

(22) (i)   **Introducer + X**

Examples:

(ii)	see boy	(Braine, 1963b; Brown & Fraser, 1963)
(iii)	it ball	(Braine, 1963b)
(iv)	here bed	(Braine, 1963b)
(v)	there ball	(Braine, 1963b)
(vi)	there book	(Braine, 1963b)
(vii)	here more	(Brown & Fraser, 1963)

(viii)	there my nails	(Brown & Fraser, 1963)
(ix)	's bird	(Brown & Fraser, 1963)
(x)	that blue	(Miller & Ervin, 1964)
(xi)	's a truck	(Miller & Ervin, 1964)

7.8 LOCATIVES

The word indicating where something is located or where the action takes place is usually placed in the second position. The rule produces:

(23)   (i)   **X + locative**

Examples:

(ii)	sat wall	[= He sat on the wall; (Brown & Bellugi, 1964)]
(iii)	baby highchair	[= baby is in the highchair; (Brown & Bellugi, 1964)]
(iv)	baby room	[with the accent on the second word; (Miller & Ervin, 1964)]

"Here" and "there" in first position might best be regarded as introducers. In (22)(iv)–(viii) one has the impression that these words might just as well have been replaced by "this," "that," or the like. On the other hand, there are examples in the published data of "here" and "there" in second position which strike one as being truly locative, i.e., they serve to indicate a place:

(24)	(i)	I put bucket here	(Brown & Fraser, 1963)
	(ii)	blanket in there	(Brown & Fraser, 1963)
	(iii)	milk in there	(Braine, 1963b)
	(iv)	more down there	(Braine, 1963b)

7.9 POSITION RULES VERSUS PIVOTS

It is proposed, then, that a child learns how to place words relative to each other so as to express certain relations. For instance, he hears the adult expressing a modifying relation by expressions such as

(25)   (i)   my coat

       (ii)   big dog

       (iii)   Evie's doll

These expressions may or may not be embedded in sentences. What they have in common is that the modifying word comes first. It is this rule which the child comes to learn from many examples presented to him in adult speech that refer to concrete situations in which the modifying relation obtains.

Position rules can account for most of the two-word utterances in the published records of child language. So can pivot theory, that is, the theory that the child learns certain words are P_1—i.e., belong to the class of pivot words appearing in the first position of the two-word utterances—and other words are P_2, and belong to the class appearing in the second position (see Slobin's introductory chapter). The two theories converge on the same set of data, because pivot words tend to appear in combinations exhibiting certain relations and, hence, in certain positions. Thus, "more" is a modifier, and, following (17), comes in the first position. Pivot theory states the same fact by saying that "more" is a P_1.

The present approach seems to have a slight edge over pivot theory in its ability to explain the data. Sometimes a P_1 will appear in second position, or a P_2 in first position. Such deviations may in some cases be explained as due to the fact that a different relation is expressed. For instance, in Braine's (1963b) list of Steven's utterances we find among others:

(26)   (i)   more ball

       (ii)   more book

       (iii)   want more

In the first two utterances the position rule is: modifier + head; but in (iii) it is: action + direct object.

On the other hand, Braine (personal communication) has pointed out that in the first stages of language acquisition the number of pivots is very small (unlike the number of "open class" words), and this argues against the operation of realization rules at this stage. This is because the child who has acquired a rule such as, e.g., modifier + head should

he expected to have other modifiers in his vocabulary of which there
are quite a few—appear as P_1, and not only a small subset of these. Realization rules thus have more generative power than necessary for the
linguistic data of this period.

All this suggests that we might conceive of the two theories as comple-
menting each other. Pivot theory accounts for the first stage, in which
the position of a restricted number of words is learned. This prepares
the ground for the learning of realization rules. Several M_1 words might
be modifiers, for instance, and the child thus learns how the modifier–head relation is expressed.

A. Category Rules

In the child's two-word utterances, relations are expressed in much
the same way as in adult language, as far as relative position is concerned. Acquisition of position rules seems to precede that of category
rules. While the child knows how to express a relation by relative position, he has yet to learn which grammatical classes may occur in the
two positions. This results in "errors" from the point of view of adult
grammar, such as

(27) (i)   more wet   (Braine, 1963b)

      (ii)   allgone sticky   (Braine, 1963b)

      (iii) allgone outside [= the outside is all gone; when the
                               door is shut; (Braine, 1963b)]

      (iv)   more outside   [= I want to go outside again;
                               (Braine, 1971, Section 2.22, Table
                               2)]

Gradually, the child comes to learn that in the *modifier + head* construction the head is a noun, and thus he avoids such mistakes. Eventually the more complicated rules of adult language are acquired.

How are these category rules learned? A category rule is based on
word classes: given a certain relation, only words of such and such
a class may appear in the given position. Word classes are perhaps
learned as acquired stimulus and response equivalences, in the manner
described by Jenkins and Palermo (1964), Jenkins (1965), and Palermo
in this volume. After word classes have been formed, a category rule

may operate alongside the position rule, e.g.,

(28)   **modifier + head**

adjective   noun

It is not surprising, in view of the above, that category rules are learned later than position rules. For a two-word utterance there are only two permutations possible, and the position rule contains therefore little information (in the technical sense of the term). Much more is required of the child in forming word classes, and still more in learning a category rule like (28).

9. Further Developments

9.1 INFLECTIONS AND AUXILIARIES

Presumably it is much easier to learn the relative positions of two elements than to learn the rule that results in an element (such as an inflection) being added. Learning the former, the child must distinguish between only two possibilities of order—*a,b,* or *b,a,*—while in the latter case there are many possible elements that might be added and one of which he must add. Moreover, if the child is to learn how to express a relation by inflecting one of the words in the utterance, he must not only learn which element is to be added, but also to which word it is to be added. In other words, he must also learn a position rule. Therefore one should expect it to be easier to learn how to express relations by word order than by inflection.

In Russian, where word order is much less restricted than in English, relations are usually expressed by inflections. The Russian child, however, also seems to learn position rules first (Slobin, 1966a; in press a). No doubt he acquires these rules from the word order which happens to be prevalent in those sections of adult speech which he comprehends. Inflections are learned only later, because they are more difficult to learn. The same seems to hold for most auxiliaries in English: for a long time utterances of three or four words with few, if any, inflections and auxiliaries are the child's principal means of expressing relations.

Interestingly, the possessive "_____'s" and the third person singular present "_____s" are among the inflections learned relatively late (Bellugi, 1964). In a sense, these inflections are redundant. Thus, the possessive may be indicated in the entire language by a simple position rule, as in (17)(vi) and (vii). The plural "____s" and the past ending "____ed, by contrast, carry semantic information that cannot be expressed by position rules, and these inflections appear earlier.

9.2 HIERARCHICAL UTTERANCES

Utterances of more than two words usually have hierarchical structure. They may be regarded as the result of applying two or more position rules. Table 1 shows how a few position rules jointly may account for such utterances.

TABLE 1   Hierarchical Utterances Obtained by Two or More Position Rules

(a)	Position Rule	(22)	introducer +	X	
	Position Rule	(17)		modifier + head	
	Hierarchical utterances[a]		see	Evie	car
			that	mummy	book
			that	my	cup
(b)	Position Rule	(14)	agent + action		
	Position Rule	(15)		action + direct object	
	Position Rule	(23)		X	+ locative
	Hierarchical utterances[b]		I	put	bucket	here
			Lucy	go		nursery
			You	hold	this	

[a] The first two examples are from Brown and Fraser (1963), and the last is from Brown and Bellugi (1964).

[b] Examples are from the following sources (in this order): Brown and Fraser (1963), Miller and Ervin (1964), Braine (1971, Section 2.22).

Position rules operate on I markers, and it is the latter which specify the relations that have to be expressed. In the first example of Table 1(a), the I marker includes the information that "Evie" modifies "car" (and not "see car"). Thus, the order of applying position rules is determined by the I marker. If it were not, we would obviously get a scrambled word order. Similarly, in (29) the I marker determines that the position rule assigning the position of the article must be applied first—or, in (29)(iii), after rule (17)—and only then rule (22) is applied which accords to the introducer "that" its position:

(29)   (i)   that a factory

       (ii)   that a flower

       (iii)   that a your car

These examples are from Table 3 of Slobin's introductory chapter. In Section 12.3, we shall see how the order of applying position rules is formally determined.

Braine (1971, Section 1.34) has drawn attention to *replacement sequences,* in which the child produces a sequence of utterances that expand each other and are apparently equivalent in meaning, and where the longer utterance contains the words of the shorter. Such sequences may often be explained as the result of the child's starting with a simple utterance (i.e., one word, or two words learned as a unit) and applying one position rule after another, till a full-fledged hierarchical utterance is produced. This is illustrated in Table 2 by a replacement sequence quoted in Braine (*loc. cit.*)

TABLE 2   The Production of a Replacement Sequence

Position (14)	agent + action	
Position Rule (23)	X	+ locative
Simple utterance	stand up	
Application of (14)	cat	stand up
Application of (23)	cat	stand up	table

9.3 Interrogations and Negations

Learning the correct structure of interrogative and negative sentences is much more difficult for the child than learning other hierarchical structures. At first he simply adds "no," "not," or any word expressing negation, to the previously learned form of utterance. The following examples are from Stage I described by Bellugi (1964, and unpublished):

(30)   (i)   no drop mitten

       (ii)   no sit there

       (iii)   not a teddy bear

The negative morpheme of the English speaking child in Stage 1 stands outside the sentence. The same holds true for Russian and Japanese children, according to the evidence summarized by McNeill (this volume); likewise, my observations of Hebrew speaking children show that in the beginning stages the negation always precedes the sentence. McNeill argues that this fact describes "an aspect of the linguistic predisposition of children." I suggest that the child simply follows the adult model. He is often exposed to English (or Hebrew) adult utterances where the negation precedes the first word incorporated in the two-word utterance. [My knowledge of Russian does not extend beyond the examples given by Slobin (1966a, p. 133).] Hence he learns position rule (19): negation + X.

Next he applies the same rule (incorrectly, of course, from the point of view of adult grammar) in longer utterances such as those in (30). Here "drop mitten," "sit there," and "a teddy bear" are formed according to previously acquired position rules. In the I marker the negation must be assumed to apply to the whole utterance (it is not true that "drop mitten"), and the utterances in (30) are arrived at by applying position rule (19) to the above.

To obtain the correct structure of adult language, the child has to learn another set of position rules for the case when negation is expressed. Likewise, he must learn to insert the auxiliary "do," and to use "any" instead of "some," etc. What the child must acquire, then, are *conditional* realization rules: if the I marker contains a negation, one set of rules is to be applied, and if not, another set. The same holds for questions which, like negations, are represented in the I marker. The parallel of realization rules to transformation rules, mentioned in Section 3, should be obvious here. An alternative solution is proposed in the following.

10. Underlying Structures Revisited

Transformations may be acquired in either one of two ways:

1. The child learns conditional realization rules which are applied directly to I markers (see Section 9).

2. Following the suggestion made independently by McNeill (1966) and Braine (1971, Section 3.33), a rule is learned which converts a previously acquired incorrect structure into another one:

(31)   Why not he eat → Why does he not eat?

According to the latter alternative, the realization rule is a two-stage rule: in the first stage the I marker is converted into an underlying structure ("why not he eat"), and in the second, this structure is converted into the output sentence. The underlying structures posited here are *not* abstract structures which are never realized in speech. In this they differ from McNeill's structures. Instead, they are the result of previously acquired realization rules (and may actually have occurred in the child's speech at a certain stage). Therefore this explanation does not raise the vexing problem of how the underlying structure is acquired. (It will be remembered that this problem was claimed to be nonexistent within our theoretical framework of I markers and realization rules.)

An explanation in terms of a two-stage realization rule might also be appropriate for the explanation of discontinuous constituents. Thus,

(32)   I called up him → I called him up

may be the result of first applying the usual position rules to the I marker—which results in "I called up him"—and then permuting the word order by an additional rule. This does not presuppose that the child ever be exposed to "I called up him" or that he has ever produced this utterance. It is sufficient that he has learned rules which can generate such an utterance.

11. The Role of Semantics

Semantics plays a central role in the present approach, and in this it contrasts with other views of language learning. It is not that the importance of semantics has failed to be recognized, but so far it has not been incorporated into an explanation of language acquisition. The reason for this is, as Fodor (1966) has pointed out, that there is not enough systematic knowledge about semantics.

Syntax, on the other hand, has gone a long way toward formalization. Psycholinguists have therefore concentrated on syntactic models, trying to show how the child acquires abstract sentence forms, and have let the sense take care of itself. Yet it is not very plausible that the child should learn to produce empty structures which he subsequently stuffs with meanings. As far as sentence comprehension is concerned, recent experiments suggest that syntactic and semantic processes are not separable (Schlesinger, 1968; Stolz, 1967). The present proposal asserts the reverse: meanings come first—in the form of I markers—and the child learns how these are realized in linguistic form. Similarly, we have seen

in the production of sentence production, that it is quite improbable
that the syntactic frame should be produced in isolation from meaning.

It might be argued, though, that in laboratory situations, syntactic
processes can be shown to operate on meaningless material. Thus, it
has been found that of two strings made up of nonsense words, the
one having grammatical ones, (33), is learned more easily than one
which has none, (34):

(33)   The maff vlems oothly um the glox nerfs

(34)   Maff vlem ooth um glox nerf

(Osgood, 1957a; cf. also Epstein, 1961.)

I would argue that even in such sentences there are *semantic* cues
which may help the subject in learning them. In (33), but not in (34),
there is something (maff) which is singular and carries out an action,
called vlemming, in a certain manner (oothly, to be more exact), etc.
(But perhaps I misunderstood, and it is umming which is done by
maff vlems.) Any grammatical cue renders some information about content, and this in itself would account for the greater ease of learning
"grammatical" nonsense strings.

It is suggested, therefore, that hearing (33) one tends to construct
an I marker. To be sure, this is a curious kind of I marker where the
relations are all there but the elements between which these relations
hold are vague. "Vague" is really not an understatement, because most
of us tend to invest nonsense words with some meaning. Carnap's

(35)   Pirots karulize elatically

invokes in me quite a vivid I marker: there are several birds (parrots?)
talking (garrulous) in an animated and elated manner. While this particular interpretation is certainly idiosyncratic, some such process seems
to be common to all of us. Human nature abhors a semantic vacuum.

It is true that college students manage to learn grammars of artificial
languages which consist of letters of the alphabet instead of words
(Hunt, 1965). But all that is proved by such experiments is that subjects
are capable of solving this particular type of problem; there is no shred
of evidence that children go about learning their native language in
the same way. Indeed, already the fact that semantic cues are supplied
to the child in abundance, is sufficient to make it implausible that they
should learn language without using these cues.

The meanings which form the basis for constructing utterances are not merely those of isolated words. It has been pointed out that semantic correlates of word classes might have a part to play in their acquisition. Braine (1971, Section 2.32) has criticized some simplistic notion of this sort. It appears that these do not apply to our approach which accords an important role to the semantics of *relations* between words rather than to that of single words. Actually, some of Braine's suggestions (*loc. cit.*) are very similar in outlook to the point of view of the present paper. Likewise, McNeill's treatment of grammatical relations in this volume bears many similarities to the present approach; cf. Section 14 for a comparison.

Recently, semantics has begun to be accorded a place in linguistic theory. Katz and Postal (1964) have presented a model which comprises also a semantic component. Their syntactic component, however, operates independently of the semantic component. In the models described by Lamb (1966a,b), Weinreich (1966), Fillmore (1966, 1968), and Sgall (1966), the semantic and syntactic aspects of linguistic description are no longer segregated. While these writers do not discuss performance models in any detail, their theorizing should be expected to have an impact on psycholinguistics.[8]

12. Toward a Formalization

So far, only an informal description has been given of an utterance producing model. To show the feasibility of this model, a more formal description would be desirable. Some tentative steps towards such a formalization are made in the present section.

It is important to point out that a description of a speech production model does *not* amount to a generative grammar. An utterance production model must of necessity start from the speaker's intentions. It will show therefore: (a) how the linguistically expressed aspects of these intentions are formalized, and (b) how the latter are converted into the linguistic output. The formalization has to start, therefore, with (a), i.e., with I markers. Not so the generative grammar, which has the task of accounting for all grammatical sentences of the language. Here

---

[8] I have made use of some of Fillmore's notions. Sgall's paper, which came to my attention only after the draft of the present paper was finished, presents an approach that in some of its aspects is similar to the present one. More recently, Kelley (1967) has proposed an acquisition model which is based on functional relations. Renira Huxley and others at the Nuffield Language Acquisition Project, University of Edinburgh, are currently engaged in analyses of child speech which make use of similar notions.

intentions may not be taken for granted: if these are to figure at all in the grammar, it must be shown how they are generated. This is not the purpose of the present discussion, which confines itself to the speech production model, and does not probe further into the psychology of thought by trying to enumerate the set of possible intentions. Hence unlike the grammarian, we do not have to start with any primitive symbol (such as S for sentence). However, the following sections should make it apparent that the present approach towards formalization may ultimately provide a basis for constructing a generative grammar.

12.1 I Markers

Table 3 shows the relations holding between elements of the I marker of

(36) John catches the red ball.

The words of this utterance appearing in the table should be taken to refer to "concepts" in the sense discussed in Section 5. The table also shows the notation to be used henceforward.

TABLE 3   The Relations in an I Marker

a	Relates to	b	Notation	
red	is attribute of	*ball*	Att	(a,b)
the	determines	[*red ball*]	Det	(a,b)
[*the* [*red ball*]]	is object of	*catches*	Ob	(a,b)
John	is agent of	[*catches* [*the*[*red ball*]]]	Ag	(a,b)

In addition (at least in English where number and tense are obligatory), the I marker must contain several linguistically relevant specifications, such as the fact that "John" is singular, "catch" occurs in the present, etc. This information will be disregarded for the time being, so as not to complicate the exposition which follows.

Following the above table, the I marker of (36) may be formally described as follows:

(37) Ag (*John*, [Ob ([Det (*the*, [Att (*red, ball*)]))], *catches*)])

In writing, a left-to-right order is imposed on the elements, but remember that temporal sequence is not a property of the I marker, for reasons stated in Section 2.

12.2 REALIZATION RULES

Realization rules accord each element in the I marker a *position* and determine its grammatical *category*. Further, these rules must be assumed to accord a grammatical category to each constituent of the sentence. To produce the above utterance, the following realization rules are employed:

(38)   R1   Att $(a,b) \rightarrow N\,(ADJ\,a + N\,b)$

       R2   Det $(a,b) \rightarrow N\,(Da + N\,b)$

       R3   Ob $(a,b) \rightarrow V\,(Vb + N\,a)$

       R4   Ag $(a,b) \rightarrow S\,(Na + V\,b)$

R1 states that if a is an attribute of b, then a is an adjective, and is followed by b, which must be a noun.[9] The N before the parenthesis indicates that the resulting combination is to be regarded as a noun. The remaining signs are to be read: V—verb, D—determiner (*a, the, this, that,* . . .), S—sentence.

R1 is only one of the ways Att (a,b) can be realized. Another one is given by

(39)   R5   Att $(a,b) \rightarrow ADJ(ADV\,a + ADJ\,b)$

Thus in "very good," "very" modifies "good," and the whole phrase may serve as an ADJ in R1, above (e.g., "very good boy"). Still another example of how Att (a,b) may be realized is given in R6 below (Section 12.5).

[9] See footnote 7 on this point. While I have deviated from current conceptions of generative grammar with respect to attribution, I have in other details followed these conceptions closely. The exact form of realization rules remains of course to be determined and all that has been attempted here is to show how they might work. Crucial to their operation is the correct bracketing; this bracketing is given in the I marker and accords with the speaker's intentions. Note also that R1, or possibly some other realization rule, also permits *reddening ball,* but this will not be a realization of I marker (37), because "reddening," having a different meaning than "red," does not belong to the same concept.

12.3 PRODUCTION OF UTTERANCES

Regarding the order of applying the realization rules there seem to be several possibilities. An obvious way would be to start with the elements of the innermost brackets of the I marker and the relations holding between them e.g. with "Att (red, ball) in (37). Leaving out of account questions of grammatical agreement and the operation of the phonological component, the steps of producing (36) would be as described in Table 4.

TABLE 4   Production of "John catches the red ball"

Step	Rule	
1	1	Att (red,ball) → N(ADJ red + N ball)
2	2	Det (the, [Att (red, ball)]) → N(D the + N(ADJ red + N ball))
3	3	Ob ([Det (the, [Att (red, ball)])], catches)
		→ V(V catches + N (D the + N(ADJ red + N ball)))
4	4	Ag (John, [Ob (. . . catches)])
		→ S(N John + V(V catches . . . + N ball)))).

Another possibility is illustrated by Fig. 1. Note that the "tree" in the figure contains all the information of the I marker (37) and the realization rules that have to be applied to it. Incidentally, the figure is suggestive of the way a generative grammar might be constructed which is in accord with the approach outlined in this chapter.

In producing an utterance, the speaker may be assumed to work from the top of such a tree to the bottom. In Fig. 1, he first applies R4, which realizes the agentive relation in (37). This renders "John" on the one hand, and the rest of the I marker on the other. This rest is then further realized by applying R3, R2, and R1, in this order. The order of application is, thus, the reverse of that in Table 4.

At present it cannot be decided which of these descriptions is preferable. Empirical findings on the utterance-production process are too sparse to lend support to either one. It is quite likely that we usually follow neither of these courses in its entirety, but rather move alternately from top-to-bottom and from bottom-to-top of the tree in Fig. 1. Thus, one might start with R4, producing "John," and then go on realizing the remainder of the I marker in the manner indicated by the first three lines of Table 4. Whatever the sequence in which realization rules are applied, the bracketing in the I marker acts as a safeguard against incorrect word order (cf. Section 9.2). For instance, "red the ball" is ruled out by the bracketing in Table 3.

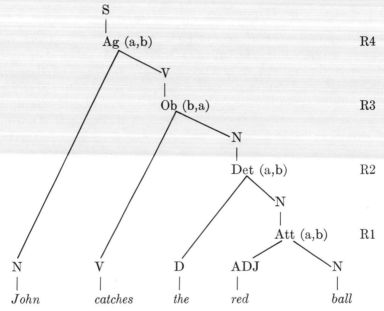

FIG. 1. The tree representing "John catches the red ball." The first and second letters in parentheses refer to left and right branches, respectively, and the notation is that introduced in Table 4.

12.4 COMPREHENDING UTTERANCES

The process of decoding may be hypothesized to be the reverse of the production process described in Table 4. Table 5 shows the first four steps of comprehending (36).

In the steps following those given in Table 5, "the red ball" serves as N in V (V *catches* + N . . .)

What words are singled out in Step 1 will depend largely on the

TABLE 5   Steps in Comprehending "John catches the red ball"

Step		
1	Single out part of utterance	*red* + *ball*
2	Assign categories	N (ADJ *red* + N *ball*)
3	Apply R1 in reverse	N(ADJ *red* + N *ball*) → Att (*red*, *ball*)
4	Single out part of utterance including that chosen in Step 1	*the* + *red* + *ball*
5	Assign categories.	N (D *the* + N (ADJ *red* + N *ball*))
6	Apply R2 in reverse	. . . → Det (*the*,[Att (*red*,*ball*)])

listener's previous experience. In the light of this experience, "the red" will not be a likely candidate to start the process with. But this description of decoding is certainly not an algorithm. At any step something might go wrong. A wrong set of words might be singled out in Step 1, the wrong categories might be assigned in Step 2 (the same word often belongs to different categories, e.g., "swim"); and applying a formation rule in reverse (Step 5) does not always have a unique result; see, for instance, (41) below. All these would be severe shortcomings in a grammar. Yet as a general blueprint for the operation of a decoder, the above seems to be sufficient. If the listener makes false starts, he subsequently corrects them. Some false starts will be avoided because of his language habits which lead him to assign greater probabilities to certain solutions than to others; some others will be obviated by semantic constraints.

Needless to say, the actual process by which a sentence is comprehended may differ considerably from the step-by-step procedure described here. The sequence of steps might be a different one (cf. also Section 12.3). Probably, several of these steps are taken simultaneously, and at any rate, the listener is hardly ever aware of the grammatical categories involved.[10] What is attempted here is an account of steps which *may* lead to appropriate decoding.

Category symbols that belong to constituents (preceding parentheses) are the same as those belonging to elements. For example, N is used instead of the more customary NP. As becomes evident from Table 5, this ensures the functioning of the process. If "red ball" would have been called NP in Step 2, R2 (which is formulated in terms of N) could not operate on the outcome of Step 5. The same holds, *mutatis mutandis*, for the first three steps in Table 4. This notation, and the process described in Table 5, are in some ways parallel to the syntactic procedure suggested in an early paper by Bar-Hillel ("A Quasi-Arithmetical Notation for Syntactic Description," in Bar-Hillel, 1964).

12.5 Transformations

Transformations are introduced by present-day generative grammarians so as to account for certain linguistic phenomena. Specifically, it is claimed that (a) different deep structures may result in the same surface structure through the application of transformation rules, an example being (4) in Section 3; and that (b) different surface structures may have the same deep structure.

[10] The heuristics of the decoding process have been subject to much recent research which has been summed up by Bever (1970).

The facts on which these claims are based can also be explained within the present framework. Consider first the case of utterance phrases with two possible interpretations, like

(40) visiting relatives

There are two different realization rules, both of which result in (40):

(41) R6   Att $(a,b) \rightarrow N(V_{ing} a + N b)$

R7   Ob $(a,b) \rightarrow N(V_{ing} b + N a)$

The "visiting relatives" resulting from R6 *are*, perhaps, a nuisance, whereas the visiting of relatives resulting from R7 *is* a nuisance. It appears, then, that a syntactically ambiguous utterance like (4) may have different I markers underlying it.

Conversely, the same I marker may result in different utterances. One explanation of this may be that different realization rules can be applied to the same I marker. Alternatively, one of the utterances may be the result of applying a realization rule (permuting word order and, perhaps, adding auxiliaries) to the other utterance, i.e., to the outcome of a set of realization rules another rule is applied. The latter solution has been discussed in Section 10.

Each of these two solutions may account for the utterance of active and passive sentences. However, the fact that the utterance is passive should perhaps be represented in the I marker [cf. also Katz and Postal (1964, p. 72)], and if so, there would have to be two conditional realization rules, and the instructions in the I marker as to the form of the utterance—active or passive—will determine which of these two rules is to be applied (see Section 9.3).

13. I Markers and P Markers Compared

The present approach is based on a conception of deep structure which differs somewhat from that which figures in current linguistic theory. Much of the foregoing discussion may be summarized by comparing these two conceptions.

I markers—which are the deep structures suggested here—differ from the P marker of the deep structure in that they are defined in terms of relations and not in terms of grammatical categories. Chomsky has shown (1965, pp. 68 ff.) that grammatical relations can be derived

from the grammatical categories appearing in the P marker. Note, however, that it is also true that categories can be defined in terms of the
relations appearing in the I markers. I markers and P markers, then,
contain essentially the same information; but I markers contain this
information in a form which is appropriate for a performance model
This is because we perceive our environment in terms of relations (like
agent and action), and not of, e.g., verbs and verb phrases (cf. Sections
2 and 4).

This redefinition of deep structure has further consequences. Consider
the following sentences:

(42)   John closes the door.

(43)   John feels well.

(44)   John enjoys himself.

(45)   Flowers please us.

(46)   The stamp sticks.

In each of these the first rewrite rule in the P marker is: S → NP + VP.
If relations are defined in terms of these grammatical categories, each
one of the above sentences must be said to exhibit the same relation.
Intuitively this is not so. In (42) we have the agent–action relation,
but not in (43)–(46), however far we wish to stretch the notion of
"action." This seems to be another reason for formulating deep structures
in terms of relations, rather than in terms of grammatical categories:
the latter obliterate important distinctions which the speaker presumably
is aware of.

Not only are there no grammatical categories in the I marker, but
the items between which the relations hold are neutral in regard to
grammatical category. In Section 5, it has been shown why the I marker
contains not words—which belong to classes such as noun, verb,
etc.—but more general "concepts," "meanings," or "referents" (all terms
that suggest themselves seem equally infelicitous). This enables us to
deal with some phenomena of reflexivization [see Chomsky (1965, pp.
145–146)]. Consider the following:

(47)   John hurt John.

(48)   John hurt himself.

Whether (47) or (48) is correct depends on whether John, the agent, and John, the object, are identical; i.e., whether we are dealing with the same referent. There is no rule which makes reflexivization dependent on the appearance of the same *word.*

Finally, the proposal that the deep structure contains general concepts rather than specific words seems to be in line with Morton's (1964) explanation of the locus of hesitations in speech. If individual words which make up the utterance are selected before the application of realization rules, one would expect hesitations to occur at phrase boundaries, and not, as actually is the case, mainly before content words (even when these occur within phrases). Morton has therefore suggested that the speaker decides first on "thought units," and only after applying the syntactic rules he chooses the exact words to express these units.

Still another difference between I markers and P markers is that the latter assign order to grammatical categories and to morphemes, whereas the terms of the relations in the I marker are not ordered (cf. Section 2 for a discussion of this point). The view that deep structures are ordered gives rise to serious difficulties for any theory of language acquisition, whether nativist or empiricist. This can be seen from McNeill's treatment of this problem (this volume). Since the order in the deep structure is apparently not universal, the conclusion is forced on McNeill (who represents the nativist position) that it is learned. But the order in the deep structure is unobservable and it often differs from that in the surface structure. Therefore the problem arises of how the order, which the child is never exposed to, in the deep structure, can be learned (cf. Section 4).

The changed conception of deep structure proposed here is motivated by an attempt to account for language learning and linguistic performance. The present proposal, which aims to achieve this, involves essentially the following:

1.   It relegates to deep structure (I markers) only that information which one must ascribe to linguistically expressed intentions of the speaker and his way of looking at the world. Therefore, the problem of how one learns what is in the deep structure does not arise.

2.   Aside from the above, it involves only processes that appear to be amenable to an explanation within a learning theory framework.

14. Additional Remarks: A Comparison with Other Approaches

The contributions in this volume fall into two distinct groups. On the one hand, there are those writers who, under the influence of recent work of generative grammarians, attempt to show *what* rules of grammar the child acquires, and on the other, there are the learning theorists, who, by applying learning principles set out to explain how these rules are acquired.

Generative grammarians have done a great service to the psychology of language not only in stimulating most of recent research in this area (cf. Section 1), but also in providing a solid basis for a theory of language learning. A grammar not only describes which utterances are acceptable to the speaker of a language (Palermo, this volume), but also what types of utterances are most likely to be produced by the speaker. Hence, it provides the theorist of language learning with a plan of action: it describes the behavior which he must explain. Therefore the approach of the new look psycholinguist who takes his lead from the generative grammarian and that of the learning psychologist should, ideally, complement each other.

In actual fact, the work of these two groups does not show such compatibility. The pictures they draw of language acquisition, each from his vantage point, do not fit together too well. Among the jagged edges there is the conclusion arrived at by some psycholinguists of the former group that learning theory is incapable of providing an adequate explanation of the acquisition of grammar, a conclusion which seems to be based on a very questionable view of the implications of linguistic theory (cf. Schlesinger, 1967; Staats, this volume). Learning theorists, on the other hand, have paid relatively little attention to problems of language acquisition (as pointed out by McNeill, this volume), and this may have contributed to the bleak view taken by some writers of the chances of applying learning principles in this area.

The contributions of Palermo and of Staats in this volume seem to go a long way toward closing the gap between what is now known about child language and what learning theory has to say about it. One might wish, though, that they would have gone further, instead of stopping short at just those phenomena which seem to be most intriguing—at least to those who have come within the pale of generative grammar—and which have given rise to the feeling that a radically new approach is required. Staats, for instance, explains how in a certain stimulus situation "Put the red hat on" is emitted. His presentation raises the question why this word order should be preferred to that in "Put on the red hat," or why one should say "Call the man up" instead of "Call up the man." Such discontinuous constituents are a phenomenon well accounted for by transformational grammar. Two alternatives are open to the learning theorist. Either he may account for the acquisition of such transformations (perhaps by showing how the child learns to reorder, add, and delete elements; cf. also Section 10 above), or else he might try to explain utterances of this kind without viewing them, behaviorally, as transformations from other structures. Neither of these approaches is taken by Staats and Palermo, who just do not deal with these problems explicitly. It would be unfair to reproach them for what they have failed to do, especially in view of what they have achieved in their chapters, but it should be recognized how much there is still left to do for learning theorists.

Still another problem concerns the correspondence of the stimulus world with syntax. To take Staats' own example, how does one set of stimuli come to elicit "The golf ball hit John," and another set "John hit the golf ball." This is perhaps the most important lacuna of the learning theorists' account in the present book. Obviously, it is not enough for the child to distinguish between these two utterances involving golf balls and John; rather, he must learn to master the linguistic expression of the subject–object relationship in *any* sentence. It is this problem of the relationship between language and the stimulus world which is a focal point of the present chapter. In view of the enormously large number of sentences in which the subject–object relationship, for instance, occurs, it is out of question that the child should learn the relationship for each sentence separately. Instead, he must acquire certain generalizations, or "realization rules" in our terminology.

As far as I can see, an elaboration of Staats' approach might cover the learning of realization rules. Principles of conditioning which account for the sequencing of two words belonging to two sets of words, "the car," for instance, might also account for the conditioning of the agent–action sequence or any other position rule. True, the stimulus situation which controls *agent* or *action* is a rather abstract one, but hardly more abstract than that which controls such words as "other," which, to quote Staats, is one " . . . where one person or object has been or done something and then another one is or does the same thing." There is one important difference here, however. According to the present chapter (Section 8), word classes are acquired through realization rules, and do not appear in the I marker. It follows that in the case of the agent–action relation the child does not learn to sequence classes of words—as he does in those cases treated by Staats—but rather the word associated with the agent and that associated with the action at the time the utterance is produced.[11]

To summarize, there seems to be no inherent contradiction between the views of the present chapter and those of Staats and Palermo. A

[11] These ideas have subsequently been further developed (Schlesinger, to be published).

l............ ....,
in that it describes the mechanism by which the child learns realization
rules.

This conciliatory attitude is apparently not shared by McNeill, who
has declared learning theory to be *hors de combat* as far as the acquisition of grammar is concerned. He subscribes instead to the theory that
language development is due to species-specific innate propensities. The
difference between McNeill's view of deep structure and that of the
present chapter (cf. Section 13) may serve to explain why his pessimism
concerning a learning theory account of the acquisition of language
is not shared by the present writer.

The I marker contains only concepts and those relations which are part
and parcel of our way of viewing the world. In a sense, of course, this
way of viewing the world is innate; it is part of our intellectual outfit
(but it is not very meaningful to call it species specific as long as there is
no possibility of describing an alternative way of viewing the world which
might conceivably be that of another species; cf. Section 4). Note, however that it is one thing to state that a modification relation is perceived
by the child in the environment (e.g., when he sees that a ball is red),
and quite another to agree with McNeill's claim that, in addition,
" . . . if one word is understood as modifying another in parental
speech, one of them is *inevitably* classified as a N and the other as
Det" (McNeill, this volume, italics mine). McNeill believes that this
classification appears in the deep structure. If this is so, there are indeed
difficulties for an explanation in terms of conditioning principles. This
leads him to the conclusion that this classification is not the product of
learning, but occurs "inevitably," i.e., as a result of the child's innate propensity. This is a very strong claim to make. It is not clear why we
should be born with a bent for classifying in such a particular manner.
By contrast, it has been suggested in the present chapter that grammatical categories do not appear in the deep structure at all, but are ascribed
to realization rules, which are learned.

McNeill's approach leads to additional difficulties which have been
mentioned in Section 13, where it has been shown how these can be
avoided (cf. also Section 9.3).

My conception of deep structure, then, deprives McNeill's attack on
empiricism of its foundation. It is curious, therefore, that he should
claim that there is no essential difference between our theories. If they
are alike, why should they lead to such diverse conclusions? McNeill
seems to be faced with the following alternatives: He can either criticize
the concept of the I marker (not showing its essential similarity to
the concept of a P marker, as he does, but rather) showing its weak-

nesses and the wrong conclusions it leads to. Or else, he can renounce the nativist position which he has been identified with for some time now. Since he is apparently not yet ready to do the latter, let us see what he has to say in regard to the former.

I markers are not identical with intentions. This seems to sum up several things McNeill has to say, which are both true and obvious. It is true that there are more things between intentions and I markers than are dreamed of in this chapter. I markers, to repeat, are merely those aspects of the speaker's intentions "which are expressed in the linguistic output" (Section 2). They are hypothetical constructs just as P markers are, and both I markers and P markers can be judged in terms of their value as constructs in the model of the human user of language. My discussion of intentions has attempted to show the insufficiency of P markers in this respect, and has led to a suggestion of deep structures which may be operative in the model. I have not attempted to go beyond this by establishing a formalization of the connection between intentions and I markers (this would presuppose a psychology of cognition in a more advanced state than the present). Nor have I tried, as McNeill seems to suppose, to abolish linguistic structures altogether and to jump directly from intentions to speech (this would presuppose a much less advanced stage of knowledge than linguists have arrived at by now).

The manner in which McNeill perceives of the difference between I markers and P markers seems to be due to some misunderstandings. In Section 13 (which was not yet written when McNeill wrote his Additional Remarks), I have tried to correct some of these.[12] The issue is not, as McNeill puts it, which aspects of deep structure belong to intentions and which to syntax, but rather what aspects serve as the input to the model on which the realization rules operate. Throughout this chapter, arguments have been adduced to the effect that neither the initial symbol S nor the underlying P marker can be considered as the input, and that a changed conception of deep structure may prove a

[12] There are, in addition, some minor misunderstandings in McNeill's Additional Remarks. Due to McNeill's urge for unanimity, not only does Staats willy-nilly become a nativist, and my position become identical with McNeill's, but my proposal for a performance model in Section 12 becomes "indistinguishable" from such theories as that of Yngve (1960). Actually, an acquaintance with both these models is required to make them quite distinguishable. While, in McNeill's view, everybody agrees with everybody else, there is a discordant note struck in this harmony, since I am claimed to have contradicted myself on at least one occasion. But this allegation stems from a failure to distinguish between the correct claim that a grammar is not a performance model and the incorrect statement that a grammar does not function in a performance model.

viable alternative, McNeill does not deal with these arguments directly and it seems that they are not weakened by anything he says in his Additional Remarks.

This brings us back to McNeill's nativism. As has been shown above there is nothing in the present proposal which bars an empiricist explanation of language acquisition. There can be no question, of course, that the organism comes to any learning task with some innate equipment; the question is only how much is innate. The soundest approach seems to be to make as few assumptions as possible, and to try to explain with these as much as possible. Currently, the nativists seem to be in favor of a much easier approach: they put down as much as possible to the organism's innate propensities. It has even been argued that all universals of language are innate (without seriously considering the possibility that these may be due to experiences common to children growing up all over the world). Explaining human behavior by invoking instincts has long ago become disreputable in psychology, because it does not constitute an explanation at all. But it seems that we are again faced by an invasion of noun-phrase instincts, verb-phrase instincts, and many others. Such is the outcome of a wholesale renunciation of empiricism.

McNeill accepts P markers as they are currently described by generative grammarians. This approach is well motivated in that it provides a firm basis for his analysis. It would be a highly desirable state of affairs indeed, if exactly those structures arrived at by an independent linguistic analysis could be shown to be operative in the human language acquisition device. However, at present, such a unified description can be bought only at the price of very strong assumptions regarding the innate intellectual abilities of the child. As stated, this is a very high price to pay.

This chapter, by contrast, attempts to sketch the outlines of a theory of how grammar is learned and utterances produced, and while it is based on a minimum of assumptions about innate ways of perceiving the world, it necessitates leaving the relatively firm ground of current linguistic theory. Hence, there arise a host of questions awaiting further study. If only for this reason, our account of language learning and production must be regarded as highly programmatic; but, all in all, it seems justifiable to deviate somewhat from the current linguistic model if thereby prospects are opened up for a performance model. Psychological theorizing about language learning is in its infancy, and generative grammar is not yet fast frozen. For the time being, the psycholinguists should be permitted a little fanciful theorizing, unfettered by the dictates of any particular linguistic theory. The unification of the two models will be a result of further developments in both areas of endeavor.

Acknowledgments

This paper owes very much to the many helpful suggestions and criticisms offered by Professor Y. Bar-Hillel. These have helped me in developing the ideas expressed therein, and in refining many of the formulations. I have also had the benefit of long discussions with Dr. Martin Braine, and the opportunity of reading, before its publication, his important critical review of the literature on child language (Braine, 1971). Dr. Braine's comments on a preliminary version of this paper have led to my revising a part of Section 7. I am also indebted to Mrs. Ruth Clark for her helpful comments on a preliminary version, and to Dr. Dan I. Slobin for his valuable comments on the content and style of this paper and for suggesting the quotation from William James in Section 1.

Linguistic–Mentalistic Theory versus an Explanatory S–R Learning Theory of Language Development[*]

ARTHUR W. STAATS

University of Hawaii
Honolulu, Hawaii

There are several general features to be outlined in introducing the present learning approach to grammatical speech development in children. The general features must be touched upon to give the analysis context and to indicate that what is involved is part of an approach that concerns various areas of language. There is a philosophy of science underlying the approach, a new basic learning theory, and research on and theoretical analyses of complex human behavior in general as well as language behavior in particular. Most of these topics cannot be dealt with herein in any detail—but it is suggested that this type of generality is necessary if one wishes to deal comprehensively with language.

Specific learning interpretations of language have been successfully criticized and the implication has been made that learning theory in general is being challenged (for example, see Chomsky, 1959; Fodor, 1965; Miller, 1965; Weinreich, 1958). It should be noted, however, that criticism of a particular learning theory of language does not disqualify learning approaches in general. The fact is the traditional basic learning theories have been separatistic; even as the field of learning has been lumped together by its critics, major efforts within learning have been expended in developing and maintaining separate experimental methods, separate general (philosophical) methodologies, and separate terminologies.

1. Limitations in Traditional Learning Theories of Language

It is thus to be expected that learning theories of language that are based upon the traditional learning theories will suffer the limitations

[*] This paper was prepared under partial support of the Office of Naval Research, Contract N00014-67-C-0387-0007 with the University of Hawaii.

of this separation. There are numerous examples. Thus, there have been people interested in the operant conditioning of verbal behavior who often eschew the experimental results and conceptions of investigators of word meaning and semantic mediation. And, many times these latter investigators reject the importance of operant conditioning in the area of language. A third approach has focused upon verbal learning, including serial and paired-associate verbal learning. And this approach has ignored the findings of the former two areas—an action that has largely been reciprocated. To continue with the example, another group has been concerned with the mediational properties of word associates. In the latter two cases, in fact, there has been almost no contemporary articulation even with basic learning principles. At any rate, even though these various approaches spring from the same general tradition, they have been theoretical competitors rather than contributors to a general learning approach. Obviously, complex language behaviors cannot be accounted for solely on the basis of word associations, or word meaning, or the operant conditioning of speech.

Furthermore, besides the separatism of the field, the strategy of theory construction in learning has not been conducive to the development of a theory of human behavior. Learning theories have been developed largely to explain the principles of conditioning. It is suggested, however, that the conditioning principles themselves are basic—not to be explained—the theory comes in deriving principles not yet observed from those already observed. Moreover, the theory construction further occurs in elaborating the learning theory as a theory of the various aspects of human behavior. The inadequacies of traditional learning theories as well as the inadequacies of traditional theory construction strategies suggests the need of a "third generation" learning theory (see Staats, 1965b, 1968b, 1968c, 1970). A more sophisticated learning theory provides a much better basis with which to compose a theory of language.

Thus, extensions of traditional learning theories to language have made important contributions—but have in many ways been short of the mark. For example, Osgood (1953), while inspiring a great deal of research in the measurement of connotative word meaning, has based his analyses on Hullian theory, which has several weaknesses. Among other things, Hullian theory does not adequately distinguish classical and instrumental conditioning—and thus as a basic learning theory does not provide a structure within which to adequately differentiate the different aspects of language. The basic theory is thus a one-factor learning theory. Moreover, Osgood's extension of basic learning theory has been largely restricted to the consideration of only one aspect of language; that is, the manner in which words come to elicit implicit connotative meaning responses. His later excursions in language theory (Osgood, 1957a, 1957b, 1963) have tended to abandon a learning approach in favor of neurological theorizing and linguistic conceptions.

Mowrer (1954) has dealt with similar matters—extending the analysis in a classic paper to a consideration of how word meaning may be conditioned from one word to another when the words occur in a sentence. Mowrer suggested that the principle of classical conditioning was involved in the acquisition of meaning responses by words and that higher-order classical conditioning was involved in the transfer of meaning responses from word to word. In addition, Mowrer (1952) suggested that vocal responses can be learned because of their secondary reinforcing properties. Again, however, these extensions of learning principles to language behavior do not constitute a comprehensive account.

Skinner (1957) has employed his own basic learning theory in an analysis of restricted aspects of language. Although his basic learning theory is nominally a two-factor theory, he has almost completely ignored the principle of classical conditioning in his treatment of human behavior. While Osgood and Mowrer have dealt only cursorily with speech, Skinner has hardly touched upon classical conditioning in his consideration of language. Actually, Skinner has never developed or employed the principles of classical conditioning in either his basic theory or in his extensions of theory to human behavior. His approach thus suffers from the crucial weakness of being a one-factor theory in practice—a crucial weakness.

Moreover, in restricting his analysis to selected aspects of the conditioning of speech, Skinner's approach to language has also been less than comprehensive. Furthermore, his atheoretical methodology in general and his rejection of detailed S-R analyses constitute grave handicaps. Such a learning theory cannot deal with many of the complex aspects of the development and function of language.

The fact is, in summary, the basic learning theory employed must include clear presentation of the principles of both classical and instrumental conditioning, as well as *the manner in which the principles interact*. Although it is not possible to present the full formulation here (see Staats, 1959, 1963, 1965b, 1968b, 1968c, 1970), it should be indicated that classical conditioning and instrumental conditioning interact—and the symbolic form of the theory should indicate the interactions. That is, as one example, the principle of classical conditioning underlies the formation of conditioned reinforcement. Thus, in the process of becoming a conditioned stimulus, ^{c}S, which will elicit a response, the stimulus will also become a conditioned reinforcer when the unconditioned stimulus is also a reinforcer. Such a ^{c}S will also function as a reinforcer, capable of strengthening any instrumental response of the subject involved, when the stimulus is applied in a response-contingent manner. Besides being an important basic principle in learning, the principle has important implications for language. As will be described, as a word becomes a conditioned stimulus which will elicit an affective or meaning response, the word also becomes a conditioned reinforcer. The word can then be used to affect the strength of any instrumental behavior when applied in a response-contingent manner.

It is also the case, as another example of the interaction of the basic principles in human behavior, that the conditioned reinforcing value of a stimulus is related to its discriminative stimulus value, as the author has indicated (Staats, 1963, 1964b, 1968b, 1970). Thus, as a word comes to elicit an evaluative emotional meaning response, and thus acquires conditioned reinforcing value, it should also have an increased strength as a discriminative stimulus that will elicit (or control) instrumental behavior.

It is suggested that to serve as an adequate foundation for a learning analysis of language the basic learning theory must indicate in a detailed way the principles of classical and instrumental conditioning and their interrelationships. Furthermore, the basic theory must also indicate the general ways that stimuli and responses can be formed into complex constellations. It is suggested that although the basic principles must be separated to distinguish and study them, in actual life the principles function in concert. That is, although the conditioning principles themselves are simple, the S–R mechanisms that are formed in real life consist of exceedingly complex arrays and constellations of functionally connected stimulus–response events. Critics of learning are customarily aware only of some of the basic principles, and few or none of the complex S-R mechanisms that can be formed on the basis of the principles.

It is not possible to present here even a brief summary of the complex S–R mechanisms. [See Staats (1955, 1959, 1963, 1965b, 1968b, 1970) for additional discussions.] As an illustration, however, responses (since they produce stimuli themselves) can come to elicit other responses. Thus, through conditioning (either classical or instrumental or both) sequences of responses may be formed such that the occurrence of one response leads to the next and so on. In addition, one stimulus may come to control more than one following response in what may be called a response hierarchy. In such a case, whether or not a particular response will occur when a stimulus is presented will then depend not only upon the strength of the conditioning involved, but also the strength of the other competing responses the stimulus tends to elicit.

In addition, more than one stimulus can come to have control over a response. This control may be facilitating, when two or more stimuli present in a situation tend to elicit or control the response, or the control may be inhibiting, when one stimulus tends to bring on the response and the other stimulus controls not responding, or making another response.

Just on the basis of combinations of these several general S–R mechanisms very complex repertoires of human behavior, including language, can be understood. That is, on the basis of the individual's past training complex S–R mechanisms consisting of a sequence of hierarchies of responses, with multiple stimulus control, may be formed. An example in the realm of language is illustrated on p. 138. Each word response, for example, GIVE, tends to elicit three other word responses, and each of the word responses thus elicited tends to elicit three others until the complex sequence is terminated. (It is interesting to note here that each of the three word groups tends to be in a grammatical class, a suggestion that such classes are in part based upon such associations.) It should be noted that in any particular case in which the individual with such a learned word associational mechanism emits an utterance like "Give me the small shirt," there will be additional situational stimuli besides the word associations controlling some of the word responses. Furthermore, some of the words in an utterance may elicit classically conditioned meaning responses or tend to elicit instrumentally conditioned motor responses, and so on, which may have an effect on the course of the utterance. Thus, the diagram is considerably oversimplified.

2. A Pluralistic Learning Theory of Language Is Necessary[1]

In addition to the basic learning theory and the elucidation of the complex S–R mechanisms, a learning theory of language (including theories of grammatical sentence generation) must make analyses of the *various* aspects of language. Language is not a unitary type of event. It has multiple aspects and its aspects serve many different functions. Consideration of language cannot be restricted to any one aspect or only certain functions, if the account is to be comprehensive. Theories of language, learning theories as well as others, have ordinarily made analyses of one aspect of language, or at most of a few aspects—without treating its various aspects and without being concerned about the *func-*

[1] Editor's note: Professor Staats elaborated and clarified this section in his discussion, adding additional references, in December 1970, shortly before this volume went to press.

tions of language in human behavior (Contemporary psycholinguistics, for example, restricts itself to grammatical phenomena.)

In very general terms, it must be realized that language serves in the role of a stimulus in multifarious ways which have an important function in controlling many aspects of human behavior. As such, the language of the individual and other individuals serves as an independent variable, a "cause" of the individual's actions. Furthermore, language consists of responses of great variety and complexity—and is thus a dependent variable.

It has been suggested (Staats, 1963, 1968b, 1971) that the individual's language is actually composed of repertoires of skills that he must learn. These repertoires can be considered separately. Some are learned according to different principles. The repertoire of speech responses (phonemes), for example, is learned on the basis of instrumental conditioning (which includes imitation). On the other hand, classical conditioning is the principle by which large numbers of words come to elicit emotional responses, another important aspect of language.

While the learning of the repertoires may be analyzed separately, the learning of the language repertoires may occur in the same experimental situation. Moreover, it is the various repertoires of language that when functionally combined, constitute a functional language. Single repertoires by themselves will not constitute functional language. As an example, the child may be trained to a repertoire of imitational speech responses, he may be able to repeat phonemes, words and longer sentences. Yet this alone is not language. A child who has learned only this aspect of language has echolalia, a recognized abnormality. Similarly, a person who had learned only to say words in a language, and grammatical rules for categorizing and sequencing the words, would not have a functional language. This would be tantamount to learning a complex list of nonsense syllables.

A credible theory of language must indicate the various repertoires of which language is composed, the learning principles by which the repertoires are acquired, the specific conditions and procedures for producing the learning, and—as the next section will indicate—the manner and principles by which language functions in the individual's adjustment.

Since this conception includes a complex subject matter, it will not be possible to present a full account herein (see, especially, Staats, 1963, 1968b, 1971). However, some of the repertoires that have to be acquired for the individual to have a functional language can be briefly summarized and some of the literature can be cited that has been conducted that supports the general conception as well as the learning of the specific repertoires. Only some of the basic repertoires that go to make up language can be described in this outline—not the way the repertoires interact in functional language sequences. Some examples of the interaction of the language repertoires will be given in later sections addressed to the specific points of language development considered in this book.

1. In the child's early learning various environmental stimuli begin to come to control certain specific speech responses. Staats (1963) has described naturalistic evidence to substantiate the occurrence of this type of language learning. Experimental demonstration has been made of the child's learning such labeling responses to pictures and also to the stimuli of numerosity (Staats 1968b; Staats, Brewer, & Gross, 1970a). The principle involved in this type of learning is instrumental conditioning. The learning of labels to environmental stimuli of varying degrees of complexity yields a vast and vastly important repertoire.

2. Internal drive stimuli, and other physiological responses that produce stimuli, must also come through learning to control certain speech responses. It is by means of this learned repertoire that the individual comes to be able to verbally respond to his internal feelings and sensations.

3. The stimuli produced by one's own instrumental responses and actions must come to control speech responses. This is demonstrated when the individual describes the position of his limbs, as one example. The repertoire is central, moreover, in the individual coming to describe himself and his actions—an area important to considerations of the self-concept (see Staats, 1963, 1971).

4. Printed and written verbal stimuli must come to control the appropriate speech responses (reading). The principle is the same as that for the repertoires already described. Thus, it is important to indicate that there is strong support for the instrumental learning of this type of language. That is, the author and associates have shown that various phonemic, word, and phrase responses to printed verbal stimuli can be lawfully learned by the child according to the lawful principles of reinforcement (Staats et al., 1970a; Staats & Butterfield, 1965; Staats, Finley, Minke, Wolf, & Brooks, 1964a; Staats, Minke, Goodwin, & Landeen, 1967; Staats, Staats, Schutz, & Wolf, 1962b). (See also Whitlock, 1966.) The acquisition of a reading repertoire heavily involves this type of learning in a process requiring years of time and thousands of learning trials.

5. Verbal stimuli, or speech responses (covert and overt), must come to elicit implicit responses in the individual through classical conditioning. That is, when a word is paired with a stimulus that elicits a physio-

logical response, such as an emotional response, the word will come to elicit that response also. A most important function of words resides in their ability to elicit emotional responses in people. The primary classical conditioning of such word responses has shown experimentally (Brotsky, 1968; Staats, Staats, & Crawford, 1962a; Zanna, Kiesler, & Pilkonis, 1970). The author and associates have demonstrated that this type of learning can take place purely on a verbal level, where one word transfers its emotional meaning to other stimuli, and there have been a large number of studies that have studied the effect (see Staats & Carlson, 1970, for a bibliography). Although there is remaining controversy concerning methodology in this area (see Page, 1969; Staats 1969) various studies demonstrate this type of learning clearly (see Abell, 1969; Ertel, Oldenberg, Siry, & Vormfelde, 1969; A. Miller, 1967; Minke & Stalling, 1970; Nunnally, Duchnowski, & Parker, 1965; Phelan, Hekmat, & Tang, 1967; Staats & Staats, 1957, 1958; Weiss, Chalupa, Gorman, & Goodman, 1968; Yavuz & Bousfield, 1959).

In addition, the author first suggested (Staats, 1959) that these meaning responses could be of a sensory nature, as well as the emotional type. That is, many stimuli elicit sensory responses in the individual and these responses will also be conditioned to contiguous stimuli, including words. Mowrer (1960), Sheffield (1961), and more recently Bandura (1969), have employed this concept of conditioned sensory responses to words. Supporting experiments have also been conducted (Paivio, 1965; Staats, Staats, & Heard, 1960). The important idea to recognize in this area is that the function of many words or concepts is to elicit images (conditioned sensory responses) in the individual. These images may be general aspects of stimuli, like color, shape, types of sounds, and so on. When such words are arranged in combinations, they may elicit composite images. The power of words to elicit images, without the individual having to have the primary experience that would ordinarily elicit such sensory responses, is one of the significant functions of language.

6.   Emotional and image meaning responses have stimulus characteristics that must come to elicit speech responses (Staats, 1959, 1968b). For example, positive emotional responses will come to elicit speech (word) responses that have the same positive meaning. Lott, Lott, Reed, and Crow (1970) have recently conducted an experiment to test this hypothesis and have clearly shown that stimuli that elicit positive emotional meaning (attitudes) will elicit positive meaning words from subjects. When the attitude elicited is negative, the words elicited by the stimulus will have a negative meaning. This was conducted with social stimuli, but the principle would apply to any type of stimulus.

7. Word stimuli (or speech responses, through the stimuli they produce) come to elicit other word responses. Sequences of associations of words will be formed through various types of the individual's experience. The manner in which word associations are established has been widely shown experimentally in the rote verbal learning studies (see Underwood & Schultz, 1960). This field of study has not dealt with the learning of such word associations in actual language, or in the functions of such word associations in the individual's adjustment—both areas requiring intense investigation. The manner in which such associations of word responses can be formed in actual language development and the way these associations can function for the child has been shown by Staats *et al.,* (1970a). This was done in the context of number concept learning. As another example, it has also been hypothesized that a child could learn to read a word more easily if it was preceded by a word he could already read that was strongly associated to the word to be learned (Staats, 1963, p. 463). This hypothesis has been supported (Samuels, 1966) in a well controlled laboratory study.

8. Verbal stimuli (written, auditory, and those produced by one's own speech responses) will in the child's language training come to control certain motor behaviors. It is on the basis of large repertoires of verbal–motor units that much human interaction takes place. That is, we say things to others and they respond appropriately, under the control of our verbal stimuli—and we do so in response to what they say. The ability to follow instructions and to profit from verbal interactions rests heavily on this repertoire. Procedures for producing such repertoires in young children have been described (see especially Staats, 1971; Staats *et al.,* 1970a).

9. The child learns that it is rewarding when his vocal responses produce sound stimuli that "match" those produced by an authority source. It has been suggested that sound imitations can become rewarding (Mowrer, 1952). The way this can occur in the language learning of the child has been outlined also (Staats, 1963). Baer and Sherman (1965) and Baer, Peterson, and Sherman (1967), have employed the analysis and verified it experimentally with children.

10. The child must also learn a large repertoire of imitation speech units so that he can reproduce the phonemes of the language. The ability to imitate the sounds of the language is involved in a great deal of the child's more advanced language learning. Procedures for producing functional speech imitation repertoires in children have been described (Staats, 1971).

11. As has been suggested, a very large class of words, through the principles of classical conditioning, must come to elicit emotional mean-

ing responses of either a positive or negative sort. As a function of this process of conditioning, these word stimuli become reinforcers, either positive or negative as the case may be. When individually delivered contingent upon an instrumental behavior these words will either strengthen (if positive) or weaken (if negative) the tendency of the behavior to occur again in the future (Staats, 1968). This early theoretical analysis has been supported in experiments by Golightly and Byrne (1964) and Byrne, Young, and Griffit (1966), with "agreed with" attitude statements; and by Finley and Staats (1967), Reitz and McDougall (1969), and Staats, Carlson and Reid (1970b) on a more basic level using single words. Pihl and Greenspoon (1969) have further shown how reward value can be gained by a word through pairing it with stimuli that are reinforcing. It is important to point out that humans continually reward and punish each other through language and thereby influence each other's behavior—a central aspect of language.

12. Finally, the classical conditioning process that gives a word emotional and hence reinforcing value will also give the word discriminative controlling value. If the emotional response the word elicits is positive, the word will control or elicit approach (or striving for) behaviors. If the emotional response is negative, the word will elicit avoidance (or striving away from) behaviors. Solarz (1960) and DiVesta and Stover (1962) have conducted laboratory experiments that may be seen to support this analysis. Early (1968) and Berkowitz and Knurek (1969) have shown the effect in social situations where the word is a name and it controls approach or avoidance behavior to the person with that name.

3. Language Theory Must Encompass Language Function as Well as Language Acquisition

It should also be indicated that the study of language must be concerned not only with a theory that describes how language comes about *but also how language functions in the individual's adjustment.* (This is implied, of course, when it is suggested that language is an independent variable.) It is apparent that the individual's language performs essential functions in all of his social interactions, cognitive actions, emotional actions, and motor skills. The individual's reasoning involves language as a primary determinant. Much of what we call intelligence, certainly as it is measured, involves, or is, language—as the author has indicated in detail (Staats, 1963, 1968b, 1971). Language, or its absence or disturbance, is heavily involved in many forms of psychopathology—as the author has also indicated (Staats, 1957, 1963, 1968b, 1971; Staats &

Butterfield, 1965). The study of language development in children must be concerned with circumstances that produce abnormal language, or a deficit in language, as well as with normal language development. Moreover, complex language learning is involved in reading acquisition, number concept learning and later mathematical skills, writing acquisition, and the like. These actual language tasks involve various principles of learning and must be dealt with in a theory of language— although experimental psychology as well as linguistics traditionally ignored such subjects of study. None of the other learning approaches to language has treated the *various* aspects of language, including the various functions of language in human behavior. It may be added that it makes no sense to treat one aspect of language at the expense of the others—since all are essential. This injunction applies to the linguistic focus upon the structure of language.

4. The Failure of Chomskian Psycholinguistics as an Explanatory Theory of Language

Before embarking upon the analysis of grammatical development, there is one other general issue that should be elaborated. There has been developing in the field of language a controversy (of which the present book is at least in part a symptom) which should be placed in a general context. Basically, the controversy is one that has occurred a number of times in the history of psychology—empiricism versus nativism (along with objectivism versus subjectivism). A historically recent example is that of the nature–nurture struggle that dominated the early years of developmental psychology. In fact, the lines are drawn in the present case in a very similar way.

In the original nature–nurture schism the nativists participated primarily in two types of research activities. They observed the manner in which the child's behavior developed. Upon the basis of the regularities in time and sequence in behavior development observed in a majority of children—for example, most children sit before they stand, stand before they walk, walk before they run, and so on—they inferred that there must be innate, internal, physiological and anatomical developments that produced the behavioral development. [There were also suggestive results of an indirect kind that were used to support this biological conception of behavior development. For example, anaesthetized frog and salamander tadpoles quickly swam as well when the drug had worn off as those not drugged—suggesting that the behavior of swimming was due to biological development and not learning. We also know, as another example, that lack of myelinization of certain neural fibers is related to the presence of the Babinski reflex in infants, and the like. These findings are only circumstantial, however, in the context of the development of complex human behavior (see Staats, 1971).]

Second, to counter the challenge from a nurture (learning) conception, the nativists produced research or theories whose aim was to show that learning was really not important to behavioral development. In addition, the nativists attempted to bolster their approach by citing behaviors that "could not be accounted for" using prevailing learning principles. A great deal of effort went into these experimental and theoretical activities. And much of it must be considered to be wasted.

That is, the only way to establish a nativistic theory of behavior development would be to actually find independent variables (causative conditions) that produced the behavioral development which was of interest. If the child develops anatomically or physiologically in some manner that determines his development of complex behaviors, then these biological events must be isolated. When they *have* been found, the laws by which they produce the complex behaviors could be established and statements of such laws would constitute an explanatory theory.

It is definitely the case that the *explanation* of behavior cannot be drawn from only observations of the behavior itself. No matter how regular the development of behavior is in children (and this is subject to considerable variability, which increases with the complexity of the behavior), no matter with what detail the observations are made, and no matter how elegantly formal the system is by which the observations are described, information about the behavior *itself* does not provide evidence of internal structures or processes or indeed any other cause (independent variable).

Furthermore, the discreditation of learning in no way constitutes verification of a nativistic theory. (Such criticism may have positive aspects in identifying weaknesses in a learning theory and in stimulating new research and new formulations, of course.) Discrediting learning does not in any way provide the positive identification of nativistic (anatomical and physiological) principles. It may be added that the field of learning is a growing science. Experimental and theoretical analyses are possible now which were unavailable a short time past and this progress may be expected to continue. Moreover, it is unconvincing to have individuals who are only superficially acquainted with learning theory, learning research methods, and so on—who are actually in opposition to a learning approach—act as investigators who set up the research that shows the unimportance of learning. It is too easy to set up an experiment in which learning appears to have no effect. Thus, as an example, it is rather obvious that if one twin is given training on a simple task, like climbing stairs or memorizing numbers, and the other is not, there will be slight differences after a brief training period—and at best it will only require a short time for the other twin to catch up. This type of training does not compare to the snowballing differences that training can produce over long periods of time in which one skill must be gained before the child can be trained on the next, in the cumulative acquisition of some complex skilled repertoire. [See Staats (1968b, 1971) for the complete conception of cumulative-hierarchical learning.] In any event, the studies to discredit the importance of learning in child development have been far from convincing methodologically and in fact have indicated the importance of learning in the development of complex cognitive behavior, as a recent review by Fowler (1962) shows most clearly.

Before proceeding, it should be indicated that the systematic observations made of the development of child behavior by the early developmentalists were exceedingly valuable, in their proper role. For example, the observations of child behavior development, and the various types of tests of behavior that were constructed, enable us to *place* a child with respect to his behavior development—to know if he is accelerated or retarded. This information also yields prediction of later development and enables us to take remedial steps to correct any difficulty. In addition to these important uses it should be indicated *that systematic observations and descriptions of an event are necessary before one can set about finding the determinants of the event.* Thus, detailed and systematic observations and descriptions of behavior are essential.

However, the productivity of developmental research would have been enhanced if the early child development people had been able to place their work in the context of its scientific methodology. Furthermore, much effort uselessly expended in research and theory in the critique of learning could have been saved and better directed if they had realized their work was descriptive, not explanatory.

This historical controversy is described to support the suggestion that these errors not be relived in the study of language and language development. At this point the elements exist for the same course of events to occur, however, and in recent years the nativist approach appears to be girding itself for another theoretical plunge. That is, linguists have described aspects of language behavior in detail, in a systematic and formal manner. The regularities in language behavior—as well as certain additional features such as the complexity of language, its common or universal features across languages, and its creative (or originality) characteristics—have led to conclusions that the regularities

(rules) must reflect underlying, innate, psychological structures. In addition, the booming complexity of language and the lack of development
of the traditional learning theories have led to conclusions that language
could not be learned. This has led in turn to theoretical criticisms of
specific learning approaches following Chomsky's (1959) successful
foray into the critical arena, to a general loss of confidence in the role
values of learning principles for the study of language, and is beginning
to inspire attempts to conduct research that will show that learning
principles are not relevant. While this may have a function in stimulating
additional development of learning theory—and the field of learning
has a history of building part of its generality upon the empirical findings
and challenges of its critics—it is suggested that we will progress more
rapidly if we recognize the nature of the task involved in constructing
an explanatory theory of language as well as the potential contributions
of the disciplines concerned with language.

Thus, it is well to note that linguistic information is *in principle* like
the developmentalist's observations of behavior development. The linguistic observations and systematic descriptions may be extremely productive in and of themselves. This work, for example, can help specify
the behavior that has to be accounted for in an explanatory psychological
theory. But the *determinants* of language behavior and language development must lie either in learning circumstances or in biological events
of some kind. It should be realized that linguists deal only with a certain
type of observation and their theoretical statements must be limited
by the nature of the observations. Of major importance here is the fact
that linguistic observations are of language products (behavior), almost
never of the determinants of that behavior. There are few observations
of learning variables and none of anatomical, genetic, or physiological
determinants. Linguistic observations cannot, thus, by themselves serve
as a basis for making statements about the determinants of language,
a point that Chomsky and like-minded theorists do not recognize. Nor
can this state of affairs be improved by observing language *behavior*
in children—important as these observations may be, and even if this
is done in a longitudinal fashion.

The realization of some of these limitations has been lost, or obscured,
partly, it may be suggested because of the undoubted elegance of linguistic theory. This error must be illustrated to make the point, and
the following quotation of Chomsky provides the lead.

A grammar of the language L is essentially a theory of L. Any scientific theory
is based on a finite number of observations, and it seeks to relate the observed
phenomena and to predict new phenomena by constructing general laws in terms
of hypothetical constructs such as (in physics, for example) "mass" and "electron."

Similarly, a grammar of English is based on a finite corpus of utterances (observations), and it will contain certain grammatical rules (laws) stated in terms of the particular phonemes, phrases, etc., of English (hypothetical constructs). *These rules express structural relations among the sentences of the corpus and the indefinite number of sentences generated by the grammar beyond the corpus (predictions). Our problem is to develop and clarify the criteria for selecting the correct grammar for each language, that is, the correct theory of this language* [1959, p. 49, emphasis added].

While this is a type of theory (although Chomsky's hypothetical constructs are actually just labels for an observable class of events), we should realize its characteristics and limitations—set by the nature of its observations. As will be indicated, *it should be stated unequivocally that such a theory cannot be construed to represent an explanatory theory of the individual speakers of some language.* The reasons may be explicated as follows; the observations of the linguist are of language products (responses) of some set of subjects. The theory notes the relations (laws) of the terms in its observations. Then, on the basis of the laws, predictions can be generated concerning other language products (responses) not yet observed in *additional* subjects in the same language community, or additional language responses of the same subjects. It should be noted that we are dealing, in psychological terms, with an R–R (response–response) type of law—or an R–R theory. The limitations of such theory in the study of behavior have been discussed by Spence (1944) and the present author in the context of complex human behavior (Staats, 1963). The central point is that the type of theory Chomsky describes is not explanatory, it tells us nothing of the determinants of the language responses of the original subjects, nor of the subjects whose language is to be predicted. As a consequence, Chomsky's R–R type of theory cannot produce scientific control of the events being studied. There are no independent variables indicated which when manipulated will produce or change the language behavior of an individual. Nothing can be done on the basis of the theory to produce desirable language behavior, correct undesirable language behavior, or to in any way affect this most inportant aspect of human behavior. Until observations are made of manipulable biological events that actually produce language development, a biological theory based upon linguistic observations must remain as the weakest of hypotheses.

The fact is that Chomsky has completely misunderstood this—his scientific methodology in the area of psychological explanation (not in linguistics) is actually a philosophical mentalism. That is, Chomsky does not leave his linguistic theory in its justified realm. He also attempts, in a very erroneous manner, to suggest that linguistic theory is an explanatory psychological theory. Probably because of his stature as a linguist he has provided a very potent, but misleading, influence in the psychology of language.

Chomsky's inappropriate psychological theorizing can be illustrated with various examples, for he uses a number of circular, mentalistic concepts which are based solely upon inferences from behavior itself or from R–R relationships. Thus, Chomsky uses supposedly causative (explanatory) terms like "mind," "deep" versus "surface" language structures, language universals which are innately given, grammatical rules which are causative in a psychological sense, "competence" (as opposed to performance) as an internal innately given mental process, and so on. As one example, take the following quotation: "the grammar proposed by the linguist is an explanatory theory; it suggests an explanation for the fact that . . . a speaker of the language in question will perceive, interpret, form, or use an utterance in certain ways and not in other ways" (1967b, p. 3). He goes on to suggest that the *particular* grammar is not as "deep" as the universal grammar. "Universal grammar thus constitutes an explanatory theory of a much deeper sort than a particular grammar . . . [1967b, p. 3]."

Chomsky's competence and performance distinction—which Fodor and Garrett (1966) call a major methodological clarification—is another example of the fallacious reasoning involved. That is, the linguistic description of a limited set of utterances (corpus) can be used as a theory to predict the structural relations of *future* speech of the individual (and of other individuals in the language community). In this sense, then, the linguistic theory is *more than* the sample of the individual's speech from whence it was derived. It is, unfortunately, an easy step to infer that the linguistic theory thus represents the individual's "competence"—that there are internal mental structures that correspond to the linguistic theory—and this is why we can predict additional grammatical speech characteristics of an individual from the linguistic theory. However, this step is circular, mentalistic reasoning. Our observations do not justify the step.

The same error in reasoning occurs in language universals. The finding that an aspect of various languages can be described by a common statement (grammatical rule) is used as the basis for inferring that there must be innate mental structures that correspond to the "universals." Again, this is a response inferred concept which is thus circular. The systematic nature of language, the universality of grammatical characteristics, or the fact that our descriptions of that system have uses which the language sample itself does not have, and so on, should not induce us to feel that our description of the system has some counterpart in a supposed innate mental structure of the individual. We would be no more justified in doing so than we would be in inferring that there are innate mental structures corresponding to the rules of mathematics, chess, or hopscotch.

Linguistic theory of this type may be illustrated by indicating that it is like an algebra. Let us say that a culture has a certain number "language." That is, the individuals in the culture make number responses in various ways—they count, add, multiply, and so on. When the algebraist describes their behavior—the number responses—in formal properties in terms of general statements (laws or rules) this has many useful products. It may be possible to derive new numbers from the algebraist's rules (his theory), for example, as negative numbers were derived (Stevens, 1951). It is also possible to teach a child the rules more easily in some cases than to teach the child all the specific number manipulations directly, since there are fewer of the former.

But the algebra is not an explanation of the behavior. The algebraist does not have contact with the independent variables that determine the child's acquisition of a number repertoire. Nor does he study the principles of acquisition (learning actually, but conceivably biological in nature). He can make no statement about such determining events or principles. Of course, in the area of mathematics behavior (which is a type of language), it is quite obvious that the behavior is learned—for it was not long ago that mathematics was not a feature of human behavior and then children did not "develop" the behavior simply through "maturation." Furthermore, we see today people who cannot train their children (informally, or formally) to math behavior and their children do not develop the behavior.

I would suggest that the linguist is analogous to the algebraist in this example. The linguist observes language and creates a grammar or theory, like an algebra, which systematically describes some of the properties of the language in general statements, or rules. These rules, the theory, may have the same uses as the algebra. For example, the person who is learning a new language—who has only partially learned the language himself—may use the rules to generate statements in the language which follow the rules. However, grammatical rules, like algebraic rules, are themselves learned skills—not explanations of grammatical skills.

Thus, the present analysis should not be construed as a criticism of linguistic theory in its own realm. The analysis does, however, seek to remedy the error made in extrapolating from linguistic theory in an attempt to produce an explanatory (in a psychological sense) theory of language behavior. The value of linguistic theory is to be assessed

In its own realm rather than one in which we are concerned with the actual events that produce language products. This has not been understood by Chomsky and the psycholinguists who have been most influenced by his approach. Thus, the present analysis may be considered to be an answer to the general criticism of learning approaches made by Chomsky.

The preceding has dealt only with the weaknesses of Chomsky's approach in terms of the principles of explanatory theory construction. While it cannot be elaborated here because of the limitations of space, it should be noted that the approach fails on other grounds that are of even greater importance. Centrally, Chomskian psycholinguistics does not deal with the *various* important aspects of language. His approach is restricted to only one aspect of language, the description of grammar within and between languages, and the way these logical rules are involved in predicting grammatical utterances. The various repertoires that constitute a functional language for the individual are not dealt with in any way. Yet these are the bases for some of the most powerful functions of language in human learning and in human interaction. There are no principles within the Chomskian psycholinguistics theory for studying how the child learns his *various* repertoires of language or how they function in the individual's behavior and in social interaction. Moreover, there are no methods for conducting such study. These are insuperable obstacles in a theory that claims to understand language acquisition and the functions of language—that is, a comprehensive, explanatory theory.

5. Learning Principles and Grammatical Development

Having said this it becomes clear that it is the task of any explanatory conception of language to indicate the events that produce language as well as the principles by which this is accomplished. This is true for those who hold a biological conception and thus must isolate biological events directly and relate them to language development, and it holds true for those who place their reliance upon a learning conception and who must isolate environmental events that produce language development. This task, in either case, demands that we are able to observe the presence or absence of the determining events and the related presence or absence of language development. This means experimental research.

The author has described his experimental results obtained in research on various aspects of language (see Staats, 1963, 1968b, 1971), and other references have been listed in the previous section. A primary suggestion is that research on a new phase of language learning must be preceded by an S–R analysis. Since the principles involved are empirical, experimental hypotheses may then be derived from the analysis. Observational data on the progressive development of language responses in children have been given in Slobin's introductory chapter. The first step in a learning analysis is to suggest tentatively the S–R mechanisms that appear to be involved. The S–R analyses can then be employed to suggest empirical hypotheses by which to test and extend the analyses.

5.1 Two-Word Utterances

The first of the important observations of language development to be dealt with herein concerns the two-word utterances that Slobin describes (this volume). Before discussing these observations in learning terms, it may be indicated that a great deal of important language learning takes place prior to this stage, and there is much additional language learning occurring not included in the observations of two-word utterances. The restrictiveness of the focus on grammar can be seen here. Because grammatical relations cannot be described until the child makes multiple-word utterances, language development and function prior to this point are generally ignored in the psycholinguistic approach.

To continue, however, it may be suggested that there are two ways, at least, in which S–R principles can produce two-word utterances in the child and lead to the formation of interrelated classes of pivot and open class words. The author (Staats, 1963, 1965b) has described one of the mechanisms already in discussing how original speech can occur—on the basis of specific past conditioning.

The child might say "bread" in asking for the object and be told by the mother "bread *please*." This is a usual middle class type of training; the verbal stimulus of the word "please" would serve as a ^{D}S (discriminative stimulus) and control the child responding "bread please." (Suitable training is of course necessary before the child will match, or imitate speech.) This process would be expected to result in the establishment of the word–word sequence

$$R\underline{\quad}s-------R\underline{\quad}s$$
$$\text{word}_1 \qquad\qquad \text{word}_2$$

If the mother provides this type of training for several different words, "apple please," "milk please," and so on, the child will acquire a more complex S–R mechanism of the following sort.

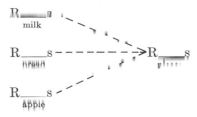

This of course corresponds to a pivot-open class in the present terminology, with a reversed order. The multiple stimulus control over one response has been called a convergent hierarchy by Hull (1943). It should be indicated that a more detailed analysis of this type, which indicated the other stimuli which are operative—for example, internal drive stimuli (deprivation caused), external reinforcing objects, and so on—would show how this type of two-word utterance could occur to *new* objects on which the child had never received training. That is, after the child has said "_____please" in the presence of a sufficient number of objects he "wants" (which have reinforcing value) such an object (and the presence of a person who responds to his verbal requests), and the response of labeling the object, will as stimuli acquire control over the response "please." This might be described as the following of a rule by a child. But the term is empty (and circular) unless we state the learning determinants of the rule behavior. In the present case it can be suggested that such rule behavior is to be accounted for by the principle of instrumental conditioning and the manner in which a discriminative stimulus can transfer its control to other potential discriminative stimuli with which it is paired in a process labeled instrumental higher-order conditioning (see Staats, 1964a, 1965b, 1968b). That is, the mother saying the word "please" to the child acts as a discriminative stimulus which elicits the child repeating the word response. As a consequence of this training the other stimuli present (for example, the words "bread," "milk," or "apple," as well as the actual objects) come as discriminative stimuli to control the word response "please" of the child. When stated in this manner, the analysis constitutes an experimental hypothesis which could be easily subjected to test.

A similar analysis may be made of another example that will indicate more clearly how original utterances (novel sentence generation) may emerge from specific S–R training. A frequent criticism of learning approaches (treating one as if it spoke for all) is that they cannot account for novel behavior. G. Miller (1965, p. 18) has presented such a challenge to learning analyses in the context of the study of language. He states, for example: "Since the variety of admissible word combinations is so great, no child could learn them all. Instead of learning specific combinations of words, he learns the rules for generating admissible combinations." The challenge is well taken, if the concept of rule is not. Traditional learning theories have not indicated how novel language behavior can arise.

This, however, is a critique of fragmented, simplistic, learning theories. There is nothing in principle that suggests an S–R learning approach is not capable of accounting for novel sentence generation, as well as other novel behavior—*based upon the past learning of the individual.* Actually, with the concepts of response hierarchies, word associations, and complex environmental stimulus control, the way in which past learning produces novel sentence generation can easily be seen. The following simple example will suggest how a child could have learned specific S–R connections, and on this basis emit entirely novel combinations of words in generating a two-word sentence.

Let us say that the child has been reinforced for saying "man" in the presence of different "man stimulus objects" and such a stimulus has come as a discriminative stimulus to control the vocal response "man." Let us also say that the child has also had the same experience with respect to the vocal response "running." That is, in the presence of a running dog, a running boy, a running girl, and so on, the child has been reinforced for saying "running." This response, however, has never been reinforced in the presence of a man running—nor has the child ever heard or said the two words together.

Let us also say, however, that the child sees a man who is running. Under these circumstances of the combined stimuli the child would be likely to say "man running" or "running man." The *total* response would be entirely novel—a case of original sentence generation—since the child would never before have emitted the sequence. Nevertheless, the emission of the two words would establish an association between them. If the child has similar experience with a running dog and a running horse, and so on, he will acquire a pivot–open construction without formal training, but on the basis of S–R mechanisms acquired through conditioning principles.

This mechanism is easily studied experimentally in various ways. The author, for example, using straightforward instrumental conditioning procedures, trained a child to make a vocal response (a syllable) in the presence of one stimulus and another vocal response (another syllable) in the presence of another stimulus. When both stimuli were presented together the child made the two vocal responses, a novel combination, under the control of the compound stimulus (Staats, 1965b). This type of learning is also readily observable in everyday life—it is the basis for the phonetic teaching of reading. The child is trained to respond to single letters and syllables. Later on, when he encounters a new word, a new compound of verbal stimuli, he responds to the units and sounds out a novel word. The child is continuously reading *novel* combinations of verbal responses (novel words, sentences, paragraphs, and so on) controlled by specific stimuli to which he has learned specific responses. (Many times hierarchies of responses are involved, of course. In the response to any one stimulus unit, and there are many other controlling stimuli which cannot be enumerated here.) Thus, the child should be able to generate an infinite and of novel constructions (sentences) on the basis of a finite set of stimulus–response language elements.

At any rate the examples like "allgone shoe," "allgone bandage," "allgone outside," and so on are easily accounted for in S–R terms. The controlling stimulus for "allgone" is the absence of something which has recently been present. The specific object involved controls the other word in the two-word utterance. That children can be directly trained to make such two-word responses under this stimulus control could be easily demonstrated experimentally. Moreover, it could be seen that the stimulus control could be made to function to produce novel two-word utterances.

One problem many people have in the application of learning principles to complex human behavior is in trying to think in terms of the elements manipulated in the laboratory—a bell, buzzer, light, and so on—as the only examples of stimuli. Many types of events, simple and complex, can constitute controlling stimuli in the conditions of everyday life. For example, the absence of something, or the recent removal of something is a stimulus event also and can come to control language behavior, an hypothesis that again could be readily tested empirically.

Slobin has indicated that many of the child's utterances "do not directly correspond to adult utterances, and do not look like reduced imitations of adult utterances" (this volume). The above analysis suggests several ways that S–R mechanisms can produce such novelty, and additional ways are yet to be described. It may be generally suggested that *the child's "system," like the adult's, consists of the S–R mechanisms that he has learned.*

One more suggestion may be made concerning the pivot–open constructions of two-word utterances in the young child—a suggestion that seems to have general implications. It appears that in many pivot–open constructions the pivot words are learned in response to stimulus events that occur with or are part of many other different stimulus objects. Thus, with the word "on" the child is trained to verbally respond to the stimulus event of a type of position. This stimulus event may occur with a ball on the ground, an apple on the table, and so on. When the child is trained to label the stimulus of position in each case, plus the stimulus object involved itself, this would produce the following type of S–R mechanism which would constitute a pivot–open construction of utterances.

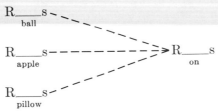

It is also the case that there are many stimulus characteristics inseparably combined with many different objects. Thus, red is part of the stimulus complex of red apples, red balls, red cars, red houses, and so on. The child's straightforward labeling training will produce a pivot–open construction in which the word response "red" comes to tend to control the various nouns. In other languages, of course, such as Spanish, the child will learn the same pivot–open construction in reverse where the class of noun words each comes to elicit the adjective word— in this case

R_____s_ _ _ R_____s   R_____s_ _ _ R_____s   R_____s_ _ _ R_____s
   apple   red   car   red   house   red

and so on.

This analysis is made because identification of the types of stimuli that control this type of language development is a step towards suggesting the training that must be involved in producing the development. In these examples labeling responses are acquired by instrumental discrimination training and can easily be produced experimentally in young children—if one employs appropriate methods. The author (Staats, 1968a, b, 1971) has described an appropriate experimental methodology for working with the language learning of very young children.

Finally, setting the pivot–open description in its most general context, the concept of word class should be discussed. The (sometimes implicit) conception of some psycholinguists is that there are cognitive classes of words (each presumably based upon a cognitive structure). Once a child has an experience with a word in its class role, so the conception goes, he "puts" the word into the cognitive class and thereafter uses the word in novel ways that obey the "rules" of the class. Actually, this is a circular concept with no explanatory value—unless independent observations can be made of the cognitive structure or process supposed to be involved. Unless such observations are available it is simply a concept inferred from the behavior that has been observed—and it is that behavior that we wish to explain. An S–R approach must ask for an analysis that shows the effects of the presentation of the word in terms of bringing the word under stimulus control. The controlling stimuli would later govern the appropriate (according to rule) elicitation of the word. To illustrate this, an example of psycholinguistic research will be cited and an S–R analysis made of the observations. The analysis, paraphrased from one previously made by the author (Staats, 1968), will illustrate the demands of explanatory empirical statements in accounting for word classes. The example is taken from Brown and Berko (1960).

The linguistic scientist defines the parts-of-speech in purely syntactic or formal terms. He has shown that the English teacher's semantic definitions (e.g., "a noun is the name of a person, place, or thing") are imprecise approximations to the underlying but less obvious syntactic facts. The noun, in descriptive linguistics, is a class of words having similar "privileges of occurrence." Nouns are words that can follow articles and can occur in subject and object positions and, in this respect, are distinct from such other classes of words as the verb, adjective, and adverb [p. 2].

As an example, Brown and Fraser (1963) show how "count nouns" may be defined in the following description.

Hearing *car* as a new word in the sentence: "See the *car*" a child could use this context as a basis for listing *car* with count nouns and so be prepared to hear and say such additional sentences as: "I own a *car*"; "The *car* is new"; "This *car* is mine"; and a multitude of others. Of course the particular sentence uttered on a given occasion would depend on semantic and motivational factors, but the population of sentences from which the particular could be drawn would be established by the syntactic kinship linking *car* with *house, barn, table,* and *fence* [pp. 162–163].[2]

The linguistic theorist in treating the psychology of language infers a cognitive structure or process to account for the "syntactic kinship." Such a concept, however, would have no independent observations to define it and would thus be circular in an explanatory sense. However, the straightforward description of the language behavior itself can serve as the basis for an investigation in terms of learning principles. For example, the term "privileges of occurrence" seems to refer to the fact that certain groups of words occur in certain circumstances, or rather,

[2] From *Verbal Behavior and Learning* edited by C. N. Cofer & B. S. Musgrave. Copyright 1963, McGraw-Hill Book Company. Used with permission of McGraw-Hill Book Company.

in a certain relationship to other words. That is, what a child reads and hears and what he is reinforced for saying will be of a certain form. From our knowledge of S–R principles of word associations, for example, it could be said in general that such experiences should produce a systematic set of grammatical habits.

If that is the case it should be possible to discover the principles and the particular controlling variables underlying the formation of these classes Brown and Fraser describe. The following fairly complicated set of S–R mechanisms is offered to explain the finding that having heard "See the car," a child can then emit the response "car" in other syntactically appropriate sentences, such as "I own a car," "The car is new," and "This car is mine."

First, let us say that the responses "the," "a," and "this," among others, have come to have extensive associations with many words. For example, the child has heard, read, and been reinforced for saying "the horse," "the house," "the dog," "the table," and so on. The stimuli provided by the vocal response "the" should come as a consequence (according to the principles of conditioning) to tend to elicit many word responses.

In turn, however, one could expect "the" to be elicited by the stimuli produced by many other word responses. "see," "own," and "what," should for example, all come to elicit "the" through being in contiguity with "the" in sentences "See the blank," "I own the blank," "Do you know what the blank is?" and so on. Thus, let us say, the word "the" is elicited by many words and tends to elicit many other words.

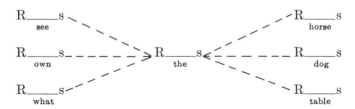

The term "privileges of occurrence" may be thought to refer to the learning conditions that produce such hierarchies of responses. It is suggested that as a consequence of these associations, formed through conditioning during one's extensive language experience, an individual will say such things as "See the horse" but not "Horse the see."

The generality of word usage Brown and Fraser describe would be expected to occur according to this interpretation, in the basis of such S–R mechanisms. That is, a new word, through being paired with "the," would become associated with "the," in other words, "the" would tend to elicit the new word. The sentence "See the car," for example, would establish the sequence "the car." As a consequence, the response "car"

would tend to occur in all situations that elicited the — for example,
"I own the car." The key to the syntactically appropriate novel uses
of "car" would depend upon the association

[In addition to these associations, the child
also forms associations between "the," "a," and "this," among others.
[A more complete analysis of this would involve the implicit elicitation
of all three of these responses by stimuli like "see," "own," and "what."
As a consequence of this implicit elicitation (see Russell & Storms, 1955),
the words the, a, and this would occur contiguously and would
become associated.] As a consequence, any one of these word responses
would have a tendency to elicit either of the other two. Because of
this there would be even greater generality of novel usage of the word
car, produced by the associations among "the," "this," and "a." It would
be expected that when "car" was associated to "the" it would also become
associated with "this," and "a," among other words. Thus, any time "this"
or "a" was elicited by the experience of the individual, "car" would
also have tendencies to occur, as one of these words' associates.

These, of course, would constitute some possible syntactic associations.
In the emission of any particular sequence of verbal responses (such
as a sentence) the specific words emitted would be under the control
of the particular stimulus objects and stimulus events that were acting
at the moment.

With these concepts in hand, the important observational results of
Brown and Berko (1960) can be described in terms of behavior principles. They discuss the research in the following manner.

The general plan of this test is to introduce to S a new word (actually a
pronounceable nonsense syllable) by using it in two sentences. The two sentences
are adequate to place the word in one of six parts-of-speech: the count noun,
mass noun, transitive verb, intransitive verb, adjective, or adverb. After this introduction to the word, S was asked to use it in sentences of his own creation, and
these are scored as correct if the new word was used as it ought to be in view
of the part-of-speech implied by the introductory sentences.

As "new words" 12 nonsense syllables were used. . . . There were 12 problems
in all with two syllables assigned to each of the six parts-of-speech. . . .

For each problem, S was shown a colorful picture of either a girl, a boy, a
man, a woman, a cat, or a dog, and E read text of the following kind: "Do
you know what a *wug* is? This is a picture of a little girl thinking about a *wug*.
Can you make up what that might mean?" This was the presentation identifying
wug as a count noun. Where *wug* was to be identified as an intransitive verb,

E would say: "Do you know what it means to *wug?* This is a picture of a little boy who wants to *wug*." With *wug* as a mass noun there would be such sentences as: "This is a cat thinking about some *wug*." With *wug* as a transitive verb such a sentence as this was used: "This is a woman who wants to *wug* something." Where *wug* was to be identified as an adverb *E* spoke of a dog thinking of doing something wuggily [p. 6].

Actually, all these cases may be considered in terms of S-R mechanisms that are very similar to the one already described—not in terms of placing a word in a grammatical word class. The analysis of the first case, concerning the noun count, really is precisely the same. That is, "wug" is conditioned to "a" let us say, and the type of generalization already described should take place. The same is true of the mass noun. When "wug" is conditioned to "some," any set of verbal stimuli that will elicit "some" should now tend also to elicit "wug." It would be expected that the child, after being told "This is a cat thinking about some wug," would say such things as "I would like some wug," "When do I get some wug," "Everyone here enjoys some wug," and so on. The same is true of the intransitive verb. The sentences should produce in the child the response sequence

$$R\underline{\quad}s\underline{\quad} \underline{\ } \underline{\ } R\underline{\quad}s$$
$$\text{to} \qquad\qquad \text{wug}$$

Thus, whenever a set of verbal stimuli that will elicit "to" is presented, it will tend also to elicit "wug." After having heard such sentences, the child would be likely to say, "I like to wug," "My sister tries to wug," "Where do you go to wug?" and so on. As the reader will be able to see by this time, a similar analysis can be made for the transitive verb (in which case, however, additional associations are involved), the adverb, and the adjective. The present author's analysis of the learning and function of grammatical word classes (Staats, 1963) was followed by a similar analysis stated in mediation word association terms (Jenkins & Palermo, 1964). It may be added that the analysis could be tested experimentally very readily.

This interpretation may also be used to consider the additional important result of Brown and Berko's experiment that children showed an ability, increasing with age, to construct grammatically correct sentences using new words. This finding would be expected on the basis of the present behavioral analysis. Since the S-R mechanisms involved seemed quite complex, it would be expected that many conditioning trials would be required to establish all the associations involved. Ordinarily, the older the child, the more such trials he would have an opportunity to experience. Again, learning experimentation could readily be conducted to test this analysis.

5.2 HIERARCHICAL CONSTRUCTIONS

It is not necessary to apply the term hierarchical to the phenomena that have been discussed under this heading, but an S–R analysis seems quite at home in this area. There are several points to be made in this context. First, it is quite apparent that sequences of vocal (or other) responses that occur together repeatedly become like a unitary response. Although each component response was in the young child hesitatingly acquired, and the tendency of the first response (or its stimulus) to elicit the next was not at first smooth, after conditioning experience the two can function smoothly—that is, word responses can come to occur as a unit. (This should be apparent since individual words may also be acquired originally as separate syllables, as is the case when the child hesitantly sounds out a novel word in reading—but after repeated trials says the word fluently, as a unit.) Let us say, for example, that the following S–R mechanism has been acquired in speech where the child says the word "other" followed in various instances (because of appropriate stimulus elicitation) by one of several other words. The mechanism may be written as follows:

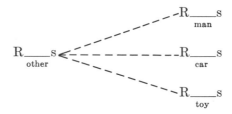

After these pairs of words had occurred together a number of times, the pairs should come to function not as a response hierarchy structure, but as individual units and could be depicted in this manner. It would be expected that any stimulus circumstance that tended to elicit the word "other"—for example, where one person or object has been or done something and then another one is or does the same thing—will tend to elicit smoothly one of the other word responses right along with "other." The particular one, of course, will depend upon the stimulus (person or object) involved.

In terms of phrases functioning as units, it should be indicated that the manner of learning the phrase and the stimuli controlling the phrase should also be important items of study. That is, following the examples of Brown and Bellugi (1964), "the red hat" should function as a unit because it is learned under the control of a particular stimulus which is both red and a hat. Brown and Bellugi suggest that analysis of the pauses in the sentence "Put the red hat on" indicates the three center words function as a unit. This would be expected from an analysis of the controlling stimuli. Thus, "put" is controlled by the stimuli, let us say, of a bare-headed child going out into the snow. The phrase "the red hat" is under the control of the specific object among the various pieces of apparel available to the mother making the statement. Depending on the occurrence of the controlling stimuli there may be a greater or lesser pause between "put" and the noun phrase. The word "on" is under the control of the preceding words plus the position cues involved—the head in one place and the hat in another.

It may be generally suggested that phrases are many times learned under stimulus elicitation, with some words occurring together. As a result the co-occurring words are more likely to be learned as units.

5.3 REGULARIZATIONS OF IRREGULAR VERB FORMS: LEARNING VERB INFLECTIONS

The main thrust of the psycholinguistic (cognitive or biological) argument here is that the facts go against a learning interpretation. Even though strong (irregular) verbs *should* be learned more strongly, but they are not—it is suggested. That is, the irregular verbs occur more frequently than the regular forms, but the child inflects the irregular like the regular, for example, "comed," "breaked," and so on. This occurs even though the child has said the irregular forms correctly at an earlier period.

This type of observation is then used to conclude that the observations do not support, in fact militate against, the importance of learning principles in language acquisition. That conclusion may then be followed by another, namely that the child because of innate mental structure accepts only patterns, and functions according to the rules involved—not according to S–R principles. As stated, however, any such analysis is circular unless one points to potentially observable independent variables. *If one is interested in seeing what the determinants of the child's language behavior are, then rigorous and detailed observations of the experience of the child, even on a naturalistic level, would be a starting place. We cannot be content with observing samples of adult speech because adults speak differently to each other than they do to children.* (In addition to the study of the child's language experience the language behavior of the child should be *produced* in experimental studies. These topics will be discussed further on.)

Actually, even rudimentary consideration of the learning task and the learning experience suggests that it is not at all clear that the inflection "anomalies" are not to be expected on the basis of elementary conditioning principles and the S–R structures that result—quite the reverse. To begin a more appropriate learning analysis, if ten different irregular verbs (which have no, or almost no, commonality) are each presented ten times, that yields ten conditioning trials on each of the ten competitive and mutually inhibiting responses. If ten different regular verbs, on the other hand, are presented only once each, a stronger regular (than irregular) form ending will be produced, not in the root form of the verbs, but in the ending. The following examples, shown in Table 1, are illustrative; the first will involve irregular and the second regular verbs.

TABLE 1

Irregular verbs		Regular verbs	
He spoke up	He drank up	He looked up	He traveled up
He sat up	He drew up	He scrambled up	He lumbered up
He came up	He swam up	He talked up	He hobbled up
He ate up	He hung up	He gathered up	He flipped up
He went up	He swung up	He limped up	He pushed up

The nature of the conditioning clearly suggests that even with fewer regular verb conditioning trials the child will learn the following:

$$S \_ \_ \_ \_ \_ \_ \_ \_ R\_\_\_s$$
$$\text{He (blank)} \qquad \text{ed}$$

In addition, of course, there would be individual associations between the word "he" and each of the irregular, or regular forms (response hierarchies), and between these words (or their stimuli) and the word response "up." This analysis suggests several thing, in addition to the facts of the development of inflections. That is, because of the greater number of conditioning trials of the irregular verb forms, "he" should elicit the irregular verb responses more strongly. Thus, in a word association task, if "he" was presented the child would be more likely to respond with an irregular verb.

However, because of the strong conditioning of the response "ed" to the word "he" when followed by another word (or root word), the child should tend to add "ed" to any presentation. (This should push out his former correct irregular verb form use.) Presented with a task in which he had to use new nonsense words as verbs in the past tense he would regularize the inflection, for example, he would say "He wugged up." Thus, it is suggested that the three stages—(1) first correct use of the irregular forms, (2) incorrect regularized inflections, and (3) later correct use—are a function of the extent of completion of what amounts to a very complex training task.

The advantage of an analysis in terms of explanatory (learning) principles again can readily be seen. Experiments are suggested by which the behavior can be produced and thus studied. We do not have to be content with the circular inference that there is some rule inside the child that accounts for the performance—a concept that is by definition beyond observation and can only be inferred from the behavior we wish to explain. We *could* set up an experiment to test the above *learning analysis.*[3]

For an additional analysis of inflections, the reader is referred to the author's previous discussion (Staats, 1963, pp. 177–178) and another discussion in the context of reading acquisition (Staats, 1968b). Prepublication articles by Montrose Wolf and associates, and James Sherman and associates (both at the University of Kansas) contain results that verify these analyses.

5.4 NEGATION AND TRANSFORMATIONAL DEVELOPMENT

The observation that the child's saying of "no" is different from the adult's may be used as an example to indicate that the adult speaks differently to a child than to an adult. This is a fact psycholinguists have missed. Although in a phrase like "No, I won't sit there," the adult

[3] This is another example of the general suggestion made throughout this article; that is, that since learning principles are empirically established antecedent–consequent principles (S–R), each analysis in terms of the principles constitutes an experimental hypothesis. In the present case, evidence to this effect has already begun to accrue. That is, this paper was circulated to the participants in this book in April of 1967. Palermo and Eberhart (1968) have already conducted a very interesting study that verifies the present analysis of the learning of verb inflections. The study was conducted with adults, however, instead of children. Moreover, there were more regular response cases than irregular—although the regular were repeated less frequently. Slobin (see Appendix) has criticized Palermo and Eberhart's study because of the use of adult subjects and because the procedures did not follow the frequency relationships of the regular and irregular verb forms in natural language. These are justified criticisms—but they are idiosyncracies of this particular experiment. The criticisms are irrelevant to the present author's learning analysis. It is thus suggested that an experiment with child subjects which followed the features of this analysis would demonstrate clearly how the child's verb inflection development proceeds according to learning principles. As was first outlined herein, the verbal stimulus inputs to, as well as the behavioral development of, the child's language must be studied systematically. Slobin has now begun such naturalistic observation and has found, as one example, that adult-to-adult speech is different than adult-to-child speech, in the ways hypothesized herein (Fillenbaum, 1971, p. 265).

may use a falling intonation in ordinary speech, this is not the type of utterance used by the adult with a young child, when training the child to respond to the word "no." When the child's language is only beginning to develop, in fact even before the child learns to speak, the parent will [illegible] [illegible] [illegible] [illegible] [illegible] [illegible] [illegible] it is hypothesized. The child acquires this form in multiple word utterances until he learns the more adult form through additional experience.

The main feature of the second period of the negation that has been described, for the purposes of the present issues, is that the child uses double negatives, whereas adults do not. This would be expected if we examine the types of learned stimulus controls that are operative in the language learning of the child. The child learns to say "no" in situations where something is occurring, or about to occur, that he does not like (is not reinforcing). His verbal response comes to occur under the control of these stimulus situations because the response results in many cases in preventing, delaying, or removing the offending stimulus. The same would be true of such a response as "You can't do that." This verbal response could also become strongly elicited by certain stimulus situations because it would delay or remove certain aversive stimulus events. The child also learns to say "none" in response to requests—such as "How many pieces of candy may I have?"—that would otherwise result in the loss of desired objects. At any rate, when the child has learned several such negative verbal responses, a particular stimulus situation may have control over two or more of the verbal responses. The elicitation of both verbal responses in sequence could constitute a double negative, which may also be more effective in controlling another child's behavior than a grammatically correct single negative. Later, after the child has been corrected for double negatives, he learns not to make such verbal responses.

It may be generally suggested that one of the deficits in developmental psycholinguistic observations of child speech is neglecting to study the stimulus situation in which the speech occurs. It is as though the speech occurs in a vacuum, unaffected by the stimulus events which are so important to the content *and the order* in which child and adult speech occurs. A child says certain things when he is "hungry," that is, has been deprived of food which produces characteristic internal stimuli. He says things depending upon the objects that are present, and events that occur. The order of the speech is controlled in some cases by the order of events, or the order in which objects occur. It is not possible to elaborate this here, but it must be realized that the complexity of the responses involved in language must be analyzed in psycholinguistics, as well as the complexity of the stimuli that control those responses. This must be done experimentally as well as theoretically.

It was also suggested that there are two additional stages of the development of the proper (adult) use of negatives. These stages are not characterized on simple dimensions—but rather the improvement occurs in several different ways. In any event, the conclusions that are drawn from these examples of language acquisition are (1) that there are stages in this type of language development, and (2) categorization of *behavior* into stages supports a conception of maturational or cognitive stages that correspond to the behavioral development.

It may be suggested, on the other hand, that the observations of the child's speech could be examples of progressively learned complexity in speech. This includes the fact that new stimuli come to elicit speech responses—so that they occur in the appropriate order and form— whereas other stimuli had formerly controlled the verbal responses. The observations of the child's language do not lead this writer to conclude that the child is advancing to new stages of maturational development each of which has its set of cognitive rules. As already stated, this conclusion is not tenable without independent observation of such biological or internal cognitive structures.

5.5 ADDITIONAL AREAS OF LANGUAGE DEVELOPMENT

There are several other issues which may be productively touched upon before concluding. It may be suggested in each case that the S–R approach may contribute to an understanding of the psycholinguistic observations of language that have been made.

5.5.1 Language Training and Telegraphic Speech. It has been shown in various observations that the length and inclusiveness of children's speech develops in a manner that has been called telegraphic speech. For example, Brown and Fraser (1963) have systematically observed and described the natural speech habits of children between 24 and 36 months of age. They found that the number of word responses included in each separate sentence (complete sequence of verbal responses) increased as the children grew older. In addition, they noticed that the speech of these young children was systematically abbreviated, and the extent of abbreviation was related to the number of word responses they produced in their average utterance. Children who produced a low average number of word responses per complete utterance tended to say "I going to town" rather than the complete "I am going to town," for example.

These investigators further studied the abbreviation effect by having the children match, or imitate sentences produced by the experimenter. They found that with increasing age the match made by the child in included more of the individual words pronounced by the experimenter. In addition, they found that when words were excluded, they tended to be the less essential words:

that occur in intermediate positions in the sentence, words that are not reference-making forms, words that belong to such small-sized grammatical categories as the articles, modal auxiliaries, and inflections; words that are relatively predictable from context and so carry little information, and words that receive the weaker stress in ordinary English pronunciation [p. 199].[4]

This led the authors to describe the speech of the children as "telegraphic English" and to attribute the increased ability to match sentences to an increase in "memory span" (which again is a nonexplanatory maturational term). Although these authors interpret their findings in these other terms, the present analysis of children's speech development in terms of learning principles suggests the determinants of the "telegraphic" English, as well as the development of the increased ability to repeat sentences ("memory span").

In discussing this aspect of speech, it is appropriate to introduce an issue that is general to various aspects of language development. The primary point is that the training conditions for the child's language are not from the speech of adults to each other—the observations that are usually the data of linguistics. The speech of adults to one another may ordinarily be considered for the young child to be "background noise." Adult speech of this type is important as it acquires conditioned reinforcing (reward), value—however, actual training of children's speech is quite different from ordinary adult communication.

When speaking to the young child, the adult's speech is ordinarily appropriate to the listener's skill development. Thus, with preverbal infants and young children, the adult will emit many more one-word utterances, or utterances that are very simple. The parent will many times say simply "Daddy . . . , Daddy" when he walks into the child's room and the child looks at him from the crib. The parent will say "Doll . . . , Doll," when the child looks at a doll. And the parent gives similar training with other objects. When the parent knows the child is hungry (that is, has not eaten) and sees the child reach for an apple on a table the parent will say "Apple . . . , Can you say apple?" In these and many other ways, the child receives a great deal of single word training.

[4] From *Verbal Behavior and Learning* edited by C. N. Cofer & B. S. Musgrave. Copyright 1963, McGraw-Hill Book Company. Used with permission of McGraw-Hill Book Company.

Furthermore, even at a later stage of advancement, *much of the child's language training will consist of the parent naming an object or event as the child experiences the object or event.* Since the primary type of training at first involves labeling stimulus objects and events, it is to be expected that certain classes of words (for example, some nouns, adjectives, and verbs) will be acquired more quickly than others.

It is thus suggested that the child receives training which will give him a repertoire of certain words *before* other types of words and that many times these more frequent words are learned singly or in short multiple-word utterances. The parent who is a good trainer presents experience that will most effectively train the child—and this means presenting training that is not too complex for the child to respond to appropriately. For example, the parent of the child who has *just* learned to say "bread" appropriately (that is, under the control of bread and not other objects) among a very sparse repertoire of word responses, should not say to the child "If you are hungry you may have a slice of bread." The child would be unable to respond appropriately to this communication stimulus and would learn little or nothing besides. The more effective parent–trainer will simply say "Bread?" or "Want bread?" and hold up a slice for the child to see. If the child says "Bread" or "Want bread" the parent will then give the slice to the child—a very important training action that will help ensure that the verbal response will be well learned, under appropriate stimulus control.

The verbal stimuli provided the child, along with other training supports, may be gradually increased in complexity as the repertoirial skills of the child make the progression appropriate. It is a long time before the adult can converse with the child in the same manner that he would with another adult. Furthermore, adults who have more extensive language development than some other adults have to modulate their speech in accord with the person being addressed. As an example, any professor who is a good trainer will present to his students material to which they can appropriately respond—a display of inappropriate erudition has little training value.

It may be helpful to illustrate a possible progression from single word utterances, through telegraphic speech, to more standard sentence production. That is, let us say that a young child has just been conditioned to say the single word "ball" as a label, as a request, or in imitation. At this point, the child will of course not be able to repeat the sentence "Give me the red ball" solely on the basis of the training with the single word. (It would thus be said that his memory span was small.) In time, however, through similar training, the child will be able to emit two-word utterances such as "red ball." Each time he does this the tendency for the first response to elicit the second will be strengthened. In time the child will also, through conditioning, come to make

the response "give," under appropriate stimulus control and may make
the statement "Give red ball" through prompting or in the novel manner
previously described. Later, let us say, because of training opportunities
he will learn to say "give me," and thus "Give me the red ball." Each
new verbal response so far has increased the cue value of the child's
speech and thus the specificity of the responses that the listener can
make to the child (thus enhancing the reinforcement value of the listener's response and its immediacy). The child will also be trained to
say "the ball" and "the red ball," and may emit the utterance "Give
me the red ball"—a sequence of word responses.

5.5.2. *Memory Span and Extended Stimuli in the Control of Word
Associations.* To continue, this type of training, starting from the conditioning of simple responses up to the formation of the complex response
sequences, appears to take place over a period of years. This type of
language acquisition, as well as many others, is by no means complete
in the short period of time up to the age of four. The length and complexity of the verbal response sequences the child can make and profit
from have by no means attained the maximums by this age. It is decep-
tive to suggest in any way that a child's language learning comes any-
where near being complete at four—or that the progression may not
be a never-ending process. Such a suggestion stems from the oversimplified conception that considers only simple grammatical classifications
in language, to the exclusion of other important aspects.

It should also be indicated in the above example that other word
responses would be learned in combination with each other and would
acquire tendencies to elicit each other in certain orders. That is, not
only would "give" come to elicit "me," but also "him" and "her," and
so on. It is suggested that at each point in the response sequence there
would be a hierarchy of responses which would tend to be elicited,
not just one single response, and these hierarchies could vary in the
numbers of responses included, with some, as in the case of count nouns,
being very large. An example of these sequences of hierarchies of responses which would include the sentence in the example might be
as follows.

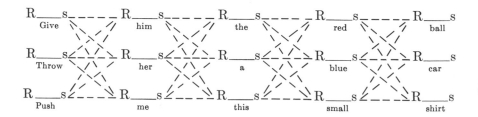

After such sequences of hierarchies of responses had been formed the child would find no difficulty in repeating a sentence that was composed of any of these alternatives; the associations would already be there. This would be true even though the new sequences of responses (the new sentence) had never occurred before in that particular combination. As long as "give" tended to elicit "her" and "her" elicited "this" and "this" elicited "small" and "small" elicited "shirt," the sentence "Give her the small shirt" could be readily emitted, controlled either by environmental stimuli, or imitated, controlled by verbal stimuli, even though the child had never heard or repeated such a sentence before. For example, the same sequential hierarchies of previously learned responses could enable the child to answer grammar test items correctly. That is, asked to underline the correct statement, the child would select "Push him the blue car" rather than "Push he the blue car."

It is thus suggested that an important source of the child's "memory span" for words consists of the skilled vocal responses *and the various associations between (sequences of) hierarchies of these responses.* An example may be taken from the literature to further illustrate this conception and to show also that the verbal stimuli that control a word association response may consist of more than just one other word. That is, the word sequence "The maff vlems oothly um the glox nerfs," is learned more readily than the word sequence "maff vlem ooth um glox nerf," even though there are fewer words in the latter (Osgood, 1953).

To see the function of the associated verbal stimuli in this case—"The," " . . . ms," " . . . ly," and " . . . fs"—it is necessary to understand that a verbal stimulus plus another verbal stimulus may be the controlling compound stimulus for a following verbal response. To illustrate, let us say that the child in the course of his language training will go through a large number of experiences involving word–response sequences which are in part the same and in part different—"the girl is fat," "the dog is running," "the car is big," and so on. As a consequence of this type of experience, the word response "is" should, in part, come to be elicited by the stimuli produced by the response "the"—but not *solely* by these stimuli. That is, in the presence of the stimuli produced by "the," *plus* the stimuli produced by another word response following "the," the word response "is" would occur frequently. However, in the presence of "the" and the absence of another word response, the response "is" would not be reinforced. The controlling stimuli for "is," in this case, would thus come to be those produced by the response "the" *plus* another word response, such as "the ball," "the girl," or "the house." The combined stimuli would have strong tendencies to elicit "is," whereas "the" alone would not.

It would be expected on the basis of this interpretation that "the" plus the stimuli produced by a novel (therefore, nonsense) word response would tend to elicit the response "is." For example, if subjects were given the stimulus "the Wuh" in a word-association task it would be expected that the response is would (among others) tend to occur. The stimulus properties produced by "the" and another word response would tend to elicit "is" on the basis of stimulus generalization. It is suggested that it is this type of word association which accounts for the fact that "The matt vlems oothly um the glox nerfs" is more easily learned (remembered) than "maff vlem ooth um glon norfu." That is, "the" plus a word response has been paired with verbs such as "swims," "climbs," "sums," "slums," "bums," "rams," "jams," and so on, and as a result tends to elicit responses ending in the verbal response " . . . ms." If that is the case there would already be associations between "the maff vlems": on this basis, learning this sequence *should* require fewer trials than verbal response sequences which are completely unconnected. This same type of mechanism would operate in other parts of this sequence.

In any event, the concept of what verbal stimuli can be involved in learning verbal sequences must be elaborated theoretically and experimentally. *The above suggests that various inflections, as well as other compound or part stimuli, may be involved in the order of emission of word sequences. It should also be noted at this point that experimental hypotheses are suggested by the S–R analysis.*

5.5.3. *Imitation.* There is a tendency in psycholinguistic statements to consider imitational behavior of children, and imitational learning, to spring from a basic characteristic of the organism involved. [Actually, this error had been made by people other than cognitively oriented psycholinguists. For example, Bandura (1962), in an influential analysis, considered imitation or modeling as a basic principle rather than as behavior *derived* from basic conditioning principles, although he has more recently begun to accept a learning analysis of imitation (Bandura, 1965).] This leads to the hypothesis—which can be readily rejected by those inclined to an antilearning orientation—that imitational *learning* is not importantly involved in language development. That is, as the psycholinguistic approach suggests, it can be seen easily that the child's speech is quite different from that of the adult's. If the child learned by imitating adult speech, then his language would be more like that of an adult.

It has already been suggested, however, that adult communication is not like the communication that occurs between adult and child. This is also true in the case of imitation. It should be noted that a child does not imitate *any* stimulus that impinges upon his sensory apparatus. A child comes to imitate through learning, not because of innate propensity. As a consequence *some* stimuli come to control imitational responses, but not others. It is not possible to go into this topic fully. However, it may be suggested that in the realm of language, as one example, the child will imitate the speech of an adult who is looking at him more than an adult looking elsewhere. The child is trained to do so. Certain verbal stimuli will also come to control imitational behaviors, such as, "Can you say . . . ," "Try and say . . . ," and so on. Furthermore, the child will learn to imitate some people more than others. Other things being equal, and for reasons that cannot be described herein (see Staats, 1968b, c), the child will imitate more strongly people who have more positive attitude value. This reinforcement value may be acquired in ways that have nothing to do with imitation.

The point to be made here, however, is that a non-learning conception such as a faculty of imitation can lead to hypotheses that are thought to challenge a learning approach, but which do not. It points up the difficulty involved in having individuals whose primary area of study is not learning derive the hypotheses upon which the value of learning is to be tested. In the present case any test of the importance of imitational learning in language development must utilize a sophisticated learning conception of imitation. Otherwise incorrect expectations may be derived. Furthermore, it is necessary upon the basis of such a conception to examine the actual imitational learning of the child—to assess actual examples of such training.

5.5.4 Language Universals. A brief word may also be said about the interpretations which language universals justify. It has been suggested herein that the regularities within the language responses of the individual, and among the language responses of individuals in the same language community, are incorrectly taken as evidence that there must be internal cognitive processes or structures that are common to man that determine his language development. In the same way the fact that there are common characteristics evident in different languages has led to the same erroneous conclusion. Staats (1968b) has suggested a contrary interpretation of language universals which may be mentioned here.

In general it is suggested that language is not only learned by the individual child, but also that *the original acquisition of language by primitive man occurred on the basis of learning principles.* Furthermore, it may be suggested that languages evolve and change according to the same principles operating within one individual and over a number of individuals. It would be expected that language would not be a static behavior, but would evidence considerable historical development, in the various aspects of language.

Because language is learned in response to the features and principles of the world in which man lives, one would expect considerable similarity in the features and principles of different languages in areas in which the language must be isomorphic with the features and principles of the world. That is, as an example, much of language has its function in being isomorphic with worldly events. By means of language responses which parallel these worldly events the individual may better deal with these events—solve problems concerning the events, predict events that have not yet happened and take account of them in various ways, and so on.

Thus, it is suggested that languages should have communalities in their terms and in their rules for relating the terms, because *the different languages have evolved to be isomorphic with the same world of events.* These events follow the same physical, chemical, biological, and psychological (learning) laws everywhere. Language universals can thus be expected on the basis of the learning theory of language.

This is not to say that there should not be large differences among languages. Many aspects of language are surely arbitrary—such as the particular sound that will refer to an object or event of the world. One language may also have terms that refer to dimensions of the empirical world that another language does not have, because of environmental or social differences, and so on. The linguistic categories of speech and their rules of relations may also differ in some ways. The basic point here, in any event, is that such general features as language universals and differences can be examined within the context of a sophisticated learning theory of language in, it is suggested, a productive manner.

6. Conclusions

In summary it may be stated that it is important to indicate the nature of theory in the context of language. There are antecedent–consequent (S–R, or causal) theories. These could conceivably be of two types—learning or biological. In either case it is necessary to observe the antecedent conditions and their relationship to language. An even more convincing act is to manipulate the antecedents and thus produce the language behavior. When this has been done in detail the result is a theory by which the behavior can be manipulated, and thus explained, as well as predicted.

In addition, there is the R–R type of theory in which observations of language behavior are formally systematized (described) and the formal theory used to predict other language behaviors. However, these linguistic theories or generative grammars cannot lead to one of the most important products of a causal theory—namely scientific control. It is in thinking that the R–R linguistic theory is explanatory in the above sense—that the linguistic theory constitutes the set of independent variables that *produce* the individual's language behavior—that the error is made in the present learning versus linguistic controversy (see Chomsky, 1967a, b, 1968). Linguistic observations and linguistic theory are important scientific products—but only in their appropriate realm.

It is important to indicate this in a definitive way—because the biological conception of human behavior is one that has considerable social significance. When we accept that a human behavior is biologically determined, then we attribute problems of human behavior to the personal defects of the individuals involved. If language comes from biological determinants, then the child who does not develop normal language is biologically inferior. It is but a short step to consider groups of individuals, or races, inferior when we observe that they do not display the behaviors we desire. Certainly, the type of indirect evidence that has been used to support the biological conception of language (Lenneberg, 1967; Chomsky, 1967a, b, 1968) could, by the same rationale, be mistakenly applied to other types of social behavior.

Furthermore, acceptance of a biological conception of complex human behavior aims to turn our attention away from environmental or learning causes (an effect which again has social significance). Although the biological view has not approached the state where it can account for the vast individual differences in behavior that exist, or solve problems of complex human behavior, in the present case, language, it has a primary thrust in directing us not to attempt to find learning principles that can potentially produce the necessary type of knowledge. The fact is that learning principles are much more advanced as an explanatory theory than is biological theory. Learning principles have already been applied to solving problems of language development. (See for example Lovaas, 1965; Wolf, Risely, & Mees, 1964; Staats, 1964b, 1965a, b, 1968b; Staats, *et al.*, 1967; Whitlock, 1966.) It would be unfortunate not to extend and accelerate this progress. The biological–maturational theories of child development had this obstructional effect in the area of child development. We are, partly as a consequence, just beginning to accept the fact that deprived or inappropriate environments produce deprived or inappropriate human repertoires, and we are just beginning to investigate ways to produce enriched repertoires through environmental manipulations.

The writer is quite willing to grant on a hypothetical level that there may be neurophysiological variables that through maturation produce language behavior. But it is quite legitimate to ask for a demonstration before considering this anything more than a weak hypothesis, and before turning away from an approach that has already found causative principles. This is not a place for a review of the literature. However, it may serve to indicate, as examples, that Rheingold, Gewirtz, and Ross (1959) have increased vocal responding in infants through rein-forcement. The author and associates (Staats 1965b, 1968b, Staats et al., 1970a; Staats & Butterfield, 1965; Staats et al., 1964; Staats, Minke, Finley, & Wolf, 1968b) have produced reading, writing, and number concept skills in children prior to the age they are thought to be maturationally capable of the behavior. This work has been done in controlled circumstances based upon explicitly stated S–R principles. Normal children and children considered to be biologically defective have been included. This is also true of the work of others, for example, Birnbrauer, Bijou, Wolf, and Kidder (1965); Lovaas (1965); Wolf, et al. (1964). There is no comparable linguistic or biological finding in which specific antecedent conditions are manipulated to *produce* language behavior according to specifically stated empirical principles. The above type work, on the other hand, suggests that learning is very important, that conditioning principles are relevant, and that we need to know much more about what children—normal and otherwise—are capable of learning under maximal conditions. Furthermore, we cannot gather this type of information by simply observing the language behavior in the naturalistic circumstances that life provides for children. We have to study these behaviors in circumstances where the behavior is *produced*.

Actually, it should be patent, even from naturalistic observations, that the child learns vastly important aspects of his speech. Only a narrow focus on the grammatical aspects of language and disregard of the various types of stimuli that elicit language behavior could have led to the failure to observe the effects of the past and present environment on language behavior. It is clear, for example, that various stimulus events and objects come to elicit specific labeling speech responses (nouns, verbs, adjectives, and adverbs). The process of the acquisition of a repertoire of such responses involves many, many training trials extending throughout the individual's life. This repertoire is subject to many variations in content, quantity, and precision and is extremely influential in the individual's adjustment in all spheres of activity. As another example, words come to serve as rewards and punishments depending upon one's conditioning history. There is no reason that the word *communist* could be aversive to one individual and rewarding to another except through personal conditioning history. Vastly important aspects of human motivation lie in the realm of such individual differences since many words ordinarily have rewarding or punishing properties. The principles by which these words have their effect are those of instrumental conditioning (Finley & Staats, 1967). It is also true, as the last example indicates, that many words come to control motor responses very important to adjustment in other ways. That is, one child when asked to cease an activity will do so, while another child will not. Abnormalities in this very extensive "ability to follow instructions" repertoire can incapacitate a child or adult. The major point to be made here is that there is no justification for isolating and treating only the grammatical aspects of language as if this aspect was in some way special. It should be stressed that it is possible to deal with the *various* aspects of language within the learning theory—a unique characteristic of present day theories of language.

Since it has been the linguist or psycholinguist who has been the theoretical aggressor in the linguistic versus learning controversy, the writer has felt in this paper quite free in performing a turnabout in theoretical "offensiveness"—and will continue the theme in concluding. That is, a major thrust of psycholinguistic theories has been a critical one. It might thus be expected that the response of some readers to the present paper will be a series of "Well what about this aspect of grammar?" questions. Before entering into this activity, however, the writer would suggest a moment of self-appraisal for the psycholinguist. To aid in this process several questions may be posed.

First, let us request of the psychological linguistic theorist (e.g., Chomsky) or the psycholinguist a statement of philosophy of science in which he identifies the general nature of his dependent and independent variables. What kinds of laws does he expect to establish? Will he remain on a purely descriptive level? Or does he aspire to explanatory statements in a causative sense? If the latter, how does he intend to go beyond his present observations of language behavior and his R–R laws, to make contact with the independent variables that produce control (explanation) as well as prediction? And what will his observational (experimental) methods be to obtain contact with such independent variables? Will he search for biological determinants in actuality as well as in speculation? Will he look for *direct* biological mechanisms that produce language, or continue to be concerned with "circumstantial" evidence that *suggests* biological possibilities? If he instead takes a learning approach will he attempt to establish basic learning principles from naturalistic observations of language—where simplification is impossible and thus elementary principles cannot be found? Or, will he take ad-

vantage of elementary conditioning principles that have been well ex
plored in the basic laboratory and already extended to and tested in
the realm of complex human behavior?

The writer would like to make several suggestions with respect
to further developing a learning approach. First the same types of detailed naturalistic observations must be made of various aspects of language that have been made of formal features such as grammar and
phonology. The *functions* of various types of language must be studied
as well. *In addition the same type of detail in naturalistic observation
must be made of the stimulus aspects that affect language behavior
as has been made of the language behavior itself. This must include
detailed observation of the language training environment of the
child—which will involve both verbal and non-verbal stimulus events.
In addition, detailed naturalistic observations must be made of the
present stimulus situation in which language occurs.* The statement that
"The golf ball hit John" is elicited by one set of stimuli, "John hit the
golf ball" by another. The two statements are isomorphic with different
events. It has been generally suggested (Staats, 1968b) that the nature
of the physical stimulus world in which we live operates according
to certain principles and we must expect that language—if it is to serve
the adjustment of the speaker—must to some extent follow those principles. It should thus come as no surprise that there are language universals. After all, languages are acquired in response to events that in
many respects follow the same principles everywhere.

*But, in addition to the naturalistic observations, experimental–natural-
istic research must be conducted. By this is meant studies where manipulations are made of learning variables and observations made of the
language behavior produced—but not necessarily in the controlled conditions of the basic laboratory.* The author (Staats, 1964c), for example,
tested the possibility that a word, "close," that (as a discriminative stimulus) controlled a particular motor response (closing something), could
transfer this function to a new word with which it was paired. This
would be expected on the basis of the basic learning theory. Thus,
his four-year-old daughter was first told that "Wug means close" several
times. Then she was told "Wug the door," which she did. This constitutes a simple test of the transfer of verbal discriminative control. The
manner in which grammatical forms can be produced through manipu-
lating learning principles could be studied in the same manner, as could
various other aspects of language (see Staats, 1968b).

*Moreover, there is also a wider opportunity to conduct more controlled
laboratory experimentation on language learning. This can be done at
various levels of learning beginning with the development of language*

in infancy—prior to the emergence of actual speech. It can also be done at points where the child is introduced to new types of language learning—for example, in learning reading (which includes various forms of language and various learning principles), in learning number language responses, writing, and so on. There are opportunities for conducting manipulative (causative) studies with normal children and with a variety of children whose language development is absent or defective. Thus, for example, retarded children, autistic children, and so on, could only benefit from research which would attempt to train them to normal behaviors—and learning principles could at the same time be tested and extended. (See Staats, 1968b, 1971; Staats *et al.*, 1970a).

Finally, it is suggested that the learning theory (which includes the various complex S–R mechanisms) offers a theoretical structure that has all the infinite complexity and originality that we see in language behavior. Although by no means complete, the present, more sophisticated, third generation learning approach and its findings constitute considerable impetus for continued research and theory. To end on a note of conciliation, it is suggested that the undoubted contributions of linguistic and developmental psycholinguistic observations be joined with a "causal" theoretical structure, such as the principles and methods of the present learning approach, to yield a more comprehensive understanding of language. The major attempt in this paper has been to suggest that psycholinguistic observations may be considered in the explanatory principles of the learning theory and that hypotheses and analyses for further advancement and experimentation can thus be produced.

7. Additional Remarks

There are two brief points that I would like to make regarding the response to my approach. First, it has been suggested (Ervin-Tripp & Slobin, 1966) that my learning analysis is incorrect because it accepts the Markov chain model of sentence formation, in view of Chomsky's rejection of this model of sentence generation. Palermo also makes this criticism of my approach in the present book.

I should point out that I have never suggested that my analyses of language are like Markov processes. As a matter of fact it would be inappropriate to do so. The mistaken attribution of Markov chain characteristics arises when only one of the learning mechanisms I utilize (word association chains) is referred to. I would like to stress again that language involves different learning principles, different controlling stimuli, and different responses, organized in complex but explicable ways.

Word association obtains and important in determining what vocal responses will be made by the individual, and their order—*but this is
by no means the only source of the control of speech.* The emission
of a sentence is ordinarily determined by a number of stimulus events,
some of which are the words the individual has already said, but not
all. The individual's speech is many times changed in midsentence by
stimuli that have occurred after the sentence began—in the ordinary
case such environmental and social events contribute to generation of
the sentence. Thus, my learning approach makes no assumption concerning a finite grammatical system, which generates sentences in a
left to right manner.

The variability of speech depends in part upon the constantly shifting
nature of controlling stimuli. A good example is that of a sports announcer describing a football game. Although his language behavior
is learned according to lawful principles, the stimulus events controlling
the behavior are constantly changing—not in the manner of an unfolding
chain moving from left to right. Considered in this way it is quite simple
to answer Ervin-Tripp and Slobin's criticism that my "view does not
provide for even fairly elementary phrase structure phenomena, such
as novel replacements of larger or higher order units, let alone such
matters as self-embedding and the like (Ervin-Tripp and Slobin, 1966)."
Using the football announcer as the example it is easy to see how embedded phrases occur. Thus, the announcer begins to say, "The end
is running downfield," under the control of the environmental stimulus
events involved (and the word associations and so on). As he says,
"The end," however, his eye falls on the player's ripped jersey and the
sentence becomes "The end with the torn shirt runs downfield." By
this time additional stimulus events may have occurred which further
change the sentence generation. This analysis derives directly from language learning principles I have made previously (Staats, 1961, 1963,
1964c, 1968b) and in the present paper.

I have, even in this brief paper described a number of mechanisms
which contradict the ascription of the label "Markov chain process" to
my analyses. Whatever Chomsky was referring to in criticizing the
Markov chain approach to language it was not appropriate for a sophisticated learning analysis. I would like to suggest that in my case critics
look to the various analyses I have made of language before concluding
that the formulation is simple. It is not possible to discuss each learning
principle simultaneously. It is necessary to discuss the principles and
analyses separately. However, any specific case of language may involve
various of the principles and analyses.

With respect to the other points made by Palermo, if he (or the interested reader) will look into the language learning system I have set forth (see especially Staats, 1968b) he will find principles from which to derive statements concerning the other questions posed. Having gone over Palermo's questions I can see ready answers and empirical hypotheses—of the type the original questions in the first chapter of the present book elicited. However, the principles have been stated and the method exemplified and the reader may pursue additional analyses to the limits of his interest. It is not possible in a chapter of the present scope to deal with all the cases involved in language behavior.

The previous sentence was intended to be the last—at least in these particular circumstances. As I have said elsewhere,

> In any event, the task of both a learning position as well as a cognitive position is to find the determinants of the behaviors in which they are interested. Delay of this effort in . . . [unproductive] controversy . . . is to be avoided by the experimentalist interested in investigating a particular set of principles and developing a particular theory [Finley & Staats, 1967, p. 197].

However, my good resolutions were of no avail when I later read the other reference to my work, McNeill's statement that I am a nativist. Despite the fact that I could not follow the logic by which this conclusion was reached, and am still uncertain that it is not really a "put on," I am impelled to deny the indictment. Fouler epithets were never spoken to a learning theorist than to breathe the label "nativist."

In any event, I am moved once again to reiterate that language behavior—including grammatical utterances—cannot be accounted for by only one learning principle (such as reinforcement) or only one S–R mechanism (such as word associations). Even in my early writing on grammar, from which McNeill takes his quotation, I made this point, saying the following:

> These examples [of reinforcement learning in grammar] suggest that one of the determinants of [instrumental] verbal response sequences are the grammatical habits acquired on the basis of conditioning principles. This is not to say that all the various grammatical forms of verbal response are a function of word association sequences, however. Some "grammatical" differences in verbal behavior may result from processes involved in the learning of meaning [classical conditioning]. . . . These types of "grammatical" habits would be expected to contribute to the multiple determination of verbal behavior [Staats, 1963, p. 178–179].

In these additional remarks I have indicated also that in the case of embedded phrases *one* S–R mechanism is that a new *external* stimulus, occurring after the individual has begun his sentence utterance, evokes a previously learned phrase which then occurs within the sentence. It would follow from my learning analysis that the "inserted" phrase would occur at a point in the sentence that would ordinarily be grammati-

cal—and the phrase itself will also be grammatical, to the extent of
the individual's training.

Let me add that additional mechanisms by which to account for embedding are easily derivable from the multiple learning principles and
S-R mechanisms I have proposed. The reader must peruse the system,
however, and I suggest that my most complete treatment (Staats, 1968b)
be consulted. I suspect that McNeill has read my learning theory of
language only to the extent needed to find a statement he wished to
criticize—which happened to be the first paragraph in the section relevant to grammatical word order. The value of the theory for making
new analyses of complex language behaviors cannot be gained in this
manner.

I will only add that it is interesting to see the dearth of reply, in
the parts of this book that I have had an opportunity to see, to the
challenge (of the questions of method and findings) I have posed herein
for Chomskian type psycholinguists. This illustrates by example the fact
that the major characteristic of the orientation is one of asking questions,
not answering them—a true mark of a polemicist's position. The fact
of the matter is that the *Chomskian psychology of language* has no
more ability to serve as an explanatory (psychological in contrast to
linguistic) theory of language behavior—one which provides principles
by which to *produce or modify* language development—than did the
psychology of the 18th century mentalistic philosophers who constitute
Chomsky's model (see Chomsky, 1968). Chomsky's attempt at psychological theorizing is truly circular. The theory derives solely from observations of language behavior, with little or no contact with other
determining events, and the theory once derived is turned around and
posed as an explanation of the observations from which it was derived.
Then, the major support of the theory is thought to be gained by criticism showing the inadequacy of other theories. This methodology—while
it may enjoy a brief popularity—can only lead to ultimate scientific
failure. In competition with a theory that has contact with determining
events and which therefore leads to scientific control of the events under
study, the circular theory must prove to be quite weak.

Finally, the present learning theory of language can incorporate the
various facts of language [which, oddly enough, has been criticized
(Fillenbaum, 1971, pp. 268–269)]. More importantly, the theory *generates* many experimental hypotheses and new areas of study. While
eschewing the theory, psycholinguists are beginning to accept its "generative" guidelines (Fillenbaum, 1971, p. 265). As psycholinguists also
observe the experience (learning) in the child's language development,
they will be drawn into the learning theory of language along with their
data—the predicted and proper denouement.

POST-SYMPOSIUM

On Two Types of Models of the Internalization of Grammars

MARTIN D. S. BRAINE

University of California, Santa Barbara
Santa Barbara, California

An influential current theory of language acquisition, advanced by Chomsky (1962, 1965), Chomsky and Miller (1963), G. Miller (1964), Katz (1966), and others, can be viewed as making two principal proposals. The first proposal has to do with the innate capacities that children bring to the language acquisition task, and claims that a specification of the possible form of a human language is built into the infant. Thus, according to Chomsky and Miller (1963, p. 276), "a practical language learning device would have to incorporate strong assumptions about the class of potential grammars that a natural language can have"; in similar vein, Chomsky (1965, p. 25) argues that "as a precondition for language learning, [the child] must possess a linguistic theory that specifies the form of a grammar of a possible human language." The child's situation is that he "approaches the data with the presumption that they are drawn from a language of a certain antecedently well defined type, his problem being to determine which of the (humanly) possible languages is that of the community in which he is placed (*ibid*, p. 27)." Chomsky and Miller support their proposal by arguing, first, that the universal properties of human languages must reflect the nature of the human faculties involved in language learning, and second, that language learning would be impossible without some innate restriction on the range of possible structures that the child is able to acquire. This paper accepts the essentials of this first proposal, although I shall argue later on that acceptance need not entail commitment to a rationalist viewpoint on the question of the existence of "innate ideas," as has been claimed.

The second proposal is concerned with the way in which learning occurs. It claims that the learning is a process of testing hypothetical grammars against the input data. In the words of Katz (1966):

To exhibit the explanatory power of the rationalist hypothesis, we must describe a model which specifies just how the universal features of language are imparted to speakers' internal representations of the rules of particular languages. . . . Chomsky has offered a conception of such a model. He conceives of language acquisition as a process of implicit theory construction similar in character to theory construction in science but without the explicit intellectual operations of the latter. According to Chomsky's conception, the child formulates hypotheses about the rules of the linguistic description of the language whose sentences he is hearing, derives predictions from such hypotheses about the linguistic structure of sentences he will hear on the basis of these productions against the non-confirmed hypotheses, eliminates those hypotheses that are contrary to the evidence, and evaluates those that are not eliminated by a simplicity principle which selects the simplest as the best hypothesis concerning the rules underlying the sentences he has heard and will hear [pp. 274, 275].

This paper provides a critique of this concept of grammar acquisition as a process of hypothesis testing, and suggests an alternative conception. I first present a number of arguments which make such a model implausible. A laboratory experiment is described which provides data supporting the critique, and which suggests the appropriateness of a different kind of learning model, which is outlined. The final section of the paper then returns to the question of the innateness of linguistic universals.

In general, two kinds of learning models are contrasted. According to the first kind, grammar acquisition is, as in Katz' summary above, an active process of formulating and testing hypotheses about the language being learned. According to the second kind, discussed later, grammar acquisition is a relatively more passive process of registering and accumulating properties of verbal strings and correlations between properties of strings and other events. The terms "hypothesis" and "hypothesis testing" will be used here to refer exclusively to the first kind of model.[1]

---

[1] This usage corresponds only partly with that of the literature. In the literature, the terms "hypothesis" and "hypothesis-testing" are sometimes used in connection with models of the second kind as well as the first [e.g., particularly, Kelley (1967), discussed later]. The basis of this more general usage appears to be that a learning model which proceeds by registering properties of its environment must be equipped with a mechanism capable of detecting these properties; this mechanism may then be regarded as constituting a hypothesis about what the environment might contain. In this more general usage, "hypothesis-testing" becomes essentially synonymous with "learning," and thus the term itself does not imply a specific kind of learning process. In this paper, "hypothesis" and "hypothesis testing" are taken in the narrower sense, in which they imply, specifically, a learning process in which learning occurs as a result of some sort of prediction or guess being verified or invalidated. This is clearly the sense in which Katz is using these terms in the passage cited above. Terminology aside, the basic claim in the first part of the paper is that the arguments presented make a certain class of learning models very implausible, and that the

1. Critique of the Hypothesis-Testing Model

The area of psychology in which hypothesis-testing models have been most successful is in studies of concept formation and problem solving (e.g., Bruner, Goodnow, & Austin, 1956; Hunt, 1962). In a typical concept formation experiment the subject is presented with a series of stimuli—these are often cards containing figures varying in form, color, number, type of background, etc.—and for each stimulus he has to say whether or not it is an instance of the concept to be discovered; he is told whether he is right or wrong, and the experiment ends when he consistently responds correctly, or correctly states the concept. Alternatively, an array of possible stimuli is set out, and the subject selects items in turn, being told whether or not he is correct, until he consistently chooses correctly. Various other procedures are possible. In such experiments the subject typically proceeds by making hypotheses that might characterize the concept the experimenter has in mind (e.g., "red," "two stars," "a black figure or one with a border"). He changes his hypotheses according to the feedback ("right" or "wrong") that he receives from the experimenter.

Now it is perfectly obvious that the learning in such experiments must be heavily dependent on the feedback provided: if the experimenter refrains from saying either "right" or "wrong," the subject obtains no information from his guess. If the experimenter should, with any frequency, say "wrong" when the guess was in fact right, or "right" when the guess was wrong, then one would expect the effect on learning to be disastrous; after all, the feedback is the subject's only means of discovering what the concept is. In short, it follows from the logic of the model that for hypothesis testing to be an efficient mode of learning, a nonnoisy input is required. This fact provides initial ground for reacting with some circumspection to the proposal that language learning is a process of hypothesis testing, since it is questionable that children do indeed receive a nonnoisy input.

A format reminiscent of the concept formation experiment is familiar outside psychology in the twenty-questions game. The analogy is twofold: the guesser proceeds by developing hypotheses on the basis of his antecedently given knowledge of the universe of entities (e.g., animal, vegetable, or mineral) to which the answer must belong; and a nonnoisy input is required (i.e., the guesser's questions must be answered

---

Katz–Chomsky proposals are included within this class. The term "hypothesis testing" provides the best brief characterization of this class that I have been able to think of.

correctly). An experimental format of the same general family has been used in laboratory language-learning studies (G. Miller, 1967; Miller & Stein, 1963; Hunt, 1965). These experiments show a kind of language learning taking place via the testing of hypotheses. The subject has to discover the rules of a "language" designed by the experimenter. The languages used embody simple recursive rules, e.g. in one language the vocabulary comprised the letters R and D, and the admissible strings were either RD^nR (i.e., RR, RDR, RDDR, RDDDR, etc.) or DR^nD. The subject is told to make up possible strings, and he is informed after each string whether it is acceptable or not. At first he guesses strings, until he happens to hit on one which is correct; thereafter he proceeds by forming hypotheses as to what other strings might be like, and tests these hypotheses by constructing appropriate strings and seeing whether they are labeled correct or not. A variety of strategies may govern the sequence of hypotheses that a subject chooses to test.

There are obviously many differences between a language-learning task of this sort and natural language learning, as Miller emphasizes. The difference to which I wish to draw attention is the fact that during the entire learning task the subject never gets to inspect an acceptable sentence made by someone else. The idea that language learning is a process of hypothesis testing is thus self-proving: the task design forces the learner to take a guess-and-test approach since this is his only access to information about the system.

Although Hunt (1965, p. 214) uses his results to support a hypothesis-testing model for grammar acquisition, Miller disclaims any similarity between natural language learning and his experiments and lists a large number of differences. However, the prospect of casting light on the way infants acquire their native language was one of the orginal motivations for the work. Moreover, if one starts out with the notion that language learning bears some resemblance to a twenty-questions game, one will naturally be led to some kind of guess-and-test format for learning studies. Thus, the design of the experiments is a direct consequence of the hypothesis-testing model, and so perhaps Miller's disclaimer that the experiments relate at all to natural language learning should properly be counted against the model. There does not appear to be any experimental format with a face similarity to natural language learning, in which learning does seem to occur through the testing of hypotheses.

In the procedures discussed so far, the learner always receives both positive and negative information (i.e., information both about what is, and what is not, an instance of whatever he has to learn), and the information is always accurate. These are obviously the optimal conditions under which to test hypotheses. However, it is extremely doubtful that anything remotely resembling these optimal conditions holds in the natural language learning situation. The infant's input appears to consist overwhelmingly of positive information (i.e., the sentences he hears), some of which is inaccurate (i.e., some of the sentences contain unsignaled departures from grammaticality). Learning by hypothesis testing must, at best, be very inefficient under these circumstances. It is noteworthy that Chomsky himself has repeatedly insisted on the inaccuracy of the child's input information, and has expressed uncertainty as to whether the child receives information about what is not a sentence. Why this has not caused him to have second thoughts about the hypothesis-testing model is unclear to me. Others, who otherwise appear to share Chomsky's views on language acquisition, do apparently believe that negative information is available to the learner (e.g., Miller, 1964; Saporta, 1965). The use or nonuse of negative information is a crucial issue, and one must ask the two following questions: "Could a hypothesis-testing model dispense with negative information?" and "Does the child obtain and use such information?" A negative answer to both questions would effectively rule out a hypothesis-testing model as being impossible and not merely unwieldy.

Information about what is not a sentence would appear to be necessary in order for the learner to reject hypothetical grammars and grammatical rules which are "overinclusive" (i.e., which generate all the acceptable strings, and which err only because they also generate unacceptable strings). Since such grammars generate all the good sentences to which the learner is exposed, how can he discover that they are wrong unless his input data contains information about nonsentences? In general, if G is the "correct" grammar of a language, then by judicious elimination of detail in G, it is possible to construct a set of grammars which generate all the sentences that G generates, but which also generate other strings classed by G as ungrammatical. For example, let G be a context-sensitive grammar, and G' be the context-free grammar obtained by suppressing the contexts in G's context-sensitive rules (i.e., each rule $\phi A \psi \rightarrow \phi \alpha \psi$ in G becomes $A \rightarrow \alpha$ in G'). Then G' will typically generate all the sentences of G, will assign them the same structural descriptions that G assigns, and will also generate other strings classed by G as ungrammatical. Similarly, if G is a transformational grammar, suppression of restrictions on transformations and local transformations will usually lead to a grammar which differs from G only in being overinclusive. Moreover, in such cases the overinclusive grammar would clearly be simpler than the true grammar so that any ordinary simplicity measure would favor the wrong grammar.

As concrete examples, consider an English grammar in which irregular verb forms were in free variation with regularized versions of the same verbs; children at a certain stage sometimes seem to be working with such a grammar, which generates all the correct forms. Or to take a more detailed example, consider some of the irregularities in the co-occurrences between verbs and elements introducing object complements. In the frame V Snodgrass as president, the V can be choose, envisage, expect, keep, recognize, try ("experiment with"), but not make; to be can replace as for choose and expect, but not envisage, keep, recognize, or try, although being can co-occur with envisage; nothing separates object and complement for make (in the sense of "transform," although transform requires into), or need do so for choose or keep. Make "force, oblige" is distinguished from make "transform into" by the presence of be before president, and be is also required with let; however, the near-synonyms force, oblige, persuade, and permit, allow take to be instead of be; be and to be are in free variation for help and assist. If we change the frame by putting wise, or attend the convention in place of president, we obtain slightly different subgrouping of the verbs, and then again, if we regroup the verbs according to those which can take nouns, adjectives, verbs, or various combinations of these, as object complements, we find once more a different set of subgroups. One could readily construct a series of grammars of varying degrees of overinclusiveness by increasing the amount of free variation; one grammar might permit free variation to erase only the most arbitrary differences (e.g., by making to optional after both let and allow, make and oblige), another might increase the free variation to the extent that all the subclass differences are erased and the forms generated by a single transformation. Note that the structural descriptions of the actually occurring sentences need not be much affected. To determine the correct grammar from such a series, the learner who proceeds by testing hypotheses is faced with the problem of determining which non-occurring sentences could not occur.

It is easy to see that a three-year-old hypothesis tester would find it difficult, merely by observing sentences, to reject such hypotheses as that the language contains both the forms bought and buyed, or that to is omittable in permit + Object + to + Complement. His only way would be to keep a careful watch for the appearance of sentences containing buy or permit and then count the relevant forms and compute rations, e.g., the ratio of the frequency of bought to the frequency of buyed as the realization of buy + Past, or of the frequency of the presence of to after permit to its absence. Moreover, since the learner is quite likely to encounter neighborhood children who use the form buyed, and occurrences of permit in which the to is inaudible (e.g., because it has been masked in fast speech by a previous word ending in a dental stop), a fairly large number of occurrences would have to be counted in order for ratios to be reliable and large enough to be decisive. Since there is a vast amount of irregularity of detail in natural languages, the learner would have to be perpetually in a state of keeping a careful watch out for a large number of special types of strings, and in process of computing a great number of ratios. It is very hard to imagine that hypothetical overinclusive grammars are rejected by subconscious watching out for particular types of items, counting, and computation of ratios. It follows that we must assume the learner obtains negative information—a great deal of such information—directly, i.e., he must be *told* what the non-occurring forms are.

It might be objected against the above argument that the examples used are matters of surface detail, and that the test of a grammar acquisition model ought to be whether it can handle the learning of "deep" structure. However, according to the Chomsky–Miller proposals, most aspects of deep structure are considered to be innate, and the purpose of the hypothesis-testing mechanism is, precisely, to account for the learning of aspects of structure which are not innate. Thus, in the case of the object–complement examples, the learner presumably "knows" at the outset that some form of the construction exists, and it is, therefore, the detailed co-occurrences within the construction whose learning has to be explained. In any case, it is easy to find less superficial examples of hypotheses that would be difficult to test, e.g., the hypothesis that expression of the time of an action through an auxiliary element in the verb is obligatory (false for Chinese, true for English).

Since it seems clear that a great deal of negative information must be included in the input to a reasonable hypothesis-testing model, let us consider whether the child obtains and uses such information. Several lines of evidence suggest that negative information cannot be necessary for first language acquisition. First and foremost, there is the universality with which language is acquired at a fairly rapid rate beginning at around 18 months or earlier, despite a wide variety of cultural conditions and child-rearing practices. It is noteworthy that even in an American middle-class culture, parents often conspicuously miss obvious opportunities to provide negative information. A case in point occurs on a tape of one of my subjects, Stevie, aged 26 months. Stevie complains to his mother about his elder brother, Tommy, and says "Tommy fall Stevie truck down." His mother, a little harassed, responds by turning to Tommy and saying somewhat threateningly "Tommy, did you fall Stevie's truck down?" Obviously, his mother has concerns more pressing than the possibility that Stevie may be testing the hypothesis that *fall down* is a transitive verb. When one considers the difficult circumstances under which huge numbers of children are raised, it becomes clear that correcting their infants' speech must be among the least of the concerns of very many human adults.

Another fact worth noting is that it would often be difficult for even the best-intentioned parent to know precisely what correction to make in response to many errors. Consider, for example, an utterance like "Want other one bread." One can tell the child that he should have requested "the other piece of bread," but this gives him little information about what precisely was wrong with what he said. A great many errors by young children seem to be such that it would be difficult to find a correction which would neatly pinpoint the nature of the error; it is probably only in older children (say, four years and over) that the preponderance of errors are of easily correctable types like *mouses, tooken,* etc.

Regardless of the extent to which corrections actually occur, there is little to indicate that young children are able to use such information when it is given, even in apparently simple cases. Consider the following interchange between mother and child, cited by McNeill (1966). Child: "Nobody don't like me." Mother: "No, say 'nobody likes me.'" Child: "Nobody don't like me." The dialogue is repeated eight times. Then, mother: "No, now listen carefully; say 'NOBODY LIKES ME.'" Child: "Oh! Nobody don't likeS me." The mother clearly has had to work quite hard to cause any change at all; when she finally manages to bring about some change, it is a moot point whether the change represents a grammatical step forward or backward; and it is hard to believe that the correction will have any lasting effect on the form of the child's negative constructions. For experimental purposes, I have occasionally made an extensive effort to change the syntax of my two children through correction. One case was the use by my two-and-a-half-year-old daughter of *other one* as a noun modifier.[2] Over a period of a few weeks I repeatedly but fruitlessly tried to persuade her to substitute *other* + N for *other one* + N. With different nouns on different occasions, the interchanges went somewhat as follows: "Want other one spoon, Daddy"—"You mean, you want THE OTHER SPOON"—"Yes, I want

---

[2] This very common back formation seems to derive from the fact that children's early NP structures usually have the property that noun modifiers can serve as complete NPs, the head noun being left understood: *want Mommy's plate—want Mommy's, more water there—more there, I see some milk—I see some,* etc. When he hears forms like *other one,* he construes them similarly as noun modifiers with the noun omitted. He is then naturally led to alternations like *here other one—here other one truck, want this one—want this one piece bread,* etc.

other one spoon, please, Daddy"—"Can you say 'the other spoon'?"—
"Other . . . one . . . spoon"—"Say . . . 'other'"—"Other"—"Spoon"—
"Spoon"—"Other . . . spoon"—"Other . . . spoon. Now give me other
one spoon?" Further tuition is ruled out by her protest, vigorously supported by my wife. Examples indicating a similar difficulty in using
negative information will probably be available to any reader who has
tried to correct the grammar of a two- or three-year-old child.

Although the evidence that young children do not use negative information is indirect or anecdotal, the argument, that children acquire
grammar without benefit of the negative information that seems required
by a hypothesis-testing theory, is consistent with a considerable amount
of laboratory work which indicates that human subjects do readily acquire certain grammar-like relations merely from exposure to sentences.
The laboratory work has studied the learning of simple artificial semantically empty systems, using children and adults as subjects. In these
experiments subjects are exposed to a set of strings ("sentences"), which
are characterized by some regularities of construction that derive from
the fact that they are a subset of the possible strings generated by
a grammar. After exposure, the regularities the subjects have learned
are determined by test, e.g., the subject may be required to recall or
recognize strings. Since more strings are presented than can be learned
by rote, a subject asked to recall strings is driven to try to reconstruct
sentences which exhibit the same regularities of construction as the
strings to which he was exposed (in so far as he has learned these
regularities). Similarly, "recognition" of a string (i.e., a judgment of
whether or not a given string was one of those exposed) is essentially
a judgment of grammaticality: the subject scans the string to see if
it presents the pattern properties that he registered in the input. The
method has been called the "verbal reconstructive memory" technique.
One goal of such experiments is to define the kinds of pattern properties
of strings to which human subjects are sensitive. Although the experimental work to date—see Smith and Braine (in press) for a review—
is limited by the fact that the "sentences" are semantically empty and
contain no distinction between superficial and deep structure, nevertheless the results indicate that fairly complex distributional relations
are picked up quite readily (e.g., Braine, 1966), and that the pattern
properties learned are appropriately described by familiar types of
grammatical rules. The experiment reported now is a further study of
the above kind.

The purpose of the experiment was to study the effect on learning
of the presence of "mistakes" in the input. The experimenter first
dreamed up a grammar; he then selected a subset of the sentences

it generated, and also concocted a small set of ungrammatical strings. One group of subjects listened to the subset of good sentences, and the other group listened to this same subset along with the ungrammatical strings randomly mixed in with the grammatical ones. There was nothing to identify the ungrammatical strings as such, and both groups of subjects received the same instructions. No information about non-sentences was provided to either group. Thus the experiment provides some information on the extent to which the pattern learning mechanism that subjects bring to the experiment is robust against a degenerate input.

Before describing the experiment, it is well to consider a possible objection to such studies, namely, that they are irrelevant because of their manifest differences from natural language acquisition situations. Such an objection misses the point of this kind of experiment. Its purpose is *not* to simulate first language acquisition, but, rather, to investigate the nature of human pattern learning mechanisms for verbal (and perhaps other) material. The claim that pattern learning abilities revealed in the laboratory are actually used in natural language acquisition rests, at the moment, on the inherent plausibility of the notion that human beings will use in language learning any abilities which they demonstrably possess and which would obviously be useful in learning languages.[3]

2. An Experiment

2.1 Method

2.1.1 Materials. The "language" contained two phrase types, each consisting of a "lexical" class followed by a class marker. The symbols A′ and B′ will be used for the phrases, A and B for the classes (each

---

[3] Age of subject may of course be a factor relevant to this argument. The experiment reported employs young adults as subjects, and another experiment has used nine-year-old children. So far, the pattern-learning mechanisms of these two types of subjects seem to be rather similar for the kind of procedure and learning material used. See Smith and Braine (in press) for detailed discussion of the age variable. The acquisition of new phonological rules has not been at issue in any of the work discussed; it seems to me that it is primarily at the phonological levels involved in the acquisition of new accents that one should expect to find major age-group differences in mechanisms for learning pattern properties or rules from exposure to spoken text materials.

with six members a_1, a_2, . . . a_6 and b_1, . . . b_6), and f and g for the markers (i.e., A' = Af and B' = Bg). There were also two types of "sentence": one had the structure pA'B', with p marking the sentence type, and the other B'qA'r with a discontinous marker q . . . r. Both phrases and sentences occurred as complete utterances. The system thus comprised a set of 84 possible strings (i.e., 6 Af, 6 Bg, 36 pAfBg, and 36 BgqAfr). The realization of the system conformed to English phonotatic and intonational structure, so that no mastery of any foreign phonology was demanded. Spelled out, the "words" were: p =*eena*, q = *mo*, r = *si*, f = *uk*, g = *stoo*, a_{1-6} = *kiv, vun, seb, pow, toj, quim*, and b_{1-6} = *bew, pid, ril, leck, naf, doy*. Some examples of strings about as pronounced during the exposure period are: [táj ək # lék stuw # íynə | séb ək |ríl stuw # îynə páw ək | pid stuw # îynə kwîm ek dɔ́y stuw # byúw stuw mow | páw ək siy # pîd stuw mow kív ək siy #]. The slower pronunciations were used only during the early part of the exposure.

In addition to the above material, two kinds of anomalous strings were constructed. The first type was obtained by arranging words in random order (counting # as a word), with the restriction that the probability of selection of a word be proportional to its frequency of occurrence in the language, that strings be no more than six words long, and that no word occur twice in the same string. These strings were pronounced with normal English sentence intonation. The second type of anomaly was more subtle; it was obtained by randomly selecting running triads of words from the sentences of the language (again, counting # as a word). For instance, in any anomalous string, say j-k-l-m-n, each of the sequences #-j-k, j-k-l, k-l-m, l-m-n, and m-n-#, appeared in the regular sentences of the language. These anomalous strings ranged from 3 to 11 words in length; some examples are pAf, Afr, AfBg, BgqAf, pAfBgqAfr. They were spoken with normal intonation and the same kinds of stresss and juncture sequences as the grammatical strings. These two kinds of anomalies represent first- and third-order statistical approximations of the language, in the terminology of Miller and Selfridge (1950).

Of the 84 possible grammatical strings, 62 were selected for exposure to the subjects; these comprised 5 A', 5 B', 26 pA'B', and 26 B'qA'r. Using these 62 strings, a set of 320 strings was constructed, comprising 64 A', 64 B', 88 pA'B', and 104 B'qA'r, in no systematic order; some of the 62 strings occurred a few times, some many times. These 320 were then subdivided into 4 quarters of 80 strings each. Each sequence of 80 strings was then paired with 6 anomalous strings, 3 of each type. (Thus, 24 different anomalous strings were used altogether.) Two tapes were prepared: one contained just the grammatical strings, and in the other the anomalous strings were located at random among the grammatical strings. The time interval between successive strings was long enough to permit each string to be repeated aloud before the onset of the next string. (The tapes also contained recognition tests, to be described later.) The running time per quarter was about 6 minutes.

2.1.2 Subjects. Twenty-eight students of introductory psychology were divided randomly into two groups each containing four male and ten female students. (The sex imbalance reflected a preponderance of females among available subjects.) One group of subjects (the "experimental" group) listened to the tape containing both grammatical and anomalous strings, and the other group ("control" group) to the tape containing only grammatical strings.

2.1.3 Procedure. All subjects were told that they would be listening to a tape containing sentences from part of a new language. The material might seem somewhat strange because they would not know what the words meant. Their task was simply to listen to the tape and get acquainted with the material on it. This was not a test of any sort, and they should not specially try to memorize particular utterances on the tape; there would in any case be too many utterances for them to memorize very many; we were simply interested in finding out something about how people become progressively familiar with material of this sort. Periodically the tape would be stopped and they would be asked some questions about what was on it.

To familiarize the subjects with the vocabulary items before listening to the tape, they were shown a written list of the words in alphabetical order and the pronunciations of the words were established. To guarantee attention to the material, subjects were required to try to repeat each sentence out loud immediately after it appeared on the tape.

Various tests were given to ascertain what the subjects had learned from the tape. After each quarter, they were asked to try to recall as many sentences as they could. In addition they received two recognition tests, a "frames" test, and a "lexical class" test. The first recognition test was given after the recall following the second quarter. The "frames" test, the second recognition test, and the "lexical class" test were given following the last recall. As far as possible, the tests were designed so that correct answers involved construction or recognition of the grammatical sentences to which subjects had *not* been exposed, and thus assessed rule or pattern learning rather than rote learning. The details of construction of the tests were as follows:

Recognition Tests. The two recognition tests were of similar construction, although they presented different strings. One part of each test tested whether subjects distinguished grammatical sentences from anomalous strings containing first order errors, and the other part whether subjects distinguished between grammatical sentences and third order anomalous strings. In each part, six grammatical and six anomalous strings were presented in random order, and, after each string, the subject said whether he thought he had heard it before. "Yes" responses to grammatical sentences and "no" responses to anomalous strings were scored as "correct," although, in point of fact, all six anomalous strings had actually been heard by the experimental group, and four of the six grammatical sentences had not been heard.

In addition to the judgments just described, since the experimental subjects' "yes" answers to ungrammatical strings obviously could reflect specific memory for these strings, the items of the second recognition test were repeated for the experimental subjects; on this second judgment the subjects judged whether a string was "regular" (i.e., conformed to the predominant pattern of the sentences heard) or "irregular."

"Frames" Test. This tested for knowledge of the frames —f, —g, p(—f) (—g), and (—g)q(—f)r. The test contained seven questions, the responses being scored with points. For the first question the subject was given the four words a_6, b_6, f, and g, and asked to make up two of the short sentences that he had heard. (Neither of the usual answers, a_6f and b_6g had actually occurred on the tape.) Phrases with f or g suffixing either a_6 or b_6 received one point each. Questions 2–4 tested subject's command of the structure p(—f)(—g) and questions 5–7 of the structure (—g)q(—f)r. These groups of questions were exactly parallel, and only 5–7 will be described. In question 5 (2 points), the six items q, r, a_2f, a_3f, b_1g, b_2g were provided written one below the other, and the subject was told to make up two sentences he had heard. (Of the four possible correct sentences only one had actually occurred on the tape.) Question 6 (1 point) tested whether subjects knew that f and g were necessary to the frame; they were asked which of the following they had heard: $b_4$qa$_4$fr, $b_4$gqa$_4$fr, $b_4$gqa$_4$r, $b_4$qa$_4$r. Question 7 (1 point) tested for knowledge that A and B were necessary in the frame; subjects were asked which of the following they had heard: $b_5$gqa$_1$fr, gqfr, gqa$_1$fr, $b_5$gqfr. (In both questions 6 and 7 the correct string had not occurred on the tape.) Maximum score on the test was ten points.

"Lexical Class" Test. This required subjects to identify the A and B classes. They were told that they may have noticed that some of the words tended to precede f and some to precede g; they were then given the vocabulary list and asked to call out, first, all the words that they remembered as "going with" f, and then, all those that "went with" g. (Thus, there were 12 possible correct responses.)

2.2 RESULTS

The free-recall results will not be discussed in any detail because it is difficult to find a suitable way of quantifying them. In both groups, subjects varied greatly in the number of strings they produced and in the number of errors they made, and the amount recalled seemed to be a function of the cautiousness of the subject as well as of his command of the system.

The test results are shown in Table 1. It can be seen that scores for both groups are well above chance levels, and often close to the maximum possible. Differences between groups were small on all tests and generally not significant. The only significant difference between groups appeared in the part of the second recognition test concerned with detection of first order anomalies. Here the control group scored slightly but significantly higher when judging whether test strings had previously been presented. The difference was due to the experimental subjects' retaining some (slight) memory for the specific anomalous strings they had heard: they showed a greater tendency than the control

TABLE 1   Mean Scores of Experimental and Control Groups on Various Tests[a]

Test	Control group	Experimental group	Significance of difference
First Recognition Test:			
1st-order anomalies: No. correct	11.79[b]	11.21[b]	not signif.
2nd-order anomalies: No. correct	9.28[b]	8.86[b]	not signif.
Second Recognition Test:			
1st-order anomalies: No. correct	11.36[b]	$\left\{\begin{array}{l}10.43^b\\11.42^c\end{array}\right.$	see text
2nd-order anomalies: No. correct	10.37[b]	$\left\{\begin{array}{l}9.0^b\\9.22^c\end{array}\right.$	not signif.
"Frames" Test:			
No. correct responses	8.71	8.14	not signif.
"Lexical Class" Test:			
No. correct assignments	10.7	10.9	not signif.
No. errors	0.5	0.7	not signif.

[a] The maximum number of correct responses is 12 on the recognition tests, 10 on the "Frames" test, and 12 on the "Lexical Class" test. A subject responding at random should obtain about 50% of the maximum on the recognition tests, about 20% on the "Frames" test, and equal numbers of correct assignments and errors in the "Lexical Class" test.

[b] Judgments of whether or not presented string had previously been heard.

[c] Judgments of whether presented string was "regular" or "irregular."

subjects to accept anomalous strings, and these recognitions were sometimes accompanied by comments indicating knowledge of anomaly (e.g., "Yes, I think that was one of the funny ones.") Moreover, when the experimental group judged whether strings were "regular," they obtained a significantly higher score (11.42) than when they judged whether strings had been exposed (10.43), scoring as high as the control group (11.36). There were no significant differences between groups on any measure of a kind to suggest better learning of the structure of the grammatical strings in the control than the experimental group.

As judged from their test responses and their free-recall performance, five subjects in each group seemed to have achieved an essentially complete grasp of the system. (The others showed various degrees of partial knowledge.) These ten subjects were interviewed at the end of the experiment to discover to what extent they were aware of the rules of the system. When asked how they knew which strings were correct, only three of the ten responded by stating the system, one of them stating it imperfectly. The others made vague references to "going by the rhythm" or "picking the one that sounded familiar." Although further questioning usually elicited that these subjects could state some features of pattern (e.g., that p usually occurred at the beginning, or that r tended to occur at the end), it was apparent that their correct test responses were not due to a deliberate comparison of a test sentence against a consciously formulated structural description; not only did they deny making such comparisons, but their ability to state the rules was not good enough to explain the correctness of their responses.

2.3 Discussion and Conclusion

The results show that the 7% of anomalous strings used were insufficient to produce a learning deficit. Seven percent is of course a fairly small proportion.[4] Obviously, if noise in the input is increased without limit, it must at some point mask the structure of the part of the input that is systematic. For the language used here, I would expect that a fairly large increase in the proportion of first order anomalies could probably be tolerated by subjects without their learning being seriously

[4] For some reason I am not now clear about, I had expected a decrement in learning with this proportion, and had, in fact, planned to run two additional groups of subjects, one with $3\frac{1}{2}$% first order anomalies and the other with the same proportion of third order anomalies, in order to find out something about the amount and kind of learning decrement produced by each type. The additional groups were dropped when it became clear that it would be difficult to show any effect of the anomalies.

retarded. Since the third order anomalies can themselves be described by grammatical rules, it seems likely that the subjects would simply respond to an increase in these anomalies by learning their structure.[5]

The proportion of anomalous sentences to which children are exposed is unknown, but probably not great, unless noun and adverbial phrases occurring alone are counted as anomalous. It seems intuitively plausible that isolated phrases in the input should be very helpful to the learner. (Of course, a large proportion of the input in this experiment consisted of isolated phrases.)

To sum up, the implications of the experiment are the same as those of the earlier critique: the critique argued that humans must have a way of discovering the structure of an "impure" set of strings, and the experiment demonstrates exactly this for a limited class of structures. From now on, this paper takes it as established that an acquisition model must have the properties: that it is capable of learning—and typically learns—from positive instances only, and that the mechanism involved is robust against the presence of unsystematic noise in the positive input. Since these properties are not easily achieved in a hypothesis-testing model, another kind of model will now be considered.

3. A "Discovery–Procedures" Acquisition Model

At the present time, one obviously cannot hope to offer a detailed model which would be adequate to the task of acquiring a natural language. What is proposed, therefore, is the format for a kind of model. The description will be both sufficiently vague and general to leave plenty of room for further development, and sufficiently specific in certain respects that a model of the kind described could probably be constructed to simulate the learning of the simple semantically empty systems that have been used in the laboratory studies cited. The system of the experiment described above will be used to illustrate the operation of the model. The model is not offered as a model for the acquisition of phonological structure. While it is quite possible that the type of model could be extended to phonology, no attempt will be made to discuss any of the special problems involved in accounting for the acquisition of

[5] The set which is the union of the set of grammatical strings and the set of all third order anomalous strings can be generated by a rather simple finite state grammar with a recursive rule. One could, of course, also write a grammar which would generate first order anomalies; however, from a psychological point of view it seems best to regard random concatenations as produced without rules (i.e., as the result of forcing a "performance model" to produce strings without knowledge of the pattern properties the strings should manifest).

phonological structure. Nor will any possible bearing of the model on the acquisition of vocabulary per se be discussed.

The model has two principal components: a scanner which receives the input sentences; and a memory component which accumulates the features of sentences noticed by the scanner. For the initial description, I shall take the memory component as consisting of an ordered series of intermediate memory stores, the last of which is the permanent store which contains the rules or pattern properties which are finally learned.

The function of the scanner is to scan each input sentence, observe its pattern properties, and cause these to be registered in an intermediate store. Thus, if $a_1 f$ is the first input string, the scanner might register the properties "two words," "word $+ f$," "$a_1 +$ word," and "$a_1 + f$." At the beginning of learning the intermediate stores are empty and the characteristics of the first string are listed in the first intermediate store. Once there is some information in the intermediate stores, the properties observed in an input string are compared with the properties then listed in the intermediate stores. Those not already listed are recorded in the first intermediate store. When a property noted by the scanner is the same as one listed in an intermediate store, this property moves to the next intermediate store. Thus, if $a_2 f$ is the second input string, the properties "two words," and "word $+ f$" will move from the first to the second intermediate store. As properties recur in the input, they move progressively through the series of intermediate stores, and eventually reach the permanent store.

The intermediate stores all have a built-in decay characteristic, i.e., the information stored is lost after a period of time. This forgetting affects the learning in important ways. First, it means that unsystematic "error" in the input will have little or no effect on learning: random deviations from grammaticalness may indeed be registered by the scanner, but, since such errors are by definition dissimilar one from another, they quickly disappear without trace. Second, general properties of the input corpus will tend to be learned more readily than specific properties. This tendency follows from the fact that the properties learned fastest are those that are shared by many sentences and thus recur frequently. In general, the intermediate stores act as kind of sieve which retains what is systematic in the input. Specific properties will be subject to repeated forgetting and restorage, although those that recur often enough will of course be learned—among them, the exceptions and special cases which are so common in natural languages.

The scanner has access to the information in the permanent store. Thus, once some learning has taken place, so that the permanent store is no longer empty, the scanner is in a position to attempt a preliminary analysis of incoming strings on the basis of its partial knowledge of the structure of the input corpus. That is, the first scanning step incorporates a recognition routine. Already learned information about the structure of the shorter strings is used to group the elements of longer strings, so that these may be recorded as being composed of shorter strings. Also, pattern properties registered may be recorded as deviations from already learned properties, or as special cases of them. Thus, if the property "word $+$ f" has reached the permanent store, then the input string a_1f can be recognized as a string of the form "word $+$ f," and the specific property "a_1f is an instance of word $+$ f," can be listed in the first intermediate store, i.e., the learner can begin to form a list of the items suffixed by f. Again, suppose the input sentence is $pa_if b_i g$. Before any learning has taken place, the scanner may perhaps register only the properties "many words" and "p $+$ many words"; however, if the properties "word $+$ f" and "word $+$ g" have reached the permanent store, then the scanner can note the property "p $+$ (word $+$ f) $+$ (word $+$ g)." It follows from this mode of operation of the scanner that strings containing several words will tend to be registered as consisting of phrase parts which are in turn composed of smaller components, i.e., as having hierarchical structure.

In general, in beginning to learn a language, one would expect a model of this sort first to build up a small vocabulary, then to begin to register the structure of short strings containing familiar elements, and then to begin to analyze longer strings. Thus, in the initial stages of learning it may well be that only a small fraction of the input, e.g., single lexical items and short phrases, contributes materially to grammar acquisition. In effect, the learner is protected from being confused by the variety of the long utterances that occur in his environs because he has not learned enough for his scanning mechanism to register the structure they contain.[6]

Having sketched the general mode of operation of the model, I now discuss the function of the components in somewhat more detail, and then consider a number of issues from the standpoint of the model.

3.1 THE SCANNER

To acquire a natural language, the scanner obviously must be sensitive to a wide range of properties of sentences. Some of the properties may

---

[6] Thus, arguments about the percentage of ungrammatical sentences in the child's input are entirely beside the point: it matters not a whit to the learner whether an utterance he cannot grasp is well formed or not. Actually, if one counts fragments of sentences as ill formed, then it may well be that in the early stages of grammar acquisition, much that contributes to learning is technically ill formed.

be built directly into the scanning mechanism itself, e.g., the ability to detect temporal position and co-occurrence relations is no doubt due to perceptual mechanisms in the scanner, and it seems doubtful that these are acquired through learning. (However, the constituents whose position is registered must usually be determined by the contents of the long-term store.) Many other properties registered by the scanner— semantic properties especially—are probably taken from the long-term memory associated with the child's concept-learning mechanism (i.e., his mechanism for discovering the nonlinguistic properties of the world).[7]

Only a few properties of any particular input sentence can get registered at any one time, no doubt far less than the total number of properties that a sentence has. It follows that one must posit, not only a set of properties to which the scanner is sensitive, but also some degree of order or hierarchy among these properties, imposed, perhaps, by some processing routine in the scanner, which determines which properties of a sentence tend to get preferentially registered. That is, certain aspects of sentences will be inherently more readily acquired than others (other things being equal), because the learner is set to notice these aspects. Structures which have properties that the learner tends to register will of course be easier to learn, and thus the order of acquisition of the rules of a language is in part a function of the property hierarchy imposed by the scanner. Such a property hierarchy would play a role in language learning analogous to the role played by the "evaluation procedure" or "simplicity metric" in the Chomsky–Miller model. Both of these perform the role of determining what kinds of structures are preferentially acquired, although they perform this role in quite different ways. In

---

[7] Since we are here concerned with language learning rather than with cognitive development in general, it seems heuristically useful for the moment to distinguish the language learning mechanism from other learning mechanisms available to the child. It appears to be an open question to what extent the concept-learning and language-learning mechanisms are really separate, and if separate, to what extent they are mechanisms of the same nature. Regardless of the degree of separation, it seems apparent that the contents of the long-term memory of each mechanism must be available to the learning component of the other mechanism.

It is perhaps also worth observing that the basic learning mechanism of the concept learning device is probably not itself learned, and no doubt determines to a considerable extent the character of the concepts learned by this device, and, therefore, the semantic notions available to the scanner of the model under discussion. It follows that a complete discussion of language learning, which deals in detail with the acquisition of vocabulary and of the combinatorial semantic rules, is probably impossible without positing a model of the child's concept learning. So, ultimately, the attempt to separate language learning from other aspects of cognitive development seems bound to break down.

effect, the property hierarchy is a functional analogue of Chomsky's simplicity metric, in which "simplicity" is construed as ease of learning. That is, a linguistic description is "simple" if it represents a construction as having properties which are easy to learn (i.e., high in the child's property hierarchy and thus preferentially registered). Or again, if there is more than one possible linguistic representation of a segment of a language, the child will acquire that representation which assigns the sentences properties which he tends most readily to notice, and this is therefore the proper representation.

3.2 The Memory

More than one form of organization of the memory is possible. The form of organization described—a linear series of stores—was chosen on the assumption of the validity of current all-or-none models of learning. That is, it was assumed that an item is, at any one time, either present in a memory store or absent from it: intermediate values are not possible. If this assumption is dropped, i.e., if it is assumed that the "habit strength" of a rule or pattern property can vary continuously, then the linear array of stores can be replaced by a single store. Such a store might be organized so that newly registered properties are stored near the bottom of the store; as properties recur in the input they tend to rise in the store, so that height in the store reflects habit strength or degree of learning. The top levels of the store would play the role of the "permanent" memory, and rules near the top of the store would be available to the scanner, and in producing sentences. The forgetting principle would be that entries lose habit strength (i.e., move downward in the store) with time. A memory organized in this way would have the same "sieve-like" properties as the linear series of stores described earlier.

3.3 Some Remarks on the Registration of Semantic Properties of Strings

Development of an acquisition theory (as opposed to the mere format of a theory, as here) requires specification of the properties the learner registers. The experimental work cited has been concerned with surface positional and co-occurrence relations, and a scanner sensitive to such relations could learn the kinds of artificial systems used in these experiments. However, to acquire a natural language, the full range of pattern properties must of course go well beyond these, and among other things, must include semantic relations of many sorts. Certain very general semantic relations, which usually interpret grammatical constructions rather than particular lexical items, are clearly of special importance for explaining grammar acquisition. Since the existence of such semantic correlates of grammatical structures is controversial, it is worth emphasizing that children's language provides numerous examples of utterances which are not based merely on "analogical" extension of distributional syntactic and morphologic patterns, but, rather, are clearly the result of a grasp of semantic relations expressed by constructions. Consider the following examples:

(1)   During a recording session with Stevie (25 months), my assistant Betty blows on his neck; Stevie reports this event as *Betty h::: Stevie,* where *h:::* is an act of blowing. This introduction of an act as a linguistic element into a transitive verb slot presumably indicates that Stevie has registered some semantic value for this slot. Moreover, since he employs the order *Betty h::: Stevie,* rather than *Stevie h::: Betty,* he has presumably registered also that the doer of the act is stated as the first term of such a relation.

(2)   Between 32 and 34 months of age, I noted the following sentences from my daughter: *I don't want any more grapes; they just cough me* (="make me cough"), *I can't reach it over* (="I can't make the car seat belt reach over far enough to buckle it"), *You can only ride a young child* (="You can take only a young child, not an older one, for a ride in a baby carriage"), *I can't unscotch it* (="I can't remove the scotch tape from it"), and (after her hair was ruffled by the breeze) *Daddy, why doesn't it wind your hair, this big wind?* Again, there seems to be a construing of the transitive verb as a two-term action relation, with the first term as agent or instrument; the lexical items serving as verbs may be selected ad hoc, and are forced to take the sense required by the construction.

(3)   During a recording session, Odi, a 25-month old Israeli child, is playing with a toy telephone. Asked "What are you doing?" she replies, somewhat impatiently, that she is telephoning: *Odi hello.* It is clearly the subject–predicate form that imposed the interpretation of *hello,* and one must conclude that she has learned some general schema for interpreting subject–predicate forms.[8] An American child's *Doggie wuf-wuf* ("The dog is barking") is a similar invention.

(4)   Several children produce interesting noun modifiers. My son

---

[8] This is a Hebrew, not an English sentence; it may be relevant that *hello* usually marks the opening of telephone conversations in Hebrew, but is hardly ever used as a greeting outside of telephone conversations.

(25 months) has a book in which the characters are dogs of various breeds. He is given the names of the breeds but they become noun modifiers, not nouns, in his speech: *dachsund dog, terrier dog, poodle dog.* Another child at the same age frequently uses *Indian man* and *soldier man* rather than simply *Indian* and *soldier* to refer to his toy Indians and soldiers. My daughter's coinage *toast bread* follows the same pattern. A fourth child uses *poppa car* to refer to Volkswagens of any color or ownership; originally this was presumably a possessive— his father's car is a Volkswagen—but the extension to the make of car is immediate, and some months later he finds nothing odd in distinguishing *my poppa car* (his father's) from *Marty's poppa car* (the writer's car of that make.) Thus *poppa* in *poppa car* is purely a dummy species marker like *straw* in *strawberry,* or (for most people) *Przevalskii* in *Equus Przevalskii.* Indeed, the logical structure of these childhood compounds follows closely the schema for naming species in zoology; to the genus name is adjoined another term, which need have no independent relevant meaning. In the adult language, if one considers a set of forms like *outhouse, apartment house, bird house, mud house, Baroque house, red house,* etc., the modifier may express function, style, material, etc., or have no precise independent meaning; in particular, it often does not designate a class of objects that intersects with that of houses. However, in every case the modifier serves in context to specify a subclass of houses, regardless of how it does this.[9] What is interesting about the coinages cited is that they seem to indicate that the child registers this function of the modifier slot at a very early stage indeed. He also apparently registers the position of this function vis-a-vis the head noun: the specifier precedes the noun as is usual in English,

---

[9] This assertion might be better made in terms of properties (or semantic markers) than in terms of classes and subclasses. That is, a couplet xy expresses the properties expressed by the head word y, plus additional properties. The added properties may have no relation whatever to those normally expressed by x (or x may not occur independently of y), or there may be a rather loose associative relation with the properties normally expressed by x (as in *poppa car,* and *outhouse,* perhaps), or there may be a closer relation, the closest relation occurring when xy expresses the sum of the properties expressed by x and y separately (*red house*). Apparently, the child learns the general notion than xy delimits y before he learns to distinguish types of modifier according to the ways in which the properties of xy relate to those of x. In general, it appears that the more distant the relation between the properties expressed by x and those expressed by xy, the closer the modifier stands to the head noun in constructions with multiple modifiers (e.g., *red Baroque mud outhouse*). It seems to me that, by making assumptions about the operations of the scanner, the learning model could be developed so as to predict a relation between semantic distance and closeness of compounding.

and presumably it would follow the noun in similar child coinages in languages where modifiers follow.

In each of four above examples, the evidence indicates that the child has learned some sort of relation which correlates notionally defined entities with the positions they occupy in the surface structure. Schlesinger (this volume) argues that grammar acquisition is primarily the learning of a mapping of the terms of semantic relations into positions.

3.4 ORDERING OF RULES

From a linguistic standpoint, an important question about the model is whether the rules in the memory are ordered in terms of their sequence of application, and if so, how this ordering is learned. This question is difficult to discuss in detail because, although it is clear that there is some ordering of rules in natural languages, it is not clear just how much, and therefore not clear how much ordering of rules an acquisition model should provide for. A particular order of rules would be learned directly when pattern properties are registered by the scanner as alterations in the form of already learned structures. Thus, at a stage of development when the learner has learned enough to be able to generate sentences like *George is coming, George can come* himself, the scanner might recognize these sentences in the forms *Is George coming?* and *Can George come?*, and, computing differences, might register some such pattern property as: "a change from the normal word order to the order 'first auxiliary that has word status + subject + remainder of VP' expresses a request for information." Since questions with *do* have the same derived phrase structure (i.e., auxiliary word + subject + remainder of VP) the scanner should soon thereafter register a subproperty to the effect that *do* fills out a defective first auxiliary slot. The ordering of the rules—that the question transformation follows the phrase structure rules, and precedes the insertion of *do*—would thus be contained in the properties as registered by the scanner.

A looser ordering of rules can be guaranteed by the scanner in other ways. Thus the scanner might mark rules according to whether the pattern properties are phonological, semantic, etc., thus assuring some grouping of rules according to level or stratum. Similarly, the scanner can provide for some cross-referencing between rules, and treatment of certain rules as subrules of other rules. For example, rules generating, say, the past tenses of irregular verbs will come out as subrules of a past tense rule. In current linguistic notations such subrules are ordered, so that the subrules generating the irregular forms precede the subrule for the regular forms, e.g., "V + past → /bɔt/ for V = *buy*" precedes the more general "V + past → V-/d/"; if the subrules were unordered *buyed* would be in free variation with *bought*. In such cases, the effect of the ordering can be obtained by taking it as an organizing principle of the model, that any subrule in which an expansion is contingent on a particular lexical item is the only subrule applying to that lexical item (so that "V + past → /bɔt/ for V = buy" implies V ≠ *buy* in "V + past → V-/d/"). Where there is genuine free variation in the adult language, both forms would be learned independently; i.e., if *buyed* and *bought* did vary freely in adult speakers, their subrule for *buy* would be

$$\text{``V} + \text{past} \rightarrow \begin{Bmatrix} /\text{bɔt}/ \\ /\text{bayd}/ \end{Bmatrix} \quad \text{for} \quad \text{V} = \textit{buy."}^{10}$$

3.5 How a Discovery–Procedures Model Avoids Overinclusive Grammars

In the earlier critique of the hypothesis-testing model it was argued that such models would have difficulty rejecting hypothetical overinclusive grammars because they could not easily discover the nonoccurring forms. To see how it is that the kind of model now proposed evades this criticism, let us take the verb–complement construction used to illustrate the earlier critique, and consider how a discovery–procedures model might discover the co-occurrences between certain verbs and the presence or absence of *to* in a following complement.

Let V′ be the class of verbs that includes *make, compel, let, permit*, and *help*. Let VP refer to verb phrases of the forms *be* + NP, *be* + Adj,

---

[10] As noted earlier, in children's learning of irregular forms the developmental sequence is *buyed* > *buyed* ~ *bought* > *bought*. In principle, the period of free variation might be accounted for in two ways: (1) The subrules "V + past → *bought* for V = *buy*" and "V + past → V*ed*" are unordered; *bought* is established as the only correct form as a result of the child learning the order of the subrules. (2) The subrule "V + past → *bought* for V = *buy*" passes through a period of instability (i.e., repeated rises and falls in habit strength) before it becomes finally established in the permanent store. Thus, when he remembers, the child uses *bought;* at those moments that the subrule generating *bought* is absent from the part of the memory accessible to his sentence-producing mechanism, he generates *buyed* from the well-established "V + past → V*ed*." I would urge that (2) is the correct explanation.

Note that the question how *bought* gets established to the exclusion of *buyed* relates to the problem of overinclusiveness, discussed in the next section.

Verb, Verb $+$ NP. The forms to be considered are:

make $+$ NP $+$ VP   * make $+$ NP $+$ to $+$ VP
compel $+$ NP $+$ to $+$ VP   * compel $+$ NP $+$ VP
let $+$ NP $+$ VP   * let $+$ NP $+$ to $+$ VP
permit $+$ NP $+$ to $+$ VP   * permit $+$ NP $+$ VP
help $+$ NP $+$ VP
help $+$ NP $+$ to $+$ VP

Suppose that learning has already progressed to the point where the long-term store (LTS) contains rules that generate sequences of the form V′ $+$ NP $+$ Comp, and also contains the rule

$$\text{Comp} \rightarrow \begin{Bmatrix} \text{VP} \\ \text{to} + \text{VP} \end{Bmatrix}$$

or some equivalent rule. At this stage in learning the model has over-generalized and its rules generate the starred as well as the correct sequences listed above. The question at issue is how the model now proceeds to learn the details.

Using the rules in the LTS the recognition routine in the scanner identifies incoming strings from the above set as V′–NP–Comp sequences. The scanner then proceeds to register co-occurrences within the construction as they occur; among these it will register the co-occurrence of *permit, compel,* and *help* with *to* before the VP, and of *make, let,* and *help* with the absence of *to*. Notice that for each V′, its occurrence with *to*, or with absence of *to*, must be much more frequent than its occurrence with any other item. Since the scanner registers properties as deviations from, or special cases of, already learned rules, it will cause these co-occurrences to be stored in the intermediate store as special cases of the Comp expansion rule, perhaps in some such form as: Comp $\rightarrow$ VP for V′ $=$ *make,* Comp $\rightarrow$ VP for V′ $=$ *let,* Comp $\rightarrow$ VP for V′ $=$ *help,* Comp $\rightarrow$ *to* $+$ VP for V′ $=$ *compel,* Comp $\rightarrow$ *to* $+$ VP for V′ $=$ *permit,* and Comp $\rightarrow$ *to* $+$ VP for V′ $=$ *help.* These rules then travel through the intermediate store and eventually replace the more general rule

$$\text{Comp} \rightarrow \begin{Bmatrix} \text{VP} \\ \text{to} + \text{VP} \end{Bmatrix}$$

in the LTS. (Alternatively, the form of Comp selected by a particular V′ might be stored within the dictionary entry for the verb, rather than as a contextual restriction on the Comp expansion rule—in general, this rough outline of the course of learning could be restated for whatever types of rules are assumed for the construction.)

In general, the model proceeds only by registering and accumulating what exists—the range of what can exist for it being determined by the kinds of properties that it is able to register. Learning is a matter of acquiring more and more detail.

Before terminating this description of the model, it should be stressed that there are many important questions relevant to the operation of the model which are hardly touched by what has been said so far. These include the manner of operation of the recognition device in the scanner; how the scanner computes properties which are represented as deviations from, or special cases of, known properties; the way in which material is retrieved from the permanent store by the recognition routine in attempting to understand sentences (and by the sentence-producing device in constructing sentences); just how the order of salience among the properties is determined; the notation for pattern properties used by the scanner in registering properties in the memory; etc.

3.6 ACCOUNTING FOR LINGUISTIC UNIVERSALS

Chomsky properly points out that there must be a relation between linguistic universals and the human faculties involved in language learning. For the model described, the universal properties of natural languages are derived roughly in the following ways. (a) Some formal universals are due to the nature of the operations of the model, e.g., as illustrated earlier, immediate-constituent structure derives in part from the scanner's use of the contents of the long-term store to group the elements of novel strings; similarly, one might account for some aspects of transformational structure by positing that the scanner seeks to analyze strings (e.g., negatives, questions) as consisting of familiar structures which have been changed in some way; the structure of such transforms would then be learned in two stages—first the learning of the phrase structure, then of the nature of the change executed (see Braine, 1971, Sections 2.24 and 3.33, for further discussion). (b) Some formal universals, and perhaps also some substantive universals, reflect property-detecting perceptual mechanisms built into the scanner itself, like the mechanisms for detecting positional and co-occurrence relations discussed above. Universals which derive from these two sources can reasonably be said to be built into the learner (if the vagueness of the term "built in" is allowed for the moment). However, it should be noted that such universals are built in the form of a mechanism, not in the form of an "innate idea": they may be "innate" (in some sense) but they are not "ideas." (c) Semantic universals, like all concepts, are learned; they are jointly determined by the (unknown) character of the child's concept-learning mechanism, and by the ecological situation in which learning takes place. Substantive semantic universals presumably differ from culture-specific concepts in that the environmental determinants of learning are universal features of human ecology (e.g., the frequency of the features " +Vertical," " —Vertical," in human lexicons (cf. Bierwisch, 1967) probably reflects in part the fact that the human concept-learning mechanism operates in a gravitational field—the feature might well not arise in a weightless environment).

3.7 A Computer-Program Model

Kelley (1967) has put forward a conception of grammar acquisition in which learning is basically a process of accumulating properties of the input in memory, as in the model proposed above. Many aspects of his model are illustrated in a computer program that discovers the grammar generating a corpus of simple English sentences. The general concept is that the child recognizes functional properties of words in sentences (e.g., "subject," "modifier," these being assumed to be definable in part in semantic terms), and also categorial properties ("things," "actions"), which are assumed to define word classes.[11] The semantic nature of these properties is such that recognizing them, given recognition of lexical items, essentially amounts to finding a meaning for utterances. When an acceptable "meaning" is found for an utterance, an accumulator registers the positions of the functions in the sentence, the categories bearing the functions, the categorial assignments of the words, and co-occurrences of words with neighboring words and categories. Learning takes place by a process of confirmation by repetition and unlearning by forgetting. The program incorporates a parsing routine that is capable of skipping over unfamiliar words in sentences.

Kelley does not try to provide the semantic definitions of the functions and categories that he believes exist, and thus, unfortunately, all parts of the simulation that have to do with semantics are realized in *ad hoc* ways, on which some of the program's learning ability depends (e.g., recognition of "things" and "actions" in sentences of the input corpus is ultimately done through a component that has access to the true analyses of the input sentences and equates "thing" and "action" with Noun and Verb of the true analysis). Thus, the program itself adds

[11] These properties are referred to as "hypotheses" by Kelley; however, the model is not a hypothesis-testing model in the sense of "hypothesis-testing" used in this paper (cf. footnote 1), since the learning process is not one of making and verifying predictions or guesses.

only a modicum of useful detail to Kelley's verbal formulation of his views. Kelley emphasizes one consequence of his conception: that only input sentences that are understood (i.e., for which the child finds a meaning that is not absurd to him) contribute to learning.

4. Language Learning and Linguistic Theory

4.1 DISCOVERY PROCEDURES AND LINGUISTIC THEORY

In the terms of Chomsky's (1957) discussion, a completed model of the kind proposed would constitute neither an evaluation procedure (i.e., not a procedure for deciding, as between two grammars, which is the better), nor a decision procedure (i.e., not a procedure for determining whether a given hypothetical grammar is the best one), but a discovery procedure (i.e., a procedure for finding a grammar). Chomsky has criticized an earlier school of linguists for preoccupation with the task of building a set of discovery procedures for linguistic structure, and has proposed instead that linguistic theory accept the lesser task of finding a universal evaluation procedure. Chomsky's critique has received wide assent; for example, even Lamb, who rejects many of Chomsky's other views, praises him for his "liberation of linguistic theory from questions of discovery procedure [Lamb 1966a, p. 534]."

One can agree with much of Chomsky's criticism. It is surely desirable that the linguist be left free to develop particular grammars and test them for descriptive adequacy, make hypotheses about linguistic universals and test the descriptive adequacy of grammars embodying them, etc., without being concerned with the methods by which he arrives at the ideas tested. Moreover, it is only in Chomsky's discussions (e.g., Chomsky, 1962, 1965) that it becomes clear that the status of a discovery or evaluation procedure in linguistic theory stems ultimately from its role in explicating language learning. Nevertheless, it seems to me that the reaction against the earlier concern with discovery procedures has gone too far. Chomsky's notion of an evaluation procedure seems heavily dependent on his conception of language learning as a process of testing hypotheses: if we view the child as generating hypotheses about the language he is exposed to, it is natural to imagine that he would need some means of choosing between alternative hypotheses that cover the same data. Outside the context of the hypothesis-testing model, it is hard to see that an evaluation procedure would serve any purpose: the child would never get into the position of needing to choose between two grammars. Clearly, the child needs some procedure stronger than an evaluation procedure, something that will find a grammar and not just test one.[12]

In short, a discovery procedure of some sort is a proper part of linguistic theory. It is a requirement on linguistic theory that any human grammar be learnable, and this fact makes data on language learning and development relevant in the formulating of theories of the general form of a human grammar. Ultimately, of course, the general form of a human grammar should be derivable from the discovery procedure. Vis-a-vis proposed grammars of particular languages the discovery procedure plays a justifying role, as claimed by the neo-Bloomfieldians: the ultimate justification of a particular grammar is that it is the grammar which would be learned by a child exposed to the language.

The human discovery procedure obviously differs in many respects from the kinds of procedures envisaged by Harris (1951), and others. For one thing, it is sensitive to semantic and pragmatic categories and relations. A more interesting and particularly noteworthy difference, it seems to me, is that the procedure must be able to accept a corpus utterance by utterance, processing and forgetting each utterance before the next is accepted, i.e., two utterances of the corpus should rarely, if ever, be directly compared with each other. Unlike the linguist, the child cannot survey all his corpus at once. Note that this restriction does not mean that two sentences are never compared with each other; it means, rather, that if two sentences are compared, one of them is self-generated from those rules that have already been acquired. (The only circumstance in which it seems entirely reasonable that a child might actually

---

[12] The child may sometimes learn more than one grammar without choosing between them. The model proposed would allow for more than one grammar being acquired, although the property hierarchy in the scanner should prevent these from being radically different from each other. An interesting case where more than one description of the same set of items is clearly learned is provided by some of the phenomena associated with "restricted productivity." It has been noted (e.g., Zimmer, 1964) that the relative acceptability of derived words often appears to be determined by a factor of familiarity (e.g., we have *unintelligent* but not *unclever*). Where we have a set of derived forms, each of which individually occurs with some frequency, it would be predicted that the learner should register both the pattern property governing the construction of the forms, and also learn a listing of the forms themselves (i.e., a learner would learn two grammars, in one of which the derived forms are generated by rule, and in the other by enumeration). If the speaker has both a rule and a listing, it is understandable that he should both understand nonce forms, and also know that they are nonce forms.

It is conceivable that there are many cases in which the set of "fully acceptable" sentences is actually the intersect of the sets of strings generated by two or more slightly different grammars (cf. Bar-Hillel, 1964, pp. 196–198).

compare two input utterances with each other are such cases as question–answer or statement–negative sequences in rapid dialogue.)

Progress toward the construction of the discovery procedure will undoubtedly be slow, and, as is usual in science, will no doubt consist in the development and gradual extension of incomplete theories accounting for a restricted range of phenomena. In part, progress will depend on advances in other parts of linguistic theory. Thus, it is probably pointless to try to construct a theory of the acquisition of "deep" structure until there is better understanding of the way in which syntactic and semantic structure are integrated in natural languages. However, where ignorance of semantic structure is not a problem, there appears to be no bar to immediate progress. For instance, I can see no reason why one should not attempt, with present knowledge, to construct a partial theory covering the learning of inflectional systems and high-level morphophonemic alternations of the *leaf–leaves* type (although such a theory would, at this stage, have to take for granted the learner's recognition of such syntactic features as "accusative case," "present tense," "plural," etc.[13]) The experimental work cited earlier, on the learning of the structure of semantically empty systems, represents a step toward a partial theory covering the acquisition of arbitrary distributional regularities.

It is to be expected that work on acquisition theory will lead to results significant for other areas of linguistic work long before a worthwhile discovery procedure is formulated. Work on child language, for instance, is already beginning to throw significant light on some of the rules which are actually acquired, for a few languages. Also, work on the relative learnabilities of different sorts of linguistic descriptions may well develop to the point where it has nontrivial implications for theories of the form of a human grammar.

4.2 "Innate Ideas" versus "Empiricism"

Now I consider the claim (Chomsky, 1965; Katz, 1966) that linguistic theory requires a rationalist view of man, i.e., the view that a set of biologically given "innate ideas" exists in the human species, and that human language is one of the products of these ideas. Embedded within the current arguments for this thesis there appear to be two claims, a weak one and a strong one, which it is well to separate. The weak claim

---

[13] See Braine (1971, Section 2.29) for a review and discussion of the development of inflections. The same paper (Section 2.14) suggests a classification of different kinds of morphophonemic alternations according to the probable bases of their learning. However, questions of discovery procedure are not discussed.

is that innate structure exists which is substantially richer than that envisioned in association theory. Assuming a satisfactory gloss for the term "innate" (a matter discussed below), it could be argued that there is already a substantial body of nonlinguistic evidence in favor of this claim, e.g., the neurophysiological work on pattern detectors in the visual system (Lettvin, Maturana, McCulloch, & Pitts, 1959; Hubel & Wiesel, 1962), or the evidence marshaled by Gibson (1966). But, surely, empiricism is broader than association theory; the latter, particularly in its modern S–R form, has had a long line of eminent critics in modern psychology (e.g., the Gestaltists; Tolman, 1948; Lashley, 1951; to name only a few). No one has imagined that rejection of S–R association theory implied a rejection of empiricism in favor of a neo-Cartesian rationalism.

In addition to their attack on association theory, Chomsky and Katz often appear to be making a stronger claim, which concerns the *content* of what is innate: that what is innate does not consist of structure and mechanism only, but also of ideas and principles (cf. Chomsky, 1965, p. 48). However, it is not at all clear what Chomsky means by an innate "idea." Sometimes he and Katz speak as if they were merely positing innate mechanisms which constrain what is acquired by experience. This is a notion with which few would quarrel (again, given a satisfactory gloss for "innate"); however, in such a case it is the mechanism, not the idea, that is innate.[14] At other times Chomsky and Katz seem to be claiming that ideas as such are innate, a notion no empiricist could accept and which, taken on its face, seems rather mystical. Assuming it to be seriously intended, such a claim would be bolstered if it could be shown that children really did possess a set of inborn ideas about the nature of language, and acquired languages by a process of testing out these ideas in a manner essentially similar (apart from consciousness of the process) to the way in which intelligent adult subjects solve a concept-formation task or find the answer in a twenty-questions game. However, even if a strict hypothesis-testing model were somehow to be confirmed despite the arguments against it, one would

[14] To speak of an innate "idea" in such cases constitutes a kind of category error. The nature of the error may be further illustrated by an analogy: it is a universal property of the human eye that it is sensitive to light and dark; however, it is not light and dark that are innate, but rather, a mechanism that is sensitive to light.

When this category error is made, the term "innate" loses all explanatory value. Moreover, anyone who finds this category error harmless, and makes it systematically, will inevitably be led into a kind of rationalism, which is, again, empty of any explanatory value. In the case of linguistic primitives specifically, it follows that a characterization of what is linguistically primitive will not be a characterization of what is innate.

still need some proposal as to how the ideas are embodied in the human computational machinery in order to make clear what is meant by an innate "idea." In any case, if Chomsky and Katz do really hold that ideas are innate in some strong sense, then considerable clarification of the notions "innate" and "idea" is required to avoid mysticism. Given the clarifications, it remains to be seen whether any claim is being made that must be repugnant to a broadly interpreted empiricism.[15]

So far the term "innate" has been taken for granted. There are, however some serious problems associated with this term, which have not been brought out in the literature on the theoretical status of linguistic universals. The problems have been repeatedly thrashed out in the ethological literature (see Hinde [1966, pp. 316–321] for a compact and cogent discussion). Although some of the older ethologists, like Lorenz, have remained unmoved by criticism (e.g., Lehrman, 1953) of simplistic use of this term, others, like Tinbergen, have changed their minds (e.g., Tinbergen, 1963). Some of the problems can be indicated most directly by attempting to construct a satisfactory gloss for the term. Let us consider some possibilities.

(1)   "Existing in a person or organism from birth." This is the OED definition. It is unsatisfactory, even so far as popular usage is concerned, on four grounds: (a) because of a failure to make any reference to a genetic basis for innate characters; (b) because characters present at birth are often not considered innate (e.g., thalidomide injuries); (c) because characters not present at birth are sometimes considered innate (e.g., bipedal locomotion); (d) more trivially, because many characters which exist at birth soon cease to exist, and therefore do not exist *from* birth.

(2)   "Having solely a genetic basis." This is what I, and I believe most geneticists and psychologists, ordinarily understand by the term. According to this definition, only the genes are innate.[16] One of the

---

[15] In this connection, it should be noted that the new rationalism differs from the old in some important ways. For instance, it is taken for granted that the new innate ideas or structures have to be established empirically. Also, "innate" is now intended in a biological sense, whereas modern biology did not exist at the time of Descartes and Leibnitz. Then there existed a widely accepted theological doctrine which held that the mind entered the body at the time of quickening of the foetus. Obviously, the notion of an idea present in the mind prior to birth raises different conceptual problems in the 17th century, and in a modern embryological context. A third important change is that the new innate ideas appear mostly to have the status of attributes, whereas the old ones were propositions, usually of some philosophical interest, i.e., *"vérités innées"* as well as *"idées innées."*

[16] Derivatively, *differences* between individuals may be said to be innate, e.g., a difference in height between two individuals could have purely a genetic basis,

arguments against the simplistic innate–learned dichotomy is the obvious fact that environmental factors can influence the course of development in other ways than by bringing about learning. Since certain constancies of the uterine environment are necessary conditions for prenatal development, it follows that any character called "innate" by psychologist or linguist always has at least one set of environmental factors among its causes (according to the usual scientific definition of "cause" in terms of necessary and sufficient conditions). Usually there will be many such factors relating to the postnatal as well as prenatal environment. It follows that any claim that something or other is innate commits one to a proposition known to be false (namely, that the entity so labelled has only a genetic basis). If we wish to use the term and avoid the contradiction, we are forced to broaden the definition to include environmental factors. We might then arrive at one or other of the two following glosses.

(3)   "An unlearned character ultimately determined by the genetic and ecological universals of a species."

(4)   "A character ultimately determined by the genetic and ecological universals of a species."

Although these definitions avoid the logical problems of (1) and (2), (3) runs into the difficulty that the term "learning" is itself vague at its boundaries: some of the ways in which the environment brings about changes in competence—particularly in immature organisms—are not easily classifiable as "learning" or "not learning" (cf. the controversy in the ethological literature over whether imprinting should be regarded as learning). However, regardless of the vagueness of (3), while some linguistic universals might be innate in sense (3), it is unlikely that all could be. Consider, for instance, such semantic markers as "physical object," "animate object," "male," "female," or Katz' evaluation marker. These may well be universal since it is hard to imagine a human society which would not need to embed such properties repeatedly in the vocabulary of its language. By the same token, it is hard to imagine a society where the children would not get opportunities to learn to distinguish animate from inanimate, male from female, and things which serve well their intended purpose from those that do not. It seems unnecessary to assume that such distinctions are present prior to learning

---

even though other factors like nutrition affected (nondifferentially) the absolute height of both. The term mainly has currency in the psychological literature in respect to individual differences. This usage is irrelevant to the present discussion, since we are here concerned only with explaining similarities, not differences, between members of a species.

since any theory of cognitive development will have to provide a mechanism for the learning of a host of culture-specific relations and concepts of equal complexity. It follows that the only general claim that can be made about linguistic universals, *qua* universals, is that they are innate in sense (4). It is hard to see that this claim says anything very interesting about linguistic universals.

Acknowledgment

I am much indebted to Kalon Kelley and I. M. Schlesinger for detailed discussion of the first draft of this paper, which was written in 1967 when I was in the Neuropsychiatry Division of Walter Reed Army Institute of Research, where the experiment was done.

DISCUSSION

An Overview of Theories
of Grammatical Development

SUSAN ERVIN-TRIPP
University of California
Berkeley, California

The privilege of having the last word is a great advantage in a field of occasionally impolite controversies. The skewed distribution of contribution time since the AAAS panel that generated this book has left some authors guarding outdated positions. In particular, my comments on Palermo will refer to his views in this book, not to his current outlook which is different. The span of time has the merit of revealing certain changes of emphasis in the field over the past four years, which I hope to underline.

Nativism versus empiricism was the central theme of the panel in 1965, and it remains salient in Braine's most recent contribution. A clearer example of the tendency to polarization in intellectual controversies could not be found. While dramatic on the lecture platform, polarization can harm empirical work, and in this case it seems to have done so.

No one believes the neonate arrives as a tabula rasa, undifferentiated from other species in mental capacities.[1] On the other hand, just what is present has not been well defined, nor what the interaction with input must be to have given consequences. Indeed, as currently stated

---

[1] It is sometimes assumed that Chomsky and McNeill hold the most extreme possible position on the innateness controversy. This is not the case. In concluding a carefully reasoned reply to an examination question on this issue, a student recently wrote: "Man existed before this earth life as spirit children of God and as such he had great knowledge and language with which to communicate with other spirits. Birth simply wiped out or placed a veil over all this knowledge so that is was not readily available to him. Man therefore innately has all the capacity for language in any form that it takes. The peculiarities of the natural languages are what man learns since he came with the innate structure already available to him. Maturation is part of the plan, so each child develops totally including language in a preprogrammed manner, genetically if you wish. The capabilities of man are as you would say in the genes" (Kenneth Hoskisson, with permission).

the controversy is defined so vaguely as to involve untestable assertions on both sides. The evidence of species specificity of aspects of the communicative system they develop is one of the strongest arguments for a richer set of predisposing capacities, or orientations. The best data on this point at present may be the observations of the signing chimp, Washoe, by the Gardners (1969, unpublished). The most recent chimp texts look remarkably similar to the "pivot" stage described by Slobin, with the exception of including many verb-verb sequences. Therefore the critical test of difference may lie elsewhere in her system. Since I assume morphological features are absent in the sign language of the deaf, the place to look may be at the simplest transforms first produced by signing children, to test the chimpanzee's comprehension.

Many of the arguments used in this debate seem to be very insecure. Universality is a necessary but certainly not a sufficient condition to assume neurological preprogramming. Incest taboos are universal but not innate. Humans share an extraordinary amount of their experience of the physical and social environment, so common experience could account for many shared semantic categories, and orders of acquisition. It is tragic to cut off from the domain of research the large field of the cognitive relations which are found in early sentences—e.g., locative relations, agentives, plurality—by assuming *a priori* that there are no interesting problems in their acquisition. Dogmatism without evidence is to say the least presumptous.

The weakest argument of all is the notion that if we cannot think of a way to teach something it must not be learned or learnable. That is making a logical necessity out of our failures of ingenuity. Admittedly, some of the attempts at learning accounts in this volume are so forced as to make one wonder why we aren't all talking like second-order approximations still. But that is only a consequence of the present condition of our knowledge, not an inherent limitation.

Are we to continue to be amused by the gladiators in this arena, until we declare the topic unresolvable and forget it, or can we couch the conflict in empirically fruitful terms? Let us suppose that there are logically possible languages which someone believes to be learnable within the constraints of his theory of association, but another says must be unlearnable because they conflict with human information-processing abilities in a general or in a language-specific sense. An example might be a language in which the third word in a string was always the term for the action, the fourth the agent. It does not seem unethical to teach languages to three- or four-year-old children and empirically discover what properties are readily acquired.

At this early age, the evidence on second language learning suggests that children are still using primary mechanisms for language acquisition and that there is relatively little structural effect of the first language on the second (Ervin-Tripp, 1970b). The older the subjects, the more the results would be weighted by the employment of language processing devices from the first language in processing the new input. One could control for this relation, but it would of course make the experiment more complicated.

It does not help us to say that the universal aspects of the deep structure are a "manifestation of the child's own capacities" (McNeill, this volume p. 21). While we may leave to students of cognitive development the issue of exploration of the ontogenesis of semantic categories and relations, surely we can define our own empirical task more hopefully. The task is to find ways to specify empirically what the input to children is, or to control that input, to discover what the structures are by which the children process that input at each stage of change, and to find empirically how those structures are alterable by different features of the input. The input is, after all, all that we can manipulate, if we define input as any kind of environmental events. The "language processing structures" and the "language acquisition systems" which alter the components of these structures are necessarily inferential. Braine's analysis provides us with an example of a language acquisition system affecting certain features of syntax, namely surface order. If it turns out that nothing that we do with input, short of abolishing it, has any effects on the child's comprehension, imitation, or production of language, I believe even the "nativists" would be surprised. McNeill himself proposed some manipulations of input in speaking of how to maximize the types of social exchanges which will allow children to discover the relations between the surface structure and the meanings.

1. The Input

In several exchanges over the past few years, the input to children has been maligned without being specified. As Braine has ably demonstrated, even if input is not entirely consistent with the grammar, it can be processed if there is a predominant patterning. Human learners can find the pattern and either forget or subcategorize the exceptional cases.

But how ungrammatical is input to children? It has always seemed astonishing that men who have been parents could believe that children usually hear complex imbeddings, stuttering false starts, speakers entangled in ungrammatical strings. After all, children under three normally hear discourse to them about food, elimination, and the simple prohibitions and encouragements of child life. They do not listen to conference tapes filled with stumbling replies, as speakers search for what their ideas should be.

Fortunately, at our Berkeley Program on Language, Society, and the Child, three of my students explored existing family tapes for evidence on the grammatical features of speech to children as contrasted with speech to adults.[2] While we have known for some time that speech to children is phonologically marked (Ferguson, 1964), these features have been of interest primarily as a stylistic index of adult and children's speech to their juniors.

Children are exposed to a great deal of speech which is not addressed to them. But they probably "tune out" a good deal that is uninteresting or too complex, just as they turn off political commentators on television. There seem to be neurological bases to attention which simply eliminate from processing and storage a good deal to which we are exposed. So we have good grounds for believing that at least at the beginning the most important language in learning is the speech addressed to the child.

The syntax of speech addressed to children is simple, containing short sentences with relatively few passives, conjoined phrases, or subordinate clauses. Drach (1969) found that over two and a half times as many of these general transformations per sentence occurred in complete sentences in a woman's address to adults as to her two-year-old son, and sentences were over twice as long.

Speech to children is markedly lacking in hesitations, false starts, and errors. Occasionally, of course, adults imitate children. They do use ellipsis, as in answers, or imperatives, or in the form of subject and auxiliary deletion, as in "Wanna play a game with me?"—around half of the sentences to a two-year-old in Drach's sample. Whether such deletions are in fact more difficult to process is debatable; Fodor and Garrett (1967) have argued that perceptual complexity cannot be predicted by the derivational complexity from a generative grammar. The fact that deletions are most common in rapid, informal style makes it highly improbable that they should be more difficult to interpret or produce than their full counterparts; presumably the situation makes the deleted material obvious semantically.

There is an argument for the position that very brief sentences as input could in fact be optimal at the beginnings of language develop-

[2] The findings of these student studies have been reported in the unpublished papers by Drach (1969), Pfuderer (1969), and Kobashigawa (1969). Slobin has summarized these findings and added additional work on the issue in a conference paper (Slobin, 1968).

ment. The phrases which comprise the basic units of language would become apparent, and children would be aided in precisely the task of segmental or constituent recognition which must be present in comprehension. Shipley, Smith, and Gleitman (1969) have shown that for children around 18 months of age telegraphic input may be easier to understand than input containing articles. The deletions that we find typically leave intact units like noun phrases, predicates, prepositional phrases, which will be structurally important later. They are by no means random or arbitrary; linguistically they are consistent and rule governed. Indeed, the rules of relating the deleted and nondeleted versions might even become apparent to hearers, since often both forms occur side by side in speech to children.

Kobashigawa (1969) has shown that speech to children is highly repetitive. It contains both paraphrases and expansions of deleted material. In a sample to a two-year-old child, from a third to over half of the utterances were repeated. The general syntactic form tended to be retained, but in three fourths of the repetitions there were minor changes in order, intonation, stress, or vocabulary (see Table 1.)

Input tends to be feedback productive, since it contains many imperatives or questions. In samples of four mothers' speech to children between two and three, a quarter to half of the utterances were questions. In samples of informal family conversations of adults, the range was from 1 to 25%. The structure of the questions is often of the type described by McNeill and more fully reported by Brown, Cazden, and Bellugi (1969) as helping syntactic analysis.

Most of these samples were of speech to two-year-olds. Infants may be addressed in widely varying syntax since it is not assumed they will understand. In analyzing the texts from Brown's studies, Pfuderer (1969) found that middle class mothers increased syntactic complexity with the age of the child in the two-to-three period, showing that there may be learning by the mother as well as the child. The result may be that in certain respects the input maintains a consistent relation to the child's interpretive skill.

One kind of style to children one encounters in caricatured baby-talk was not typical of these samples, namely telegraphic speech involving copula and determiner deletion. It is possible that if this style is found it is a marker that is brief. The same phenomenon appears as a style marker at the outset of speech by some children to foreigners, as if it were an imitation of foreigners' English. Obviously in this form, as a transitory marker of relationship or social features, such changes are not important as a feature of syntactic input, in contrast to the features discussed above which are of great frequency in speech to children.

TABLE 1[a]

Sample of Adult–Adult Speech

17. An' then well now his father an' I are separated, so he sees me mainly.
18. An' then I try to do things with him and for him an' all to, kinda make up y'know for this.
19. But I can't, y'know, 'cause I can't put no man there to be a symbol for him or nothing.
20. He wouldn't have nothin' to do with Verlene.
21. An' then that child has so many problems that are jus' his or hers alone, y'know.

51. No, I really—I really believe that—that church an' the Bible an' all, that's good.
52. It gives me a certain amount of consolation which allows me to relax my mind and start thinking intelligently an' putting my efforts all in one y'know force goin' in one direction rather than jus' y'know continually feeling sorry for yourself.
53. It takes a little time.
54. 'Cause tha's bad.
55. 'N' you can't name the sort of virus goin' y'know.

65. I was on a inhalation series routine.
66. We wen' aroun' from ward to ward.
67. People are—y'know, that get all this mucus in their chest.
68. An' it's very important to breathe properly an' to be able to cough this mucus up and out an' through your chest, y'know as soon as possible.
69. And we couldn't sterilize the instruments, 'cause they were plastic.

Sample of Adult Speech to a Child

1. Come play a game wit' me.	12. Watcha been doin' today?
2. Come play a game with me.	13. What did you do today?
3. Wanna play a game with me?	14. Look at that.
4. You wanna play a game with me, *savoir faire*?	15. That's a funny picture, huh?
	16. Oh . . . wheee . . . Look!
5. Come look at Mamma's colorin' book.	17. What's that?
6. You wanna see my coloring book?	18. What's that?
7. Look at my coloring book.	19. And that's a church, huh?
8. Lookit, that's an Indian, huh?	20. Yeah, Mary goes to church.
9. Is that an Indian?	21. Mary goes to church?
10. Can you say Indian?	22. See.
11. Talk to me.	

[a] Drach (1968). Texts are from samples of Claudia Mitchell Kernan. The two samples are from the same adult speaker.

But our data are merely a beginning. We need more systematic evidence from naturalistic samples of what baby-talk styles to children actually occur at various ages and we need experimental studies to show the effects of these structural features on language change.

A precondition for language acquisition, according to John Macnamara (personal communication), is that the meaning be obvious. McNeill makes the same point, I presume, in speaking of the matching of deep and surface structure. This implies that optimal conditions at first must require that nonlinguistic events be redundant and matched quite simply with what is said. Later, of course, children learn a good deal by inference from what was said before, just as adults do in interpreting novel forms. But at first this obviousness of meaning depends, in a sense, on the adult saying what the child already knows, sees, or can see. The details of this relation demand exploration, for it implies a good deal of input is wasted from the standpoint of the acquisition of syntax or lexicon.[3] Children's learning from other children, which is the usual condition in many societies, might be efficient because of its tie to activities.

Children of immigrant bilingual parents often do not learn the first language of their parents, even if they often hear it used as the parents' private language. Lack of semantic correspondence may be the reason. We have observed two hearing children of deaf parents who heard a good deal of TV speech, but at three had not yet learned to understand or produce speech at all.

Staats' discussion lays a good deal of emphasis on responses, rather than on input. It is common, also, in discussions of language instruction to assume that getting the learner to speak a lot, to practice, is likely to accelerate learning and the development of automatic habits. Yet surely if there is one kind of evidence we already have, it is that motoric output is not necessary to language acquisition. Lenneberg's (1967) report of an anarthric child (who did not produce speech, yet developed normal comprehension of speech) makes this point very strongly. The implication of the morphological evidence both in my research cited

---

[3] The most dramatic case of prolonged absence of meaning during language learning was brought about in a self-instructional Russian program written under the supervision of Rand Morton. Intensive training occurred for 17 weeks, with over a month with no meanings, but drills in writing, discrimination, and imitating syllables and phrases in Russian. Late in the program, meaning clues were added to the workbook incidentally. At the end of the program, taken by students from the Defense Language Institute, Western Branch, the students scored below chance on the Army language achievement test for Russian. They entered the usual intensive program of the DLI for acquisition of Russian along with other students with no experience at all in Russian. The trained students remained worse throughout the program and never were able to learn as well as the neophytes. This study is cited by Postofsky (1970) in more detail in connection with an experiment on Russian instruction. He points out that the students either learned that Russian is meaningless, or they generated meanings which interfered with the conventional ones.

by Slobin, and in his reviews of Russian morphological development, (Slobin, 1966a, in press a) is precisely that neither the most frequently heard sequences nor the most frequently produced forms remain dominant. In English, before children produce any regular verb inflections, while all the verbs they actively employ are irregular in inflection, they overgeneralize the past tense suffix. How, also, can one account for the production of "handes" or "handses" after months of use of the plural form "hands"? Such forms overthrow well practiced items, frequently heard items, on the grounds that one says, after all "horses" and "glasses" and "boxes." While easily accounted for and indeed inevitable in a theory based on reorganizations of processing structures, these sudden (albeit temporary in this case) changes cannot at all be predicted from S–R theory, if we examine the accounts by Staats and Palermo.

Reinforcement appears to play a strong role in Staats' theory of acquisition. I can't imagine what kind of interaction he has been watching, but it is rarely the case that we spend much effort correcting the formal structure of children's speech, especially two-year-olds'. Listening to mothers of such children one is usually enthralled by the mother's ability to interpret what appears to a newcomer to be gibberish, and to carry on interaction satisfactory to the child. Brown, Cazden, and Bellugi (1969) examined mother–child interaction for two kinds of reinforcement, in relation to development: corrections, and failures to understand. They did not find that developmental rates were related to reinforcement at all. Corrections of formal features were rare. Instead, mothers corrected mistakes in content or truth value.

It seems, then, to be truth value rather than syntactic well formedness that chiefly governs explicit verbal reinforcement by parents. Which renders mildly paradoxical the fact that the usual product of such a training schedule is an adult whose speech is highly grammatical but not notably truthful [p. 71].

Adults listening to children speak are usually listening to the message, just as they are when they listen to adults. Our evidence is that they comment on the form only in the case of socially marked deviations such as obscenities, lower class nonstandard forms, and in the case of black families, forms believed to be "country speech." Such formal correction occurred much more when the children were five or older than at the age of interest here.

If reinforcement were the dominant factor in language development, we would expect speech of children to be primarily composed of "mands," of requests for food and services. But on the contrary, many performances requested by children are that adults look at something. And in the end the bulk of child utterances turn out to be predicative declarations, or identifications whose social function is mysterious, and for which the reinforcement is often absent.

A strong feature of Staats' account, as derived from Mowrer, is that secondary reinforcement rather than merely overt response by others controls learning. It is certainly the case that voice quality and other minute features of parent and child may become alike in ways that go beyond genetic determination. Staats assumes that secondary reinforcement gives imitation a very strong role in development, since any utterance imitative of an admired or affectionate other is likely to receive strengthening and be repeated.

There are several pieces of evidence cited by Slobin which go directly contrary to this belief. One is that children do not, at the beginning of syntactic development, imitate sentences more successfully than they spontaneously produce them, unless the imitations happen to be of expansions of their own sentences. Thus imitations, even if they were reinforcing, could not be the route to learning, since they are not any more advanced than where the child already is syntactically. Second, children say forms like "foots" for months, even for over a year, though they never hear it, and they often produce "foots" when repeating sentences containing the word "feet." Third, many utterances are regular but novel. The role of imitation in development is complex, and changes with age. But in respect to the early stage of syntax it simply is inadequate. Even if secondary reinforcement is present when sentences are imitated, the failure to imitate successfully loses it as a mechanism for language change.

2. Early Syntax

The data from several studies of early syntax have been brought together by Slobin. The evidence from the beginning phases of multimorphemic output is that the mean utterance length is surprisingly stable, increasing slowly, and that variablility in length is relatively small. Order consistencies are striking.

The arguments of Staats and Palermo to account for these phenomena seem unconvincing. If a semantic tie were learned between "bread" and some class of edible referents and "want" and a state of mind, sooner or later both "want bread" and "bread want" would occur. This happens by a simple stringing of associations. A good example of such an unordered string occurred in my nineteen-month-old son, who was frightened by costumed children on Hallowe'en and for some months could be set off into variously ordered word strings by any item on the list or by the word Hallowe'en, e.g., witch–mask–face–scared–crying. This is not a sentence, but a string. If it has any order it is like a chain association, not a sentence. It lacks the intonation and stress of sentences, as well.

The length limitations of early sentences have appeared consistently in our texts, where concordances were organized by sentence length in the early months. Imitated sentences were no longer than free speech, though surely Staats would expect them to be. Staats states that this constrained length is a consequence of training in one-word input by adults; if this were the case, we would not find such short sentences in children who learn language from older siblings who do not give them one-word training but speak in the longer sentences natural to their play. Yet we have found these short utterances to be typical of early output and to increment consistently in various societies around the world (Slobin, 1968).

The unit of length in such comparisons is the child's morpheme, not the syllable which is presumably a more superficial feature. My son learned the word "Popocateptl" quite young. Once he had mastered his version of its phonology, he produced it readily in as varied sentences as any monosyllabic word. Since for familiar words the length ceiling appears to be related to morphemes rather than syllables, the source may be some limitation on the children's ability to organize either semantic units or syntactic units. That semantic units may be to some extent at issue, and not mere syntax, is suggested by Smith's findings that at later ages deletions of material during imitation affect semantic concentrations particularly severely, such as long auxiliaries or adjective sets (Smith, 1969).

Brown (1970) has recently arranged structural features by age of appearance in various children, and finds that sentences with three basic syntactic components, such as subject–verb–object, appear at the same age as sentences with two components, but one nested, such as verb–object, with the object a possessor and a possessed. Thus "Daddy hit ball" coincides with "hit baby ball" in level of difficulty. Since the syntactic devices are quite different, but the semantic entries similar in complexity in some simple sense, one could argue that semantic rather than syntactic length limitations are present.

Staats evidently believes that the length of sentences is a simple function of training and would be easy to change. This would be an easy experiment to do. The issue goes to new sentences, of course, so that it would not pertain to drilled sequences themselves. It is conceivable that one could drill particular sequences until they were no longer produced by normal generative processes but rather by rote, like the meaningless material children sometimes recall from advertising jingles. Also, the experiment pertains primarily to children around two. As the child's grammar increases in complexity, both the variability and potential length increases, and the length ceiling disappears. The acquisition of ability to produce compounds and subordinate clauses of course most radically changes the maximum length; eventually indefinitely long strings of compounds, or right-branching sentences like "The House that Jack Built" are possible. At later ages than two, or at least after these structures are acquired, reinforcement or modeling may indeed lead to a more wordy style.

The order regularities in early sentences are not well predicted from Staats and Palermo's models. It is true that a few forms of order, such as the sentence-initial position of question words, are clearly derived from marked positions which are highly regular in adult sentences. But far more difficult are the regularities that are not based on adult models, such as the verb-final order used by Gvozdev's Russian-speaking son, or the "allgone puzzle" example. Braine's list also give many good instances of regular sequences not readily based on direct adult models.

Staats, using the example of "bread please," argues that reinforcement accounts for the order stability and the development of the sentence as a regular unit. Then we must ask several questions: Why is not "please bread" also reinforced? (Aren't parents grateful for "please" in any location?) Why does the pattern generalize to "dolly please?" Do parents reinforce form anyway? We already know that the answer to the last question is that they do not. In fact, a child is likely to get bread if the parent intends to give it to him, whatever the frame in which he supplies the word. He may even say "bread" alone and be rewarded just as often. Staats might, regarding the first question, reply that the order effects are an example of "supersititious behavior," that is that fortuitous accidents of reinforcement give that order the advantage and afterwards that order occurs more, gets reinforced more, and so on. But if that is so why should not "please dolly" suffer the same fate? There is no way, by reinforcement alone, to account for the generality of these orders across many lexical entries.

The question of the generalization of structures across lexical entries, and later to complex units like noun phrases, is at the heart of the disagreement. I do not see that Palermo and Staats have provided a means for this generalization, which is the basis of creativity in language, to take place, while retaining the sentence length and structural features of the sentence.

In typical verbal learning experiments these features are carefully isolated in the input. If the output is to be a two-item sequence, the input is two-item sequences. This is not the case in child language learning. In an experiment, if response substitutions occur, it is because they are semantically similar to the item in the particular positional slot, formally similar, or linked by mediation or direct association. These last types of response substitutions are the ones that S–R accounts must rely on to explain grammatical productivity or new lexical combinations in child utterances. They predict too much, however. They would predict that "gimme bread" might as easily generalize to "gimme eat" or "gimme big" as to "gimme dolly." And there is no way to constrain the production of longer associative strings since the input was in fact longer than two words, so no formal reason for the two-word structure is apparent to the learner. So we should get strings like "gimme bread food kitchen eat . . . ," and we do not get such associative strings, in children's first sentences, though as I indicated earlier such strings occasionally occur as a series or list.

For these reasons the S–R accounts we can at this point derive from verbal learning experiments are not a fully satisfactory explanation, though I do not doubt that some of the same intellectual processes may in fact go on in both situations. Schlesinger and McNeill explain the length limitations, the expansion without loss of pattern later, and the stability of properties of structural slots across new surface items by attributing to the child two forms of knowledge not given to him in the S–R explanation. One is a knowledge of some overall sentence pattern or relationship. The other is the recognition of categories. The details of the accounts are slightly different from each other.

While these differences are slight, they raise some valuable theoretical issues. Schlesinger views the sentences as the realization or representation of a semantic relation. In the first sentences, only one major semantic relation is realized per sentence. The sentence slots or classes involve the components of the relation, so their unity is based on common semantic properties vis-a-vis the other item. Thus, in a locational sentence, the first items must all share the property of being locatable in space, and the second must all share the property of specifying location.

In McNeill's account, as he finally develops it, the relation realized is a grammatical relation, which is one step removed in abstraction from a semantic relation. If we consider, for example, Fillmore's (1968) treatment of case relationships, or some discussions of the passive, we find that the kinds of relations which Schlesinger talks about are in fact closer to the deep structure, and those McNeill talks about closer to the surface structure. For example, the relation subject–predicate and modifier–head can in some theories of language be alternative ways of representing the relationship between an item and its attributes. The difference between the two has to do with what is salient or new information: where the redness is new, we say "The truck is red," when it is not new, but simply an identifying attribute, we say "The red truck . . . ," (e.g., Osgood, in press). In a passive, the subject is the recipient of action. So that where Schlesinger deals with the semantic relation of actor–action–patient or object, McNeill deals with the grammatical representation subject–verb–complement, which only in the unmarked condition is the realization of that semantic relation. In terms of the properties of the classes, McNeill's preferred position is to regard the lexical items as accruing features such as +V,——NP which would mark transitive verbs. The items having these features must be learned; what the features are is part of the basic grammatical features.

There are advantages and disadvantages in both of these accounts. In the grammars we have looked at for a variety of languages there is a surprising similarity in the semantic relations realized. It does indeed appear that the first orders coincide *both* with semantic relations and with grammatical relations. It is this coincidence that neither theory quite captures. If one defines early grammars purely with McNeill's formal categories, one loses sight of the regularity with which the NP in a certain position is a locative phrase. If one describes O + O sequences as N + N sequences, one loses sight of the features Bloom (1970) for example identified, and which can be found in other children, that these sequences regularly represent a finite set of semantic relations: conjunction, possession, agent–patient, attribution, location. If one added stress information, probably some of these would be for some children structurally separable, e.g., báby chair versus baby cháir. The first would be possession or attribution, the second agent–patient or location (Miller & Ervin, 1964).

On the other hand, sooner or later the kind of formal relationships McNeill discusses must be present in language, or we are unable to deal with purely formal, nonsemantic properties in the case of the *do* rule in English, or the various kinds of complementation of different verbs. Schlesinger does not fully account for the transition from semantic ordering to formal ordering, though possibly detailed realization rules could do so. Semantic ordering in the Schlesinger sense never does disappear from our sentence processing entirely, as I will illustrate later. However, by the time the auxiliary system develops in English it is clearly necessary to provide for a more abstract system as well. McNeill's is the only account which takes this requirement seriously. Braine's experimental model, of course, can handle it, in the sense of accounting for the development of finite classes defined purely formally.

It was Braine who first discovered the stability of order in early sentences and described "pivot" structures in very young children, younger than those studied by Brown and Fraser and by Ervin and Miller. Recently Bloom, using very much larger corpora from limited time periods, has shown that there is considerably more internal structure at this stage than a pivot system permits. I have reanalyzed my own data and Braine's published material from her point of view, and have found that indeed there are a great many subcategories and distributional constraints which the pivot rules do not illustrate. I also found that in my data from children with mean morphemes per utterance below 1.5, it was necessary to revise the grammatical analysis about every three weeks. For this reason, pooling of data from longer periods, as was commonly done in the earlier reported studies, seems likely to obscure structure.

Bloom's analysis, and the richer structure evident in Braine's data, suggests that the S–R explanations offered in this volume are even less likely to be tenable than if the data were limited to those available four years ago. An even more difficult challenge is presented by the presence of noun phrases and other replacement units—e.g., "There bye-bye car," "want car," "want byebye car."

Staats and Palermo assume that these longer sequences are a product of chaining. If these sequences were so produced, we would expect many longer chains, looking something like second order approximations to English, but we do not. A good example would be "see the dog." There is absolutely no reason to believe that the many children who produce this sequence as noun phrases are developing, ever say "see the" and are thus enabled to link the sequence to "the dog." For some children "big" is the first attribute. I have numerous examples from the same text of "That a truck," "That's a truck," "There's a big truck," "There truck," and "There big truck." To assume that these developed out of sequences like "There's a" and "a big" one would have to find these in isolation. On the contrary, the antecedents are sequences like "There truck," or "That truck" and the other forms are either later expansions like "There big truck," or are in free variation like "that," "thats," and "thatsa," and make no difference. The account one gives of these replacement units, of which both Braine and Bloom have given good examples, is closely related to the explanation for the early sentences in general. If one proposes that there are underlying grammatical or semantic relations, then the expansion of these by modification relations within the larger units is no problem at all. But the explanations relying on associative strings present anomalous predictions which do not fit the data. One would have thought that the string sentence was killed by numerous experiments in the past ten years.

3. Morphology

The evidence from simple morphological systems like English is probably the easiest to accommodate to various forms of extant learning theory, since essentially the issue is the linkage of two types of units. A major factor in the order of development is the emergence of the conceptual basis. For example, to generalize the suffix of "ideas" and of "pigs" one has to recognize something common to the referent or meaning of both—plurality.

There are fundamentally three types of inflectional systems in languages, of which English is the simplest. English is the type of system with zero morpheme for the unmarked form. A second type of system has suffix strings, as in Finnish. In Latin and Russian, the strings are suppletive, so that one cannot, for example, predict the form of the genitive plural feminine from knowing the rest of the matrix. This type seems the most difficult to learn. In the English plural, we typically find three stages of development. First there is no marking at all. Second, there is a stage in which, in the context calling for a suffix, less than a third of the time one occurs, but there is no suffix unless the semantic context calls for one. Third, the suffix begins to be overgeneralized and occurs first on nonsense or new forms, next on forms with irregular inflection (Cazden, 1968). It appears that at stage 3 the child can generate the form through either of two routes: either he can use his processing dictionary to locate a particular past or plural perhaps stored as if it were a single word; alternatively, he can attach a root and suffix. Children at this stage will have free variation between *fell–fall–falled* in reference to past events.

Palermo has reported his experiment with Eberhart presumably designing an experimental analog to the acquisition of past tense. As a specific analog it has many defects which Slobin has pointed out (see Appendix). The matrix structure does not match the English past tense system, one might question whether digit pairs are really like unordered semantic notions, and most seriously, the statistical features do not correspond to the natural language it is supposed to parallel. However, these are remediable defects of design, and by careful analysis of the different types of existent morphological system and of the actual input in families, one could design analogs somewhat more acceptable, do fine manipulation of various features one cannot experiment with in nature, and see if the results, when the conditions match natural languages, correspond to those we see in naturalistic studies. This kind of work strikes me as the best possible use of the experience of verbal learning researchers. It would be of great value to learn, for example, the relative role of token frequency versus variety of types in producing generalization of a suffix. The evidence from Russian, as Slobin has indicated, suggests that frequency in the input is not alone a determinant of dominance in overgeneralization.

In such experiments the age of the subjects may be important. In Berko's work (1958), children were willing to generalize the regular past tense suffix, but not stem changes. The past tense of *gling* was *glinged,* not *glang.* Adults, be they monolinguals as in Berko's work, or native Japanese learning English, as in my research, (Ervin-Tripp, 1967), are much more likely to treat stem changing as itself a generalizable pattern. The reasons for the difference are not obvious; possibly adults have greater ability to store subcategorized patterns.

In my opinion, the Klima and Bellugi material (1966) on the acquisition of the interrogative and negative in English constitutes the most serious challenge to traditional views of learning. To summarize the evidence on negation, at stage 1 the negating element is external to the sentence, at stage 2 it is internal, preceding the predicate or verb phrase (with some minor variations such as "I have any shoes"), and at stage 3 the use of modals, copula and of the dummy *do* appears, permitting a great simplification in that a common rule applies now to modals, copulas, and to *do* when the other is not present. Most dramatically, at about the same time children also begin to use general patterns in interrogative inversion and ellipsis reflecting a common underlying unit we can call auxiliary.

I believe that this material defies explanation by the models used by Palermo and by Staats in this volume in two major respects. First, the fact that a common pattern is used for the three situations, equating sentences, main verb sentences, and modals, is based upon a kind of class abstraction that is not explained on the basis of any earlier behavior of the child.

Second, while it is possible to find an underlying semantic unity in children's versions of noun phrases, and locative phrases, there is nothing that is shared by the realizations of the auxiliary. *Do,* in the sentence "Do you like potatoes" has no semantic content at all. The correlation with external events or even internal meanings cannot aid in the acquisition of its distribution. Its use reveals that the child has gone beyond direct representation of semantic categories to more abstract formal units.

A very revealing parallel to English monolingual auxiliary development appears in an excellent study by Ravem of the acquisition of English by his six-year-old Norwegian-speaking son (1968). In Norwegian, modals have exactly the same negative and interrogative patterns as English, so the child already knew the basic structure required by English. However, the sentences with simple verbs—and Norwegian has no progressive—places negatives after the verb (He likes it not) and inverts the main verb and subject for the interrogative (Saw you it?). These structures, including their use with the perfect tense, were fully mastered in Norwegian by Rune at this age. English, in a sense, gains rule simplification by using the dummy *do* which makes all classes of sentences alike; the price is a meaningless element in the surface structure.

As Rune learned English, he went through an intermediary phase syntactically, which reminds one very much of Klima and Bellugi's analysis of English, before he acquired the pattern of *do* insertion from their stage 3. In the case of interrogatives, it is apparent that though he has learned English words, at a more abstract level he continues to employ the Norwegian pattern of inversion. Essentially he produces sentences with Norwegian syntax but English morphemes:

> "Drive you car to-yesterday?"
> "Like you me not, Reidun?"
> "Say it you not to Daddy?"

Inversion of subject with the next element apparently is an important cue to the recognition of a question. Before Rune acquired *do,* he retained inversion and did not move back to the stage where only raised intonation marked questions. In one formulation at least, the rule was common to all sentences, and for this reason perhaps English syntax would not be a simplification.[4]

In the case of the negative, on the other hand, his solution before learning *do* was to go to the Klima and Bellugi stage 2, namely to insert a negator before the verb:

> "I not sitting on my chair."
> "I not like that."
> "One is not crying."

In the Norwegian negative, there is a different placement rule for main verbs and for verbs with auxiliaries. The negative follows the main verbs when they are alone, but precedes them with modals or *have.*

[4] If Rune had learned each word as a translation of an English word, the fact that he was able to produce word-for-word translations retaining Norwegian syntax smoothly would not be surprising. But if the process were indeed mediated by Norwegian words, rather than Norwegian abstract structures, would there not be interference from those words?

Thus the Norwegian rule is more complex, and moving to the English pattern constitutes a simplification. In the abstract, Rune recognized that the English rule generalizes his rule for the modal, so though he did not have *do* he adopted the negative placement feature.

Ravem pointed out that the spread to other uses of *do* was very fast, even faster than Miller and Ervin reported.[5] From the standpoint of surface structure it is not easy to see how "Do you want some" and "We don't want some" are alike. The basic issue in the development of the English auxiliary is the acquisition of an abstract unit lacking semantic parallels, and the development of permutation patterns which utilize that unit rather than its surface realizations. Unless one is willing to accept that abstract permutation in some form occurs, the generalization across the negative, interrogative, and truncated sentences ("Yes, I did") has not been explained.

The example of the development of the English auxiliary raises most clearly for the first time in the ontogenesis of language the implications of the phenomena described by linguists as transformations for theories of learning. For this reason the failure of the empiricists to account adequately for this stage of development is most damaging to their case, at least as far as their theoretical constructs are concerned.

4. Semantic Aspects of Language

One of the major changes in studies of child grammar in the past four years has been an increasing systematic attention to sentence meaning. While the students of child language early in the decade commented informally about the need for looking at semantically structured units, and taking meaning into account in writing grammars, these considerations did not fundamentally affect their theoretical approaches. The current interest in meaning, of course, in part represents a resurgence of attention to meaning in linguistics. But it also is a consequence of some despair at the lack of plausibility of the analyses reached by formal methods alone.

For example, early in the decade, I wrote grammars for five children around age two for whom Miller and I had texts. In the attempt to arrive at rigorous, replicable grammatical descriptions, I wrote explicit, distributionally defined grammars. In some cases, as Donnie (Ervin, 1964), the results were plausible, probably because the corpus was

[5] In addition, Ravem reports that Rune, like the children in other studies of monolinguals at stage 3, did not invert subject and auxiliary in *wh* questions, where inversion would be redundant.

homogeneous in time and relatively large, and because there was little variability in sentence type. In other cases grammatical class defined by distribution resulted in constructions which were so semantically diverse as to seem absurd. I am now preparing to publish a reanalysis which differs in several respects. The time periods spanned are shorter, at the price of smaller corpora. The analysis is heavily informed, on the basis of a suggestion of Braine (in press) by groupings of replacement sequences which appear to be alternative formulations of the same semantic substance, sequential in production.

Gun	Man car
Tommy gun	Man in car
Tommy give Stevie gun	Man in the car

(Braine, in press)

Bloom also gives examples of such instances, not to identify expansions of phrases, as Braine does, but to reveal that a long underlying string may, in a sense, be sampled in the surface structure.

By accepting semantic features as part of the necessary analysis, one finds that such structurally homonymous sequences as noun–noun sentences can be semantically subdivided. The relation of these sentences to their structurally diverse descendants can be more clearly seen since they occur side by side in replacement sequences. Bloom found that the list of noun–noun types was not identical for all children, and increased with age. Examples she found were conjunctions (umbrella boot), attribution (party hat), possessive (tiger tail), subject–locative (sweater chair), subject–object (cat meat).

In recent cross-cultural studies, it has become apparent that the semantic relations realized in early utterances tend to be the same in such widely different languages as Luo (Blount, 1969), Samoan (Kernan, 1969), and European languages (Slobin, 1970).

Fall baby.	Put it down.
Walks doll.	Bring candy baby.
Sleeps doll.	Put hand.
Give me baby.	Give thing here.

Who would suppose that these are literal translations of the Samoan child? They are from Kernan's texts. It is astonishing to see that the lists of children's utterances in different languages look like translations of each other for the most part. The list of these semantic relations includes: negation, repetition, possession, location, agent–action, action–object, action–indirect object, identification, attribution, and conjunction. Just how these relations are realized linguistically of course varies with language; where inflectional suffixes carry the information such suffixing may appear relatively early in grammatical development.

These early semantic relations have important implications for students of cognitive development, who must account for the knowledge of these relations very early. Some are realized in productive output as early as fifteen months of age; they are apparent in comprehension earlier. Even at the one-word stage a child could in fact be representing, for example, a possessive relation when he points to his father's coat and says "Daddy." Later he says "Daddy coat," just as later instead of saying "ball" he may say "throw ball" for identical scenes. Whether one is justified in assuming the child in fact recognizes a possessor and an object of action in the two cases would require further work.

Some of these early semantic structures have a surprising degree of abstractness, in one sense of the term. For instance, a child may at first treat "throw ball" and "want dolly" in structurally analogous ways, though from the semantic standpoint the similarity between stative and active verbs is not obvious. Also, early grammars often contain structures which group together items semantically similar as aspects or as states. Examples are the list of items following "all" in the child Andrew report by Braine (1963b): broke, buttoned, clean, done, dressed, dry, fix, gone, messy, shut, through, wet. These do not randomly overlap with items which, for example, follow "other" but represent a subclass of meanings which can be aspectually completed. Another instance is the use of "more" which several children applied equally to actions and things: e.g., more sing, more walk, more juice, more cookie.

These distributional constraints are usually represented in grammars by semantic feature markings, such as [+ animate]. This particular marker appears from the very beginning of children's sentences, for example as a feature of the possessor in the possessive constructions we find universally (to immodestly extrapolate from some small samples!).

The findings of universal, or even of common semantic features specifying subcategories or characterizing sentential relations is more than a mere curiosity, an addition to what we know. As Schlesinger has suggested, these semantic features may provide a crucial link in our understanding of how sentences develop. If it is true that language could never be learned unless meanings were obvious while sentences are heard by children, then the categories, features, and relations available to children at the onset of interpretive activity is a central issue in the explanation and prediction of language learning. For example, if we can establish the order of development of these relations, we can better account for the order of development within language; we can find which properties of input are irrelevant because incomprehensible to children on the basis of their cognitive development. The deeper investigation of the semantic properties in early sentences understood or produced by children provides a far more structured direction for research than we have had before, for the study both of the acquisition of semantic features of language, and of the experience needed to create the cognitive, non-linguistic prerequisites to language.

5. Processing Models

A major change has been taking place in psycholinguistics since the late sixties, in the direction of developing psychological models concerned with real time events, with psychological or even physiological concepts rather than logical reconstructions of sentences. Several papers discussing such models appeared in Lyons and Wales (1966); since then there have been numerous papers discussing the general need for such models (Fodor & Garrett, 1967) and describing relevant instances of processing heuristics.

It has always been a disturbing problem to psycholinguistics to accommodate grammars of linguists to the human organism. Does the grammar (at one time most of *Syntactic Structures*) reside in the brain with a battery of outputs warped by performance weaknesses? The implausibility of such an arrangement, and of the analogous notion that generative rules and transformations actually represented processes speakers and hearers go through, have finally led to some major reformulations of the relationship between linguistic descriptions of sentences and psychological descriptions of producing and understanding language. The constraints on linguists' rules include certain formal conventions about writing, the production by the rules of all and only those sentences native speakers will judge grammatical, and the use of speakers' intuitions about analogy of structure—The dog jumped : The cat fell : Did the dog jump : Did the cat fall. Since the kind of behavior predicted by psycholinguistic rules—relative latency of response, probability of understanding in a specific way, forgetting—are quite different, we can expect that the components will not be the same. Yet if the psychological models cannot account for speakers' judgments, with appropriate controls on the conditions of judging, they are likely to be suspect.

The typical processes which such models aim at accounting for are comprehension tasks, imitation, and sentence production under controlled conditions. The difference or overlap in components of Sentence Processing Structures provides a means of analyzing the nature of these components. Typically, these include phonological processors or scanners, short term memory devices, lexical access (to dictionaries with semantic and syntactic features marked, and partial morphophonemic matrices for each item), heuristics for decoding surface structure grammar, phonological production devices, and so on. I have discussed the details of some possible components from the standpoint of first and second language learning elsewhere (Ervin-Tripp, 1970b).

Such models must account for both the speed of processing under everyday circumstances, and for the power of processing under difficult conditions. Typically, psychologists have been impressed with speed but their models deal with only the easiest sorts of sentences; linguists look for the most complex cases, but either make the child out to be a phenomenal mental acrobat at birth, or leave us mired in puzzles we know we do not hear and cannot apprehend in the way we understand simple structures: "The tiger the lion the gorilla chased killed was ferocious" (Fodor & Garrett, 1967).

Current work on processing models in grammar would include ways of including the relevance of meaning in the above task. For example, the chances of "recovering subject–object relations" in the above sentence is clearly less than in "The car the man the dog bit drove crashed." While these sentences are still syntactic nonsense, the listener can guess at least from the probable relations of subject and verb. Fodor and Garrett report 15% success unscrambling the tiger and 66% success unscrambling the car. Ammon has recently reported (1970) for both adults and children that similar relating of subject to verb is easier for semantically plausible sentences like "The friendly neighbors who helped the sick man cooked the dinner" than for "The brave firemen who saved the lost kitten drank the warm milk." Slower responses and more errors occur for the implausible utterances, even in optimal conditions.

A number of studies have located a quick heuristic of assuming that NVN sequences represent agent–verb–object. There is a stage when children typically interpret (according to the selection of a picture) "The dog was chased by the cat" as meaning "The dog chased the cat." I have found that two- or three-year-olds typically complete "when" and "how" questions with transitive verbs by a suitable object for the verb: "When did he eat?" "Meat." (Ervin-Tripp, 1970a). This is not a gloss over the fact that we can in fact often go past these quick heuristics to a second analysis, under many circumstances. Just how such multiple processing occurs is one of the issues.

To understand how language changes, we need to begin with an analysis of the language processing structures at a given stage of development. Learning can effect the components of those structures quite differently; there is no reason to believe that the development of procedures for understanding relative clauses will in any way be related to the structure of phonological scanning as such, though features of short term memory influence both phonological imitation and syntactic imitation.

Models for sentence production seem to me at this stage the most difficult to produce because the input is so undefined. Schlesinger, and Osgood (in press) have both grappled with this issue. Imitation, as Slobin and Welsh (in press) have pointed out, has the advantage of providing information on both input and output. Studies of production and comprehension would have to be confined to the very limited types of semantic alternatives which can be vividly constrained by experimental circumstances.

To go from processing models to learning, we will need such Language Acquisition Systems as Braine has suggested and subjected to experimental test. As he points out, there is good reason to hope that many of the same systems are available to the child, and eventually one can test these assumptions. To exclude second language learning from exploration as *sui generis* different in all respects from first language learning one would have to assume that human mental capacity is earmarked only for certain context-defined tasks, and has no possibility of general purpose applicability.

Braine's theoretical analysis marks a valuable advance on previous treatments of learning. He includes both semantic and syntactic features, and accounts for preservation of dominant order features through his experimental work. He leans rather heavily on frequency for explanations of pattern or form dominance, so it is not clear how some of the other features beyond frequency, which Slobin found influenced morphologically predominant affixes in child Russian, could be accommodated.

While Braine's most pointed attack is on the hypothesis-testing notion of grammatical development, he has made an additional contribution by proposing some ways of handling rule ordering and transformation in a learning model, albeit a tentative one.

A few years ago Thorne *et al.* (n.d.) set out to show that other rule forms besides transformations could parse English sentences in reasonable time. A series of linear, contingent solutions of a Markov type proved remarkably successful in producing correct phrase structure. While Thorne was inclined to believe he had developed a psychological processing model, I find his treatment of the processing dictionary implausible. He relied wholly on affix and function-word classes for defining form class, with a few exceptions. Rather it seems more likely that we rely heavily, and in childhood perhaps wholly, on recognizing lexicon with distinctive syntactic features. Be that as it may, the finding of an alternative parsing route giving acceptable results frees us from incorporating transformations as such into processing models.

The advantage of the processing approach is that it is both nontrivial and empirically accessible. Braine's undertaking implies that issues about the role in learning of input structure, for example, need not be speculative alone, but are empirically testable.

Not only has the theoretical perspective changed, but methods have necessarily changed too, over the period covered by this book. The writing of grammars of children's language can only tell us that a change has occurred. Such grammars cannot tell what the changes have been in how the child processes sentences, nor how the changes came about. For these reasons, new studies are likely to develop models which can be tested. Language processing structures and language acquisition systems are going to be where the action is.

APPENDIX: An Exchange on Laboratory Studies of Language Acquisition

On the Learning of Morphological Rules: A Reply to Palermo and Eberhart

DAN I. SLOBIN
University of California
Berkeley, California

Palermo, in his Additional Remarks to his chapter in this volume, refers to research work he has done with Eberhart in which certain laboratory experiments were taken to be "analogous to the learning of past tense verb inflection in children." Since both Palermo and Staats look to studies of this sort to enrich understanding of the ontogenesis of grammar, I take the liberty of presenting a few critical considerations of such research in this Appendix. Palermo and Eberhart respond to these considerations in the second half of the Appendix.[1]

In a recent paper, Palermo and Eberhart (1968) present three verbal learning experiments which they believe to reveal something about the acquisition of linguistic rules by two-year-old children. Palermo and Eberhart (henceforth P&E) conclude:

> While the analogy between the learning of inflections for past tense and the conditions of the present experiments is not perfect, the similarity between the findings obtained in these three experiments and those reported by Ervin (1964) for children's acquisition of past-tense inflection of verbs is remarkable [p. 343].

In fact, however, the analogy is so far from perfect that the study seems to have almost no bearing on the relevant problem of first language acquisition. The "analogy" is inadequate in terms of (a) the nature of the task, (b) the structure of the materials, and (c) the frequency characteristics of the responses to be learned.

P&E had college students learn to associate pairs of digits with pairs of letters, such that (a) a given digit corresponds to a given letter, maintaining ordinal position in the associated pairs (e.g., 6 = V, 1 = M, 61 = VM); (b) some digit–letter pairs are not formed on this basis, but rather associate a unique letter pair with a pair of digits (e.g.,

---

[1] Also see Ervin-Tripp's comments on research of this sort, this volume, pp. 203–204.

61 = DL). Conditions (a) and (b) are taken to correspond, respectively, to regular and irregular past-tense inflections of the English verb. The complete set of stimuli and responses can be found in Table 1 [adapted from P&E (1968, p. 338)], where letter pairs in parentheses indicate irregular responses to be learned in the critical experiments (II and III). (Experiment I is not at issue here, as it was essentially a replication of the classic Esper experiment of 1925.) In the critical experiments the irregular pairs were presented more frequently than the regular pairs (three times as often in Experiment II; twice as often in Experiment III). In both cases, the irregular pairs were learned more quickly than the regular, and errors in responding on these pairs reflected full or partial generalization of the principle underlying correct responses to the regular pairs.

TABLE 1 Matrix of Stimuli and Responses Used by
Palermo and Eberhart

		Stimuli		
Stimuli	1	2	3	4
6	VM (DL)	VF	VG	VK
7	HM	HF (PC)	HG	HK
8	RM	RF	RG (TJ)	RK
9	XM	XF	XG	XK (WS)

P&E nowhere make explicit the analogy of this paradigm to past-tense inflections, or to the conditions of first language acquisition. Leaving aside the vast and vexing discrepancies between the college student seated at a memory drum for 25 trials and the two-year-old attempting to speak and understand thousands of sentences, the matrix of digit–letter pairs given in Table 1 does not even bear formal equivalence to English past-tense inflections. Presumably, though this is not explicitly stated, the first element of a letter pair represents a verb root (e.g., V = *walk*) and the second the inflection (M = —*ed*). There is no suggestion of what the digits may correspond to in the natural language situation. The closest evident analogy would be to assume that the first digit represents the intention to utter a given verb and the second digit the intention to indicate that the semantic reference of that verb applies to the past. Thus, following the example given above, 6 would correspond to the notion of "walking" and 1 to the notion of "past action" (though it would be difficult to defend the assumption that these notions occur to the mind separately and in fixed order). If this is the analogy intended by P&E, what might be the English correlate of stimuli 2, 3, and 4 and their associated responses F, G, and K? The regular past tense is formed, in writing, by adding a single inflection, —ed, to a verb stem. Thus the paradigm given in Table 1 must represent a number of different inflections—e.g., column 1 might be the past, column 2 the progressive, etc. However, the claim is made that the entire matrix corresponds to the English past tense only. This claim could be met only if it were the case that English had four past-tense inflections which could be applied in free variation to most verbs. I can think of no linguistic example, however, in which a given underlying marker can be realized by one of a number of freely varying surface markers in the same environment.

The claim might be made, however, that the matrix represents spoken, rather than written English, in which the past-tense inflection does admit of variant forms: /—t ~ —d ~ —ɨd/. These forms, however, are not freely varying as in Table 1, but are conditioned by phonological features of the preceding sound—e.g., *rubbed* /rəbd/ versus *stepped* /stept/ versus *seated* /siytɨd/. The paradigm of P&E, however, does not allow for influence of the first element upon choice of the second. Therefore, the use of the term "regularity" by P&E refers to a rule established for the purposes of their experiments, and does not correspond to the use of the term in a linguistic description of English verb morphology.

The notion of irregularity, as defined by the letter pairs in parentheses in Table 1, also does not correspond closely to the irregular past in English, as claimed by P&E. Irregularity is defined in their study as a totally unique letter pair—e.g., DL where VM would be expected. This pattern is true of only two verbs in English: *go–went* and *be–was/were*. In all the other cases, some phonological aspects of the root form are maintained in the irregular past. For example, there may be an internal vowel change (*fall–fell*), an internal vowel change plus suffix (*sleep–slept*), replacement of final /d/ by /t/ (*build–built*), or no change at all (*cut–cut*). This sort of irregularity is what is acquired early by the English-speaking child, and it is in no way reflected in the experiments of P&E. (The closest analogy to English verb irregularity which could be made in terms of Table 1 would be responses in which only the second element of a letter pair would be irregular.)

Such uncritical use of the terms "regular" and "irregular" leads P&E to conclude that the experimental situation relates to the learning of inflections. The experiments simply show, as Esper demonstrated over

40 years ago, that people can learn to apply a system to data, generalizing the system to new instances.

There is no support for the two other classes of analogies P&E attempt to draw between their study and first language acquisition: analogy of errors made and analogy of frequency distributions in the input. The phenomenon which P&E attempt to replicate is the fact that English-speaking children use the irregular past correctly (e.g., *came, fell*) *before* they produce overregularizations (e.g., *comed, falled*). In their study, errors of overregularization are counted whenever *one* letter of an irregular response is replaced by the corresponding letter required by the regular rule. Thus both DM and VL count as overregularizations of the correct irregular response DL to stimulus 61. The former is roughly analogous to the natural language situation (given the limitations pointed out above), but the latter has no clear analogy to the past-tense situation. The closest analogy would be to the plural, where a child might overgeneralize the irregular plural *—en,* producing such a plural form as *boxen* for *boxes.* No such examples have been reported in the child language literature. P&E report that 15 of 26 errors in Experiment II and 12 of 46 errors in Experiment III are such partial overregularizations, involving only one letter generalized from the regular case. Since these partial errors are not broken down by first or second position overregularizations, they cannot be compared to the natural language situation.

The other putative analogy is in terms of relative frequency of occurrence of regular and irregular forms. In Experiment II, 12 regular pairs are presented once each and four irregular pairs occur three times each; in Experiment III, there are again single occurrences of 12 regular pairs, but only two presentations of each of two irregulars. In both cases the number of regular types is considerably greater than the number of irregular types, and the number of regular tokens is equal to (II) or greater than (III) the number of irregular tokens. These distributional characteristics do not match relative distributions of either types or tokens of regular and irregular past-tense verbs in speech addressed to young children. I have examined four hour-long samples of adult speech to five children between the ages of one-and-a-half and four years: the three children studied by Brown's group in Cambridge (Brown, 1968; Cazden, 1968), a lower-class Negro child from the Oakland ghetto studied by Claudia Mitchell Kernan (unpublished data), and a lower-middle-class white child studied by Carolyn Wardrip near Berkeley (unpublished data). In each case there are at least twice as many types of irregular past-tense as regular past-tense verbs and about four times as many tokens. Thus, contrary to the paradigm of P&E,

children hear far more examples—both in number and diversity—of irregular verbs than regular verbs in the past tense.

It might be objected that a four-hour sample is too brief to allow the child to hear many examples of the far larger class of regular verbs. Accordingly, I surveyed the entire corpus of adult speech to Eve, one of Brown's subjects. This embraces about 49 hours of recording, spanning the age range of 18–26 months. At the beginning of the sample Eve correctly used such past-tense forms as *fell;* by the middle of the period sampled she was already producing overregularizations such as *falled.* Over the entire eight-month period she heard 40 types of irregular verbs in the past tense, but only 30 types of regular verbs. Furthermore, the irregular forms were heard almost three times as often as the regular forms, with 292 tokens of irregulars and only 99 tokens of regulars. The full data are presented in Table 2, where it is evident that the frequently occuring irregulars are *far* more frequent than most regulars (with the exceptions of *dropped, happened,* and *spilled*). Thus the paradigm of Experiments II and III is hardly analogous in its frequency characteristics to the learning situation faced by the child. The only sense in which the regular form occurs more frequently than the irregular in adult speech is that it has a single *underlying representation*—i.e., verb $+ ed$ (with the phonological conditioning pointed out above). What is involved, then, is the child's ability to make use of this underlying regularity in abstracting the regular principle. It is not yet known just what frequency characteristics the input to the child must have in order to support acquisition of this sort, but the characteristics selected by P&E are certainly far off the mark. In their paradigm the regular forms were presented less frequently but in larger numbers than the irregular, while in the natural language case the regular forms are presented both less frequently and in fewer numbers. It would be of interest to know just how small the latter number—the number of types of regular forms—can be before overgeneralization fails to occur. Clearly, the almost nonoccurring *—en* plural is never overgeneralized, though the single word *children* is of high frequency.

A more detailed examination of overgeneralization data suggests that, in addition to frequency and regularity, there is another variable at play: *partial regularity.*[2] Not all irregular verbs are equally subject to regularization; that is, overgeneralization is not a uniform phenomenon. There are five different sorts of irregular past tense formation in English, as shown in Table 3. Of these, the most interesting to the present discussion are the first two categories: (1) internal vowel change (e.g., *break–*

[2] This paragraph on partial regularity, along with Table 3, was added after Palermo and Eberhart wrote their following reply.

TABLE 2   Types and Tokens of Past-Tense Verbs Heard by Eve in 49 Hours of Adult Speech, Age 18–26 Months[a]

Irregular verbs				Regular verbs			
Types	Tokens	Types	Tokens	Types	Tokens	Types	Tokens
ate	3	heard	2	asked	1	managed	2
bit	5	hit	3	bumped	4	melted	4
bought	4	hurt	7	burped	1	moved	1
broke	8	left	1	clonked	1	pulled	1
brought	1	let	1	closed	1	saved	1
came	9	lost	3	cracked	1	slipped	2
caught	2	made	7	cried	2	spilled	11
cut	3	put	20	dropped	13	tied	1
did (main verb)	17	ran	1	dusted	1	tripped	1
drank	3	read	1	finished	1	turned	2
drew	2	said	8	fixed	6	untied	2
dug	1	saw	1	followed	1	used	3
fell	14	shook	1	happened	29	wanted	1
flew	1	slept	2	ironed	1	washed	2
forgot	20	thought	8	looked	1	wiped	1
found	3	took	5				
gave	3	tore	2				
got	12	was/were	54				
grew	1	went	29				
had (main verb)	23	wrote	1				
Total			292	Total			99

[a] The total number of past-tense utterances heard by Eve was, of course, much larger than 391, as the verb occurs in unmarked form in questions and negatives (e.g., *Did you lose it?; What did you lose?; You didn't lose it*). (Note that this complicates the general problem of learning to express the past tense in English.)

broke) and (2) internal vowel change plus final dental consonant (e.g., *lose–lost*). Note that although *broke* and *lost* are irregular, *lost* shows partial regularity in that a final dental consonant is added, as in the case of the regular verbs. Apparently such a partial regularity can act to block overgeneralization (i.e., to prevent the occurrence of *losed*). Table 3 is based on Miller and Ervin-Tripp's unpublished data, covering all speech gathered periodically from 24 children between the ages of about one-and-a-half and four. The data show a striking phenomenon: verbs with partial regularity are almost never subject to overgeneralization. It is as if the final dental consonant is enough of an anchor to the regular rule that the child can tolerate a vowel change in past tense inflection. The sample is totally devoid of forms such as *bringed, buyed,*

TABLE 3 Irregular Verbs Occurring 5+ Times in Past Tense in Miller and Ervin-Tripp Sample of Preschool Speech. (Frequencies)[a]

Verb	Correct past tense	Overregularized past tense	Input frequency[b]
Vowel change			
bite–bit	11	8	9
break–broke	102	19	10
come–came	90	7	14
drink–drank	6	1	5
eat–ate	34	10	8
fall–fell	75	8	18
find–found	14	0	6
fly–flew	10	42	1
forget–forgot	21	0	21
get–got	128	4	25
give–gave	22	0	11
run–ran	26	2	1
see–saw	20	2	10
stick–stuck	9	2	0
take–took	82	8	19
tear–tore	3	5	2
throw–threw	2	4	2
wake–woke	5	6	1
win–won	5	6	0
Total	665	118	162
Vowel change + /d $\sim$ t/			
bring–brought	34	1	4
buy–bought	20	1	9
catch–caught	15	0	3
do–did[c]	145 (?)	14	35
hear–heard	8	0	2
leave–left	29	0	4
lose–lost	17	0	11
say–said	71	0	21
tell–told	22	0	9
think–thought	11	0	20
Total	372	16	118
Final consonant → /d/			
have–had	71	0	37
make–made	54	7	12
No change			
hurt–hurt	14	0	10
put–put	68	4	40
Total Change			
be–was/were	2	0	146
go–went	80	5	48

[a] Based on a sample of 24 children between the ages of approximately 1½ to 4 years, recorded at periodic intervals (unpublished data).

[b] Based on 64 hours of speech to children in this age range by mothers and investigators under conditions of natural dialog.

[c] First column includes *do* as auxiliary; last column only *do* as main verb.

catched, leaved, losed, and the like, while it is full of examples of *bited, breaked, flied,* etc. This finding is in consonance with the experimental finding of Anisfeld and Gordon (1968) that fifth-graders, in choosing between nonsense syllables to indicate past tense, preferred syllables containing /d/ or /t/. That is, past tense meaning would be attributed to a syllable such as /dartš/ or /dardž/, with a dental consonant in the final cluster, while a syllable such as /darš/ would be rejected. It appears that children pay close attention to the fine structure of inflections, basing their generalizations on features of phonological structure—in this case, a final dental consonant. One cannot speak, therefore, of the overgeneralization of a particular inflection as a single, undifferentiated phenomenon.

Finally, it should be pointed out that the case of the overregularization of the English past tense cannot be taken as a general, cross-linguistic example of the child's overgeneralizations of morphological rules, as P&E suggest (p. 337). The simple case of one regular inflection, as in the English past tense, cannot be easily related to the successive sweeps of overgeneralizations which occur in cases of competition between *several* regular inflections offered by a language to express a given contrast. [See my discussion of "inflectional imperialism," in Slobin (in press a).] For example, in Russian, where case inflection on nouns is governed by gender and stem type, a given grammatical case will be expressed differently for masculine, feminine, and neuter nouns of different types. For example, the instrumental singular suffix on Russian nouns is realized as *—om, —oy, —oyu,* and *—yu.* The Russian-speaking child does not simply overgeneralize one instrumental suffix, and then use the entire system correctly, as in the case of the English past tense. In fact, although overgeneralizations occur, the notion of *ir*regularity is not even applicable. None of the instrumental forms is irregular; rather, the occurrence of each form is complexly conditioned by morphological and phonological features of the noun. The Russian-speaking child first overgeneralizes the *—om* instrumental suffix (masculine and neuter), using it for all nouns, just as the English-speaking child overgeneralizes the regular past (Gvozdev, 1961; Slobin, 1966a, in press a; Zakharova, 1958). However, at a later stage, the *—om* ending is dropped, and is replaced by the *—oy* ending (feminine), representing a new sort of overgeneralization. Only later are the endings correctly allocated according to noun gender. No frequency characteristics of the input can account for this change in overgeneralization, as the input remains constant. Clearly, what is involved is a far reaching internal reanalysis of the inflectional system by the child (spelled out in greater detail in Slobin, in press b). All of the determinants of such internal analysis and reanalysis of the input language are, of course, not yet known. It is my opinion that these determinants stand a far better chance of being revealed in detailed study of the speech of children and their parents than in the verbal learning laboratory. And certainly, further experimental attempts by investigators such as Palermo and Eberhart to simulate the child's acquisition of language should pay far closer attention to that process as it actually occurs in ontogenesis.

Acknowledgment

Discussion with Mr. Barry A. Gordon, Department of Psychology, University of California at Berkeley, has helped me in developing the ideas presented here, and I extend my appreciation to him. Thanks are also expressed to Professor Roger Brown for permission to cite the data presented in Table 2 and to Professor Susan Ervin-Tripp for making available the data summarized in Table 3.

On the Learning of Morphological Rules: A Reply to Slobin*

DAVID S. PALERMO
Pennsylania State University
University Park, Pennsylvania

V. LYNN EBERHART
University of Iowa
Iowa City, Iowa

Slobin (this volume, Appendix) is perfectly correct in arguing that the form of the rule which underlies correct performance in the Esper paradigm (1925) used by Palermo and Eberhart (1968) is not a good analogy to the form of the rule underlying correct performance in past tense inflection in the English language. The major purpose of the set of experiments we conducted was to show that there is nothing unique to language about the observation that the irregular forms of a rule such as the past tense inflection rule are acquired before the regular forms and that when the regular forms are acquired they overgeneralize to the irregular forms. It is this particular phenomenon which has been cited as difficult for traditional learning theories to explain (e.g., McNeill, 1966; Slobin, this volume) and which McNeill has suggested should be investigated by "concept-attainment experiments" (1966, p. 72). While we were not attempting to provide support for a learning theory interpretation, we were attempting to provide data showing the same sort of behavioral result in an experimental situation which would allow us the opportunity to manipulate the variables which might be shown to affect performance on regular and irregular instances of a rule within a concept-attainment task.

While it appeared to us that we were successful in demonstrating the analogous behaviors we were after in our variations on the Esper paradigm, we have attempted to improve on the analogy in another experiment (Palermo & Howe, 1970). In the latter experiment we presented subjects with a random selection of two-digit numbers (excluding

* Preparation of this paper and the research reported in it were supported by grant GB-8024 from the National Science Foundation and Public Health Service Research Career Program Award HD128,120 from the National Institute of Child Health and Human Development.

numbers ending in zero) to which the subjects were required to respond with one of three letters. The appropriate letter response was contingent upon the second digit of the two-digit number. In addition, there were four randomly selected two-digit numbers which were irregular in the sense that four other letter responses were required. Table 1 gives an example of the responses to be learned by one group in the experiment. On any single experimentally defined trial, the subject was presented with 22 two-digit numbers: four occurrences of one number with an irregular response (93), three of another (42), two of another (85) and one of the final number (26) plus a random selection of 12 two-digit numbers taken from a table of random numbers. The regular and irregular forms were randomly ordered within a trial. On each trial the same irregular digits were always presented the same number of times and the regular digits were randomly selected. The materials were presented aurally by tape recorder and the subjects responded orally by trying to anticipate the appropriate letter responses.

TABLE 1   Responses Learned in the Palermo and Howe Experiment (See text for explanation)

Regular Pairs	Irregular Pairs
7⎫ 5⎬—F 9⎭	93—O 42—A 85—U 26—I
1⎫ 4⎬—G 6⎭	
3⎫ 2⎬—C 8⎭	

In the Palermo and Howe experiment the analogy to past tense inflection is also not exact but it is much better than that of the Palermo and Eberhart study. There are three different forms of the regular rule analogous to the /t/, /d/, and /ɨd/ forms of regular English past tense inflection, the appropriate letter response is contingent upon the immediately preceding context and independent of the earlier context, i.e., contingent upon the last digit but independent of preceding digits. In order to learn the irregular forms, however, the subject must attend to *both* digits and learn them independently of the rule which underlies the regular form.[1] The number of irregular types was limited to four, with systematic variation of token frequency while the number of regular types was large[2] and included some random variation of token frequency.

The results of the experiment were the same in all essentials as those of the Palermo and Eberhart study. The irregular responses were learned first, the regular responses next and the rule governing the regular responses overgeneralized to the irregular forms and accounted for most of the overt errors made to the irregular digits after criterion had been reached on the irregular forms. In addition, performance on the irregular digits was a positive function of the number of presentations per trial and the number of overgeneralization errors was an inverse function of the number of presentations per trial.

The experimental procedure, the form of the rule acquired and the nature of the exceptions are quite different in this experiment than in the Palermo and Eberhart study.[3] The analogy is still not as good as it might be but the results, once again, are very similar to the behavior of young children acquiring the past tense inflection. Working with analogies is always dangerous but it is the nature of most laboratory science to work with artificial analogous situations relative to the uncontrolled natural situation. The results of these experiments seem to have captured something of the behavior in question. Future research may well demonstrate that we are wrong but dataless arguments will hardly answer the questions involved.

Some additional points should be made with respect to the comments of Slobin. He indicates that there are no examples of the overgeneralization of irregular forms in the child literature. It should be noted, however, that while Ervin (1964) does indicate that extension of the irregular patterns is "relatively rare" (as is true in our data) apparently they did occur. Ervin cites an example of the *—en* ending extended to *tooken* but that is not exactly the form demanded by Slobin.

The inference we made about the frequency of occurrence of the regular and irregular verbs in English was suggested by the writings of the various persons who have discussed this particular developmental problem (e.g., McNeill, 1966; Ervin-Tripp, 1966; Slobin, this volume)

---

[1] The form of these irregular responses does not, however, change in any manner analogous to that of irregularly inflected verbs except insofar as both deviate from the rule.

[2] The number of regular types was infinite since multidigit numbers could have been used but for practical reasons only two-digit numbers were sampled.

[3] The rules for both studies are formally specified in Palermo and Howe (1970).

with no data available to us at that time. We are indebted to Slobin for providing some data on this point. While these data were not available to us until we read Slobin's critique, we have done several experiments which bear on this problem. Our experiments on the effects of the relative number and frequency of occurrence of irregular forms in the Esper paradigm indicate that the number of irregular forms which may be included and still permit mastery of the system, or rule, is dependent upon the frequency with which the irregular forms are presented. If the irregular forms are presented frequently then larger numbers of irregular forms may be presented and the rule learned as well. In other words, if the number of irregular types is large then the number of tokens must be large for rule learning. In fact, our data suggest that if the number of tokens is large, the rule for the regular forms is learned faster than if the number of irregular tokens is small. While we have not yet worked with the ratio of regular and irregular forms indicated in Slobin's data, our results would suggest that the high frequency of irregular forms which Slobin's data reveal is essential to learning both the irregular forms *and the rule itself*. Reducing the irregular verb tokens would slow down rule acquisition and reducing the irregular verb types, holding tokens constant, should increase regular past tense inflectional rule acquisition rate if our experimental analogy is relevant here.

One additional point is relevant here. In another series of experiments (Palermo & Parrish, in press) we have found that it makes no difference in rate of rule acquisition whether a few tokens of a large number of types or a large number of tokens of a few types is presented. All that is required is that some minimal and constant number of instances, types or tokens, is presented for the rule, which will allow correct performance on all types, to be acquired. This finding suggests that verb inflection for regular verbs may be equally rapidly acquired regardless of the diversity of language input as long as the frequency of input is great enough.

Finally, Slobin points out that "overregularization of the English past tense cannot be taken as a general, cross-linguistic example of the child's overgeneralization of morphological rules . . . " And yet Slobin himself suggested that exactly this is the case using precisely the same example given in this critique. In another place, after discussing the case inflection of nouns in Russian, Slobin said,

This is very similar to the development of the past tense in English, in which irregular strong forms, like *did,* are first used correctly, only to be driven out later by overgeneralizations from the regular weak forms, giving rise to transitory though persistent forms like *doed.* [Slobin, 1966a, p. 138].

It does not seem appropriate for Slobin to turn around and use these same observations to argue exactly the opposite point when convenient.[4]

In summary, it seems that the Palermo and Eberhart studies (as well as a number of additional experiments which have since been conducted in our laboratory) go far beyond showing what Esper demonstrated forty years ago. We believe that the fact that we have used the memory drum and paired associates technique characteristic of the learning paradigm has little bearing on the significance of these research findings for the general principles relevant to language. Furthermore, we believe that research of this type allows experimental control which is not possible in the study of children's natural speech. The research strategy preferred by Slobin will provide a different kind of data than the one taken here but it will be a long time before it will be known which has the greater payoff. It may well turn out that they complement each other in a manner which will allow the most complete understanding in the shortest possible time.

[4] The question of whether the overgeneralization of rules to instances governed by other rules requires a different explanation than the overgeneralization of rules to irregular instances of those same rules is an important empirical question which Slobin makes here but he did not make that distinction earlier. We are currently engaged in research to examine this problem.

Bibliography

Abell, A. T. Words functioning simultaneously as operant and respondent reinforcers: Preliminary study. *Psychological Reports,* 1969, **24,** 123–133.

Ammon, P. R. Aspects of speech comprehension by children and adults. [Final Rept., Proj. No. 7-I-114, OEG-9-8-070114-0029-(010)] University of California, Berkeley, 1970.

Anisfeld, M., & Gordon, M. On the psychophonological structure of English inflectional rules. *Journal of Verbal Learning and Verbal Behavior,* 1968, **7,** 973–979.

Baer, D. M., Peterson, R. F., & Sherman, J. A. The development of imitation by reinforcing behavioral similarity to a model. *Journal of the Experimental Analysis of Behavior,* 1967, **10,** 405–416.

Baer, D. M., & Sherman, J. A. Reinforcement control of generalized imitation in young children. *Journal of Experimental Child Psychology,* 1964, **1,** 37–49.

Bandura, A. Social learning through imitation. In M. R. Jones (Ed.), *Nebraska symposium on motivation.* Lincoln: University of Nebraska Press, 1962. Pp. 211–269.

Bandura, A. Vicarious processes: A case of no-trial learning. In *Advances in experimental social psychology.* Vol. 2. New York: Academic Press, 1965. Pp. 1–55.

Bandura, A. *Principles of behavior modification.* New York: Holt, 1969.

Bandura, A., & Walters, R. H. *Social learning and personality development.* New York: Holt, 1963.

Bar-Hillel, Y. *Language and information: Selected essays on their theory and application.* Reading, Massachusetts: Addison-Wesley, 1964.

Bar-Hillel, Y. Do natural languages contain paradoxes? *Studium Generale,* 1966, **19,** 391–397.

Bellugi, U. The emergence of inflections and negation systems in the speech of two children. Paper read at the New England Psychological Association, Chicopee, Massachusetts, 1964.

Bellugi, U. The development of interrogative structures in children's speech. In K. F. Riegel (Ed.), *The development of language functions.* (Rept. No. 8, 1965, Pp. 103–137) Ann Arbor: University of Michigan Center for Human Growth and Development.

Bellugi, U. The acquisition of negation. Unpublished doctoral dissertation, Harvard University, 1967.

Berko, J. The child's learning of English morphology. *Word,* 1958, **14,** 150–177.

Berkowitz, L., & Knurek, D. A. Label-mediated hostility generalization. *Journal of Personality and Social Psychology,* 1969, **13,** 200–206.

Bever, T. G. Associations to stimulus–response theories of language. In T. R. Dixon & D. L. Horton (Eds.), *Verbal behavior and general behavior theory.* Englewood Cliffs, New Jersey: Prentice-Hall, 1968. Pp. 478–494.

Bever, T. G. The cognitive basis for linguistic structures. In J. R. Hayes (Ed.), *Cognition and the development of language.* New York: Wiley, 1970. Pp. 279–362

Bever, T. G., Fodor, J. A., & Weksel, W. On the acquisition of syntax: A critique of "contextual generalization." *Psychological Review,* 1965, **72,** 467–482. (a)

Bever, T. G., Fodor, J. A., & Weksel, W. Is linguistics empirical? *Psychological Review,* 1965, **72,** 493–500. (b)

Bierwisch, M. Some semantic universals of German adjectives. *Foundations of Language,* 1967, **3**, 1–36.

Birnbrauer, J. S., Bijou, S. W., Wolf, M. M., & Kidder, J. D. Programmed instruction in the classroom. In L. P. Ullman & L. Krasner (Eds.), *Case studies in behavior modification.* New York: Holt, 1965. Pp. 358–363.

Bloom, L. M. *Language development: Form and function in emerging grammars.* Cambridge, Massachusetts: MIT Press, 1970.

Blount, B. G. Acquisition of language by Luo children. Unpublished doctoral dissertation, University of California, Berkeley, 1969. (Working Paper No. 19, Language-Behavior Research Laboratory, University of California, Berkeley, 1969.)

Bolinger, D. Adjectives in English: Attribution and predication. *Lingua,* 1967, **18**, 1–34.

Bowerman, M. F. Learning to talk: A cross-linguistic study of early syntactic development, with special reference to Finnish. Unpublished doctoral dissertation, Harvard University, 1970.

Braine, M. D. S. On learning the grammatical order of words. *Psychological Review,* 1963, **70**, 323–348. (a)

Braine, M. D. S. The ontogeny of English phrase structure: The first phase. *Language,* 1963, **39**, 1–13. (b)

Braine, M. D. S. Inferring a grammar from responses: Discussion of Gough and Segal's comment. *Psychonomic Science,* 1965, **3**, 241–242. (a)

Braine, M. D. S. On the basis of phrase structure: A reply to Bever, Fodor, and Weksel. *Psychological Review,* 1965, **72**, 483–492. (b)

Braine, M. D. S. The insufficiency of a finite state model for verbal reconstructive memory. *Psychonomic Science,* 1965, **2**, 291–292. (c)

Braine, M. D. S. Learning the positions of words relative to a marker element. *Journal of Experimental Psychology,* 1966, **72**, 532–540.

Braine, M. D. S. The acquisition of language in infant and child. In C. Reed (Ed.), *The learning of language.* New York: Appleton, 1971.

Braine, M. D. S. Three suggestions regarding grammatical analysis of children's language. In C. A. Ferguson & D. I. Slobin (Eds.), *Readings on child language acquisition.* New York: Holt, in press.

Brotsky, S. J. Classical conditioning of the galvanic skin response to verbal concepts. *Journal of Experimental Psychology,* 1968, **76**, 244–253.

Brown, R. The development of wh questions in child speech. *Journal of Verbal Learning and Verbal Behavior,* 1968, **7**, 279–290.

Brown, R. Stage I. Semantic and grammatical relations. Unpublished paper, Harvard University, 1970. [Draft of first chapter for *A first language: The early stages,* to be published by Harvard Univ. Press, Cambridge, Massachusetts.]

Brown, R., & Bellugi, U. Three processes in the child's acquisition of syntax. *Harvard Educational Review,* 1964, **34**, 133–151. (Also in E. H. Lenneberg (Ed.), *New directions in the study of language.* Cambridge, Massachusetts: MIT Press, 1964. Pp. 131–162.)

Brown, R., & Berko, J. Word association and the acquisition of grammar. *Child Development,* 1960, **31**, 1–14.

Brown, R., Cazden, C., & Bellugi, U. The child's grammar from I to III. In J. P. Hill (Ed.), *Minnesota symposia on child psychology.* Vol. 2. Minneapolis: University of Minnesota Press, 1969. Pp. 28–73.

Brown, R., & Fraser, C. The acquisition of syntax. In C. N. Cofer & B. S. Musgrave (Eds.), *Verbal behavior and learning: Problems and processes.* New York: McGraw-Hill, 1963. Pp. 158–197. (Also in U. Bellugi & R. Brown (Eds.),

The acquisition of language. Monographs of the Society for Research in Child Development, 1964, **29**(1), 43–79).

Bruner, J. S., Goodnow, J., & Austin, G. A. *A study of thinking.* New York: Wiley, 1956.

Bruner, J. S., Olver, R. R., Greenfield, P. M., et al. *Studies in cognitive growth.* New York: Wiley, 1966.

Byrne, D., Young, R. K., & Griffit, W. The reinforcement properties of attitude statements. *Journal of Experimental Research in Personality,* 1966, **1**, 266–276.

Cazden, C. The acquisition of noun and verb inflections. *Child Development,* 1968, **39**, 433–448.

Chomsky, C. S. *The acquisition of language from five to ten.* Cambridge, Massachusetts: MIT Press, 1969.

Chomsky, N. *Syntactic structures.* The Hague: Mouton, 1957.

Chomsky, N. A review of B. F. Skinner's *Verbal behavior* (published by Appleton-Century-Crofts, Inc., New York, 1957). *Language,* 1959, **35**, 26–58.

Chomsky, N. Explanatory models in linguistics. In E. Nagel, P. Suppes, & A. Tarski (Eds.), *Logic, methodology, and philosophy of science.* Stanford, California: Stanford University Press, 1962. Pp. 528–550.

Chomsky, N. Degrees of grammaticalness. In J. A. Fodor & J. J. Katz (Eds.), *The structure of language: Readings in the philosophy of language.* Englewood Cliffs, New Jersey: Prentice-Hall, 1964. Pp. 384–389.

Chomsky, N. *Aspects of the theory of syntax.* Cambridge, Massachusetts: MIT Press, 1965.

Chomsky, N. Methodological preliminaries. In L. A. Jakobovits & M. S. Miron (Eds.), *Readings in the psychology of language.* Englewood Cliffs, New Jersey: Prentice-Hall, 1967. Pp. 85–103. (a)

Chomsky, N. *Linguistic contributions to the study of mind: II.* Berkeley, California (Box 27): Academic Publishing Co., 1967. (Also in N. Chomsky, *Language and mind.* New York: Harcourt Brace, 1968.) (b)

Chomsky, N. Language and the mind. *Psychology Today,* 1968, **1**(9), 48–51, 66–68.

Chomsky, N., & Miller, G. A. Introduction to the formal analysis of natural languages. In R. D. Luce, R. R. Bush, & E. Galanter (Eds.), *Handbook of mathematical psychology.* Vol. 2. New York: Wiley, 1963. Pp. 323–418.

Cromer, R. F. The development of temporal reference during the acquisition of language. Unpublished doctoral dissertation, Harvard University, 1968.

Di Vesta, F. J., & Stover, D. O. The semantic mediation of evaluative meaning. *Journal of Experimental Psychology,* 1962, **64**, 467–475.

Drach, K. The language of the parent: A pilot study. In Working Paper No. 14: The structure of linguistic input to children. Language-Behavior Research Laboratory, University of California, Berkeley, 1969.

Early, J. C. Attitude learning in children. *Journal of Educational Psychology,* 1968, **59**, 176–180.

Eisman, B. S. Attitude formation: The development of a color preference response through mediated generalization. *Journal of Abnormal and Social Psychology,* 1955, **50**, 321–326.

Epstein, W. The influence of syntactical structure on learning. *American Journal of Psychology,* 1961, **74**, 80–85.

Ertel, S., Oldenberg, E., Siry, U., & Vormfelde, D. Classical conditioning of connotative meanings. Paper presented at the Conference on Human Learning with International Participation, Prague, Czechoslovakia, July 15–19, 1969.

Ervin, S. M. Imitation and structural change in children's language. In E. H.

Lenneberg (Ed.), *New directions in the study of language.* Cambridge, Massachusetts: MIT Press, 1964. Pp. 163–189.

Ervin-Tripp, S. Language development. In M. Hoffman & L. Hoffman (Eds.), *Review of child development research.* Vol. 2. Ann Arbor: University of Michigan Press, 1966. Pp. 55–105.

Ervin-Tripp, S. An Issei learns English. *Journal of Social Issues,* 1967, **23**(2), 78–90.

Ervin-Tripp, S. Discourse agreement: How children answer questions. In R. Hayes (Ed.), *Cognition and the development of language.* New York: Wiley, 1970. Pp. 79–108. (a)

Ervin-Tripp, S. Structure and process in language acquisition. In J. Alatis (Ed.), *Bilingualism and language contact: Anthropological, linguistic, psychological, and sociological aspects.* Monograph Series on Languages and Linguistics No. 23. Washington, D.C.: Georgetown University Press, 1970. Pp. 313–353. (b)

Ervin-Tripp, S. M., & Slobin, D. I. Psycholinguistics. *Annual Review of Psychology,* 1966, **17**, 435–474.

Esper, E. A. A technique for the experimental investigation of associative interference in artificial linguistic material. *Language Monographs,* 1925, No. 1.

Ferguson, C. A. Baby talk in six languages. *American Anthropologist,* 1964, **66**(6), Part 2, 103–114.

Ferguson, C. A., & Slobin, D. I. (Eds.), *Readings on child language acquisition.* New York: Holt, in press.

Fillenbaum, S. Psycholinguistics. *Annual Review of Psychology,* 1971, **22**.

Fillmore, C. J. Toward a modern theory of case. *Project on linguistic analysis,* Rep. No. 13. Ohio State University, Research Foundation, 1966.

Fillmore, C. J. The case for case. In E. Bach & R. T. Harms (Eds.), *Universals in linguistic theory.* New York: Holt, 1968. Pp. 1–90.

Finley, J. R., & Staats, A. W. Evaluative meaning words as reinforcing stimuli. *Journal of Verbal Learning and Verbal Behavior,* 1967, **6**, 193–197.

Fodor, J. A. Could meaning be an r_m? *Journal of Verbal Learning and Verbal Behavior,* 1965, **4**, 73–81.

Fodor, J. A. How to learn to talk: Some simple ways. In F. Smith & G. A. Miller (Eds.), *The genesis of language: A psycholinguistic approach.* Cambridge, Massachusetts: MIT Press, 1966. Pp. 105–122.

Fodor, J. A., & Garrett, M. Some reflections on competence and performance. In J. Lyons & R. J. Wales (Eds.), *Psycholinguistics papers: The proceedings of the 1966 Edinburgh conference.* Edinburgh: Edinburgh University Press, 1966. Pp. 135–162.

Fodor, J. A., & Garrett, M. Some syntactic determinants of sentential complexity. *Perception and Psychophysics,* 1967, **2**, 289–296.

Fowler, W. Cognitive learning in infancy and early childhood. *Psychological Bulletin,* 1962, **59**, 116–152.

Furth, H. G. *Thinking without language: Psychological implications of deafness.* New York: Free Press, 1966.

Gardner, B. T., & Gardner, R. A. Development of behavior in a young chimpanzee (unpublished data summaries).

Gardner, R. A., & Gardner, B. T. Teaching sign language to a chimpanzee. *Science,* 1969, **165**, 664–672.

Gibson, J. J. *The senses considered as perceptual systems.* Boston: Houghton, 1966.

Golightly, C. C., & Byrne, D. Attitude statements as positive and negative reinforcements. *Science,* 1964, **146**, 798–799.

Greenberg, J. H. Some universals of grammar with particular reference to the order of meaningful elements. In J. H. Greenberg (Ed.), *Universals of language.* Cambridge, Massachusetts: MIT Press, 1963. Pp. 58–90. [2nd ed. 1966]

Gvozdev, A. N. *Voprosy izucheniya detskoy rechi.* Moscow: Akademiya Pedagogicheskikh Nauk RSFSR, 1961.

Halle, M. Phonology in a generative grammar. In J. A. Fodor & J. J. Katz (Eds.), *The structure of language: Readings in the philosophy of language.* Englewood Cliffs, New Jersey: Prentice-Hall, 1964.

Harris, Z. *Methods in structural linguistics.* Chicago: University of Chicago Press, 1951.

Hinde, R. A. *Animal behavior.* New York: McGraw-Hill, 1966.

Horton, D. L., & Kjeldergaard, P. M. An experimental analysis of associative factors in mediated generalizations. *Psychological Monographs,* 1961, **75**(11, Whole No. 515).

Householder, F. W. Phonological theory: A brief comment. *Journal of Linguistics,* 1966, **2,** 99–100.

Hubel, D. H., & Wiesel, T. N. Receptive fields, binocular interaction, and functional architecture in the cat's visual cortex. *Journal of Physiology,* 1962, **160,** 106–154.

Hull, C. L. *Principles of behavior.* New York: Appleton, 1943.

Hunt, E. B. *Concept learning.* New York: Wiley, 1962.

Hunt, E. B. Selection and reception conditions in grammar and concept learning. *Journal of Verbal Learning and Verbal Behavior,* 1965, **4,** 211–215.

Jakobson, R. The paths from infancy to language. Heinz Werner Memorial Lectures. Clark University: Worcester, Massachusetts, 1969.

James, W. *Psychology: Briefer course.* New York: Holt, 1892.

Jenkins, J. J. Stimulus "fractionation" in paired-associate learning. *Psychological Reports,* 1963, **13,** 409–410.

Jenkins, J. J. Mediation theory and grammatical behavior. In S. Rosenberg (Ed.), *Directions in psycholinguistics.* New York: Macmillan, 1965.

Jenkins, J. J., & Bailey, V. B. Cue selection and mediated transfer in paired-associate learning. *Journal of Experimental Psychology,* 1964, **67,** 101–102.

Jenkins, J. J., & Palermo, D. S. Mediation processes and the acquisition of linguistic structure. In U. Bellugi & R. Brown (Eds.), *The acquisition of language. Monographs of the Society for Research in Child Development,* 1964, **29**(1), Pp. 141–169.

Katz, J. J. Mentalism in linguistics. *Language,* 1964, **40,** 124–137.

Katz, J. J. *The philosophy of language.* New York: Harper, 1966.

Katz, J. J., & Fodor, J. A. The structure of a semántic theory. *Language,* 1963, **39,** 170–210.

Katz, J. J., & Postal, P. M. *An integrated theory of linguistic description.* Cambridge, Massachusetts: MIT Press, 1964.

Kelley, K. L. Early syntactic acquisition. P-3719, the RAND Corp., Santa Monica, California, 1967.

Kernan, K. The acquisition of language by Samoan children. Unpublished doctoral dissertation, University of California, Berkeley, 1969. (Working Paper No. 21, Language-Behavior Research Laboratory, University of California, Berkeley, 1969.)

Klima, E. S. Negation in English. In J. A. Fodor & J. J. Katz (Eds.), *The structure of language: Readings in the philosophy of language.* Englewood Cliffs, New Jersey: Prentice-Hall, 1964. Pp. 246–323.

Klima, E. S., & Bellugi, U. Syntactic regularities in the speech of children. In J. Lyons & R. J. Wales (Eds.), *Psycholinguistics papers: The proceedings of the 1966 Edinburgh conference*. Edinburgh: Edinburgh University Press, 1966. Pp. 183–208.

Kobashigawa, B. Repetitions in a mother's speech to her child. In Working Paper No. 14: The structure of linguistic input to children. Language-Behavior Research Laboratory, University of California, Berkeley, 1969.

Kuhn, T. S. *The structure of scientific revolutions*. Chicago: University Chicago Press, 1962.

Kuroda, S. Y. Generative grammatical studies in Japanese. Unpublished doctoral dissertation, MIT, Cambridge, Massachusetts, 1965.

Labov, W. Stages in the acquisition of standard English. In R. W. Shuy (Ed.), *Social dialects and language learning*. Champaign, Illinois: National Council of Teachers of English, 1964. Pp. 77–103.

Lamb, S. M. Epilegomena to a theory of language. *Romance Philology*, 1966, **19**, 531–573. (a)

Lamb, S. M. Linguistic structure and the production and decoding of discourse. In E. C. Carterette (Ed.), *Brain functions*. Vol. 3. *Speech, language and communication*. Los Angeles: University of California Press, 1966. Pp. 173–193. (b)

Lashley, K. S. The problem of serial order in behavior. In L. A. Jefress (Ed.) *Cerebral mechanisms in behavior: The Hixon symposium*. New York: Wiley, 1951. Pp. 112–136.

Lehrman, D. S. A critique of Lorenz' "objectivisitc" theory of animal behavior. *Quarterly Review of Biology*, 1953, **28**, 337–363.

Lenneberg, E. H. Understanding language without ability to speak: A case report. *Journal of Abnormal and Social Psychology*, 1962, **65**, 419–425.

Lenneberg, E. H. The capacity for language acquisition. In J. A. Fodor & J. J. Katz (Eds.), *The structure of language: Readings in the philosophy of language*. Englewood Cliffs, New Jersey: Prentice-Hall, 1964. Pp. 579–603.

Lenneberg, E. H. The natural history of language. In F. Smith & G. A. Miller (Eds.), *The genesis of language: A psycholinguistic approach*. Cambridge, Massachusetts: MIT Press, 1966. Pp. 219–252.

Lenneberg, E. H. *Biological foundations of language*. New York: Wiley, 1967.

Lettvin, J. Y., Maturana, H. R., McCulloch, W. S., & Pitts, W. H. What the frog's eye tells the frog's brain. *Proceedings of the IRE*, 1959, **47**, 1940–1951.

Lovaas, O. I. A behavior theory approach to the treatment of autistic children. Paper read at the American Association for the Advancement of Science meeting, Berkeley, Calif., 1965.

Lott, A., Lott, B. E., Reed, T., & Crow, T. Personality-trait descriptions of differentially liked persons. *Journal of Personality and Social Psychology*, 1970, **16**, 284–290.

Lyons, J., & Wales, R. J. *Psycholinguistics papers: The proceedings of the 1966 Edinburgh conference*. Edinburgh: Edinburgh University Press, 1966.

Mandler, G., & Campbell, E. H. Effect of variation in associative frequency of stimulus and response members on paired-associate learning. *Journal of Experimental Psychology*, 1957, **54**, 269–273.

McGehee, N. E., & Schulz, R. W. Mediation in paired-associate learning. *Journal of Experimental Psychology*, 1961, **62**, 571–575.

McNeill, D. Some universals of language acquisition. Mimeo, University of Michigan, 1965.

McNeill, D. Developmental psycholinguistics. In F. Smith & G. A. Miller (Eds.), *The genesis of language: A psycholinguistic approach.* Cambridge, Massachusetts: MIT Press, 1966. Pp. 15–84.

McNeill, D. On theories of language acquisition. In T. R. Dixon & D. L. Horton (Eds.), *Verbal behavior and general behavior theory.* Englewood Cliffs, New Jersey: Prentice-Hall, 1968. Pp. 406–420.

McNeill, D., & McNeill, N. B. What does a child mean when he says "no"? In E. Zale (Ed.), *Proceedings of the conference on language and language behavior.* New York: Appleton, 1968. Pp. 51–62.

Menyuk, P. Syntactic structures in the language of children. *Child Development,* 1963, **34**, 407–422.

Menyuk, P. *Sentences children use.* Cambridge, Massachusetts: MIT Press, 1969.

Mikeš, M. Acquisition des catégoires grammaticales dans le langage de l'enfant. *Enfance,* 1967, **20**(3–4), 289–298.

Miller, A. W., Jr. Awareness, verbal conditioning, and meaning conditioning. *Psychological Reports,* 1967, **21**, 681–691.

Miller, G. A. The psycholinguists. *Encounter,* 1964, **23**(1), 29–37.

Miller, G. A. Some preliminaries to psycholinguistics. *American Psychologist,* 1965, **20**, 15–20.

Miller, G. A. Project grammarama, *The psychology of communication.* New York: Basic Books, 1967. Pp. 125–187.

Miller, G. A., Galanter, E., & Pribram, K. H. *Plans and the structure of behavior.* New York: Holt, 1960.

Miller, G. A., & Selfridge, J. A. Verbal context and the recall of meaningful material. *American Journal of Psychology,* 1950, **63**, 176–185.

Miller, G. A., & Stein, M. Grammarama I. Preliminary studies and analysis of protocols. Scientific Rept. CS-2, Center for Cognitive Studies, Harvard University, 1963.

Miller, W. R. The acquisition of formal features of language. *American Journal of Orthopsychiatry,* 1963, **34**, 862–867.

Miller, W. R., & Ervin, S. M. The development of grammar in child language. In U. Bellugi & R. Brown (Eds.), *The acquisition of language. Monographs of the Society for Research in Child Development,* 1964, **29**(1), 9–33.

Minke, K. A., & Stalling, R. B. Long-term retention of conditioned attitudes. Tech. Rep. No. 6 under Contract N00014-67-C-0387-0007 between the Office of Naval Research and the University of Hawaii, 1970.

Morton, J. A model for continuous language behavior. *Language and Speech,* 1964, **7**, 40–70.

Mowrer, O. H. The autism theory of speech development and some clinical applications. *Journal of Speech and Hearing Disorders,* 1952, **17**, 263–268.

Mowrer, O. H. The psychologist looks at language. *American Psychologist,* 1954, **9**, 660–694.

Mowrer, O. H. *Learning theory and the symbolic process.* New York: Wiley, 1960.

Murdock, B. B., Jr. "Backward" learning in paired associates. *Journal of Experimental Psychology,* 1956, **51**, 213–215.

Nikkel, N., & Palermo, D. S. Effects of mediated associations in paired-associate learning of children. *Journal of Experimental Child Psychology,* 1965, **2**, 92–102.

Noble, C. E., Stockwell, F. E., & Pryer, M. W. Meaningfulness (*m'*) and association value (*a*) in paired-associate syllable learning. *Psychological Reports,* 1957, **3**, 441–452.

Nunnally, J. C., Duchnowski, A. C., & Parker, R. K. Association of neutral objects with rewards: Effect on verbal evaluation and eye movements. *Journal of Experimental Child Psychology,* 1965, 2, 44–57.

Osgood, C. E. *Method and theory in experimental psychology.* Cambridge and New York: Oxford University Press, 1953.

Osgood, C. E. A behavioristic analysis of perception and language as cognitive phenomena. In *Contemporary approaches to cognition.* Colorado symposium. Cambridge, Massachusetts: Harvard University Press, 1957. Pp. 75–119. (a)

Osgood, C. E. Motivational dynamics of language behavior. In M. R. Jones (Ed.), *Nebraska symposium on motivation.* Lincoln: University of Nebraska Press, 1957. (b)

Osgood, C. E. On understanding and creating sentences. *American Psychologist,* 1963, 18, 735–751.

Osgood, C. E. Where do sentences come from? In D. Steinberg and L. Jakobovits (Eds.), *Semantics: An interdisciplinary reader in philosophy, linguistics and psychology* (title tentative). London and New York: Cambridge University Press, in press.

Page, M. M. The social psychology of classical conditioning of attitude experiments. *Journal of Personality and Social Psychology,* 1969, 11, 177–186.

Paivio, A. Abstractness, imagery, and meaningfulness in paired-associate learning. *Journal of Verbal Learning and Verbal Behavior,* 1965, 4, 32–38.

Palermo, D. S. Backward associations in the paired-associate learning of fourth and sixth grade children. *Psychological Reports,* 1961, 9, 227–233.

Palermo, D. S. Mediated association in the paired-associate learning of children using heterogeneous and homogeneous lists. *Journal of Experimental Psychology,* 1966, 71, 711–717.

Palermo, D. S., & Eberhart, V. L. On the learning of morphological rules: An experimental analogy. *Journal of Verbal Learning and Verbal Behavior,* 1968, 7, 337–344.

Palermo, D. S., Flamer, G. B., & Jenkins, J. J. Association value of responses in the paired-associate learning of children and adults. *Journal of Verbal Learning and Verbal Behavior,* 1964, 3, 171–175.

Palermo, D. S., & Howe, H. E., Jr. An experimental analogy to the learning of past tense inflection rules. *Journal of Verbal Learning and Verbal Behavior,* 1970, 9, 410–416.

Palermo, D. S., & Jenkins, J. J. Oral word association norms for children in grades one through four. Res. Bull. No. 60, Dept. of Psychology, Pennsylvania State University, 1966.

Palermo, D. S., & Parrish, M. Rule acquisition as a function of number and frequency of exemplars presented. *Journal of Verbal Learning and Verbal Behavior,* in press.

Pfuderer, C. Some suggestions for a syntactic characterization of baby talk style. In Working Paper No. 14, The structure of linguistic input to children. Language-Behavior Research Laboratory, University of California, Berkeley, 1969.

Phelan, J. G., Hekmat, H., & Tang, T. Transfer of verbal conditioning to non-verbal behavior. *Psychological Reports,* 1967, 20, 979–986.

Pihl, R. O., & Greenspoon, J. The effect of amount of reinforcement on the formation of the reinforcing value of a verbal stimulus. *Canadian Journal of Psychology,* 1969, 23, 219–226.

Popova, M. I. Grammaticheskiye elementy yazyka v rechi detey preddoshkol'nogo vozrasta. *Voprosy psikhologii*, 1958, 4(3), 106–117. (English transl.: In C. A. Ferguson & D. I. Slobin (Eds.), *Readings on child language acquisition*. New York: Holt, in press.)

Postovsky, V. Effects of delay in oral practice at the beginning of second language-learning. Unpublished dissertation, University of California, Berkeley, 1970.

Ravem, R. Language acquisition in a second language environment. *International Review of Applied Linguistics*, 1968, 6, 175–185.

Reingold, H. L., Gewirtz, J. L., & Ross, H. W. Social conditioning of vocalizations in the infant. *Journal of Comparative and Physiological Psychology*, 1959, 52, 68–73.

Reitz, W. E., & McDougall, L. Interest items as positive and negative reinforcements: Effects of social desirability and extremity of endorsement. *Psychonomic Science*, 1969, 17, 97–98.

Russell, W. A., & Storms, L. H. Implicit verbal chaining in paired-associate learning. *Journal of Experimental Psychology*, 1955, 49, 287–293.

Samuels, S. J. The effect of experimentally learned word associations on the acquisition of reading responses. *Journal of Educational Psychology*, 1966, 57, 159–163.

Sapir, E. *Language*. New York: Harcourt Brace, 1921.

Saporta, S. Review of S. Koch (Ed.), *Psychology: A study of a science*. Vol. 6. (New York: Wiley, 1963.) *Language*, 1965, 41, 95–100.

Schlesinger, I. M. A note on the relationship between psychological and linguistic theories. *Foundations of Language*, 1967, 3, 397–402.

Schlesinger, I. M. *Sentence structure and the reading process*. The Hague: Mouton, 1968.

Schlesinger, I. M. Learning grammar: From pivot to realization rule. In R. Huxley & E. Ingram (Eds.), *Studies in language acquisition: Methods and models*, to be published.

Sgall, P. Generative Beschreibung und die Ebenen des Sprachsystems. In *Zeichen und System der Sprache*. Vol. 3. Berlin: Akademie, 1966.

Sheffield, F. D. Theoretical considerations in the learning of complex sequential tasks from demonstration and practice. In A. A. Lumsdaine (Ed.), *Student responses in programmed instruction*. Washington: National Academy of Sciences-National Research Council Publication 943, 1961. Pp. 13–32.

Shipley, E., Smith, C., & Gleitman, L. A study in the acquisition of language: Free responses to commands. *Language*, 1969, 45, 322–342.

Sinclair-de Zwart, H. *Acquisition du language et développement de la pensée*. Paris: Dunod, 1967.

Sinclair-de Zwart, H. Sensorimotor action schemes as a condition of the acquisition of syntax. Unpublished paper, University of Geneva, 1968.

Skinner, B. F. *Verbal behavior*. New York: Appleton, 1957.

Slobin, D. I. The acquisition of Russian as a native language. In F. Smith & G. A. Miller (Eds.), *The genesis of language: A psycholinguistic approach*. Cambridge, Massachusetts: MIT Press, 1966. Pp. 129–148. (a)

Slobin, D. I. Comments on "Developmental psycholinguistics": a discussion of McNeill's presentation. In F. Smith & G. A. Miller (Eds.), *The genesis of language: A psycholinguistic approach*. Cambridge, Mass.: MIT Press, 1966. Pp. 85–91. (b)

Slobin, D. I. Grammatical transformations and sentence comprehension in childhood and adulthood. *Journal of Verbal Learning and Verbal Behavior*, 1966, 5, 219–227. (c)

Slobin, D. I. Imitation and grammatical development in children. In N. S. Endler, L. R. Boulter, & H. Osser (Eds.), *Contemporary issues in developmental psychology.* New York: Holt, 1967. Pp. 437–443.

Slobin, D. I. Questions of language development in cross-cultural perspective. Paper read at Conference on Language Learning in Cross-Cultural Perspective, Michigan State University, 1968. (In Working Paper No. 14, Language-Behavior Research Laboratory, University of California, Berkeley, 1969.)

Slobin, D. I. Universals of grammatical development in children. In W. Levelt & G. B. Flores d'Arcais (Eds.), *Advances in psycholinguistic research.* Amsterdam: North Holland Publishing Co., 1970. Pp. 174–186.

Slobin, D. I. Early grammatical development in several languages, with special attention to Soviet research. In T. G. Bever & W. Weksel (Eds.), *The structure and psychology of language.* Vol. 2. New York: Holt, in press. (a)

Slobin, D. I. *Leopold's bibliography of child language: Revised and updated.* Bloomington: University of Indiana Press, in press. (b)

Slobin, D. I., & Welsh, C. Elicited imitation as a research tool in developmental psycholinguistics. In C. A. Ferguson & D. I. Slobin (Eds.), *Readings on child language acquisition.* New York: Holt, in press.

Smith, C. S. Children's control of some complex noun phrases: A repetition study. Paper read at the Linguistic Society of America meeting, San Francisco, 1969.

Smith, F., & Miller, G. A. (Eds.) *The genesis of language: A psycholinguistic approach.* Cambridge, Massachusetts: MIT Press, 1966.

Smith, K. H. Grammatical intrusions in the free recall of structured letter pairs. *Journal of Verbal Learning and Verbal Behavior,* 1966, **5**, 447–454. (a)

Smith, K. H. Grammatical intrusions in the recall of structured letter pairs: Mediated transfer or position learning? *Journal of Experimental Psychology,* 1966, **72**, 580–588. (b)

Smith, K. H. Rule-governed intrusions in the free recall of structured letter pairs. *Journal of Experimental Psychology,* 1967, **73**, 162–164.

Smith, K. H., & Braine, M. D. S. Miniature languages and the problem of language acquisition. In T. G. Bever & W. Weksel (Eds.), *The structure and psychology of language.* Vol. 2. New York: Holt, in press.

Solarz, A. K. Latency of instrumental responses as a function of compatibility with the meaning of eliciting verbal signs. *Journal of Experimental Psychology,* 1960, **59**, 239–245.

Spence, K. W. The nature of theory construction in contemporary psychology. *Psychological Review,* 1944, **51**, 47–68.

Spence, K. W. The postulates and methods of behaviorism. *Psychological Review,* 1948, **55**, 67–78.

Spence, K. W. *Behavior theory and conditioning.* New Haven: Yale University Press, 1956.

Staal, J. F. Word order in Sanskrit and universal grammar. *Foundations of Language, Supplement Series,* 1967, **5**.

Staats, A. W. A behavioristic study of verbal and instrumental response hierarchies and their relationship to human problem solving. Unpublished doctoral dissertation, University of California, Los Angeles, 1955.

Staats, A. W. Learning theory and "opposite speech." *Journal of Abnormal and Social Psychology,* 1957, **55**, 268–269.

Staats, A. W. Verbal habit-families, concepts, and the operant conditioning of word classes. Tech. Rept. No. 10, Contract Nonr 2794(02) between Office of Naval Research and Arizona State University, 1959.

Staats, A. W. Verbal habit-families, concepts, and the operant conditioning of word classes. Tech. Rep. No. 10 under Contract Nonr 2794 (02) between the Office of Naval Research and Arizona State University, 1959. (Also published in *Psychological Review*, 1961, 68, 190–204.)

Staats, A. W. (with contributions by C. K. Staats). *Complex human behavior.* New York: Holt, 1963.

Staats, A. W. Conditioned stimuli, conditioned reinforcers, and word meaning. In A. W. Staats (Ed.), *Human learning.* New York: Holt, 1964. Pp. 205–213. (a)

Staats, A. W. *Human learning* (Introduction to chapters 8 and 9). New York: Holt, 1964. (b)

Staats, A. W. Operant learning principles and communication. In A. W. Staats (Ed.), *Human learning.* New York: Holt, 1964. Pp. 191–196. (c)

Staats, A. W. A case in and a strategy for the extension of learning principles to problems of human behavior. In L. Krasner & L. P. Ullman (Eds.), *Research in behavior modification.* New York: Holt, 1965. Pp. 27–55. (a)

Staats, A. W. An integrated-functional learning approach to complex human behavior. Tech. Rept. No. 28 between Office of Naval Research and Arizona State University, 1965. Pp. 1–98. (Reprinted in large part in B. Kleinmuntz (Ed.), *Problem solving: Research, method, and theory.* New York: Wiley, 1966. Pp. 259–339.) (b)

Staats, A. W. Emotions and images in language: A learning analysis of their formation and function. In K. Salzinger & S. Salzinger (Eds.), *Research in verbal behavior.* New York: Academic Press, 1967, Pp. 123–148.

Staats, A. W. A general apparatus for the investigation of complex learning in children. *Behaviour Research and Therapy,* 1968, 6, 45–50. (a)

Staats, A. W. *Learning, language, and cognition.* New York: Holt, 1968. (b)

Staats, A. W. Social behaviorism and human motivation: Principles of the attitude-reinforcer-discriminative system. In A. G. Greenwald, T. C. Brock, & T. M. Ostrom (Eds.), *Psychological foundations of attitudes.* New York: Academic Press, 1968. Pp. 33–66. (c)

Staats, A. W. Experimental demand characteristics and the classical conditioning of attitudes. *Journal of Personality and Social Psychology,* 1969, 11, 187–192.

Staats, A. W. A learning–behavior theory: A basis for unity in behavioral–social science. In A. Gilgen (Ed.), *Contemporary scientific psychology.* New York: Academic Press, 1970.

Staats, A. W. *Child learning, intelligence, and personality.* New York: Harper, 1971.

Staats, A. W., Brewer, B. A., & Gross, M. C. Learning and cognitive development: Representative samples, cumulative–hierarchical learning, and experimental–longitudinal methods. *Monographs of the Society for Research in Child Development,* 1970, Serial Number 141. (a)

Staats, A. W., & Butterfield, W. Treatment of non-reading in a culturally-deprived juvenile delinquent: An application of reinforcement principles. *Child Development,* 1965, 36, 925–942.

Staats, A. W., & Carlson, C. G. Classical conditioning of emotional responses (meaning, attitudes, values, interests) and effects on social behavior: A bibliography. Tech. Rep. No. 5 under Contract N00014-67-C-0387-0007 between the Office of Naval Research and the University of Hawaii, 1970.

Staats, A. W., Carlson, C. G., & Reid, I. E. Interest inventory items as reinforcing stimuli: A test of the A–R–D theory. Tech. Rep. No. 7 under Contract

N00014-67-C-0387-0007 between the Office of Naval Research and the University of Hawaii, 1970. (b)

Staats, A. W., Finley, J. R., Minke, K. A., Wolf, M., & Brooks, L. D. A reinforcer system and experimental procedure for the laboratory study of reading acquisition. *Child Development,* 1964, **35,** 209–231. (a)

Staats, A. W., Minke, K. A., Finley, J. R., & Wolf, M. Reinforcement variables in the control of unit reading responses. *Journal of the Experimental Analysis of Behavior,* 1964, **7,** 139–149. (b)

Staats, A. W., Minke, K. A., Goodwin, W., & Landeen, J. Cognitive behavior modification: 'Motivated Learning' reading treatment with subprofessional therapy technicians. *Behavior Research and Therapy,* 1967, **5,** 283–299.

Staats, A. W., & Staats, C. K. Attitudes established by classical conditioning. *Journal of Abnormal and Social Psychology,* 1958, **57,** 37–40.

Staats, A. W., Staats, C. K., & Crawford, H. L. First-order conditioning of meaning and the parallel conditioning of a GSR. *Journal of General Psychology,* 1962, **67,** 167–195. (a)

Staats, A. W., Staats, C. K., & Heard, W. G. Denotative meaning established by classical conditiong. Tech. Rep. No. 13 under Contract Nonr 2794(02) between the Office of Naval Research and Arizona State University, 1960. (Also published in *Journal of Experimental Psychology,* 1961, **61,** 300–303.)

Staats, A. W., Staats, C. K., Schutz, R. E., & Wolf, M. M. The conditioning of reading responses using "extrinsic" reinforcers. *Journal of the Experimental Analysis of Behavior,* 1962, **5,** 33–40. (b)

Staats, C. K., & Staats, A. W. Meaning established by classical conditioning. *Journal of Experimental Psychology,* 1957, **54,** 74–80.

Stevens, S. S. Mathematics, measurement, and psychophysics. In S. S. Stevens (Ed.), *Handbook of experimental psychology.* New York: Wiley, 1951. Pp. 1–49.

Stolz, W. A study of the ability to decode grammatically novel sentences. *Journal of Verbal Learning and Verbal Behavior,* 1967, **6,** 867–873.

Thorne, J. P., Dewar, H., Whitfield, H., & Bratley, P. A model for the perception of syntactic structure. Mimeo, English Language Research Unit, Edinburgh University. (n.d.)

Tinbergen, N. On aims and methods of ethology. *Zeitschrift für Tierpsychologie,* 1963, **20,** 410–433.

Tolman, E. C. Cognitive maps in rats and man. *Psychological Review,* 1948, **55,** 189–208.

Underwood, B. J. Stimulus selection in verbal learning. In C. N. Cofer & B. S. Musgrave (Eds.), *Verbal behavior and learning.* New York: McGraw-Hill, 1963. Pp. 33–48.

Underwood, B. J., & Schultz, R. W. *Meaningfulness and verbal learning.* Philadelphia: Lippincott, 1960.

Weinreich, U. Travels through semantic space. *Word,* 1958, **14,** 346–366.

Weinreich, U. Explorations in semantic theory. In T. A. Sebeok (Ed.), *Current trends in linguistics.* Vol. 3, *Theoretical foundations.* The Hague: Mouton, 1966. Pp. 395–478.

Weiss, R. F., Chalupa, L. M., Gorman, B. S., & Goodman, N. H. Classical conditioning of attitudes as a function of number of persuasion trials and argument (UCS) strength. *Psychonomic Science,* 1968, **11,** 59–60.

Whitlock, C. Note on reading acquisition: An extension of laboratory principles, *Journal of Experimental Child Psychology,* 1966, **3,** 83–85.

Wolf, M., Riseley, T., & Mees, H. An application of operant conditioning procedures to the behavior problems of an autistic child. *Behaviour Research and Therapy,* 1964, **1**, 305–312.

Yavuz, H. S., & Dousfield, W. A. Recall of connotative meaning. *Psychological Reports,* 1959, **5**, 319–320.

Yngve, V. A model and a hypothesis for language structure. *Proceedings of the American Philosophical Society,* 1960, **104**, 444–466.

Zakharova, A. V. Usvoyeniye doshkol'nikami padezhnykh form. *Doklady Akademiya Pedagogicheskikh Nauk RSFSR,* 1958, **2**(3), 81–84. [Eng. transl. in C. A. Ferguson & D. I. Slobin (Eds.), *Readings on child language acquisition.* New York: Holt, in press.]

Zanna, M. P., Kiesler, C. A., & Pilkonis, P. A. Positive and negative attitudinal affect established by classical conditioning. *Journal of Personality and Social Psychology,* 1970, **14**, 321–328.

Zimmer, K. E. Affixal negation in English and other languages: An investigation of restricted productivity. *Word,* 1964, **20**(2), Supplement (Monograph No. 5).

Index